GW00541043

BUILD A BONFIRE

Build a bonfire!
Build a bonfire!
Put Bellotti on the top!
Put Bill Archer in the middle
And we'll burn the fucking lot!

(Sung to the tune of 'My Darling
Clementine' by countless thousands of
Albion – and other – fans, 1996-97)

BUILD A BONFIRE
HOW FOOTBALL FANS UNITED TO SAVE BRIGHTON AND HOVE ALBION

STEPHEN NORTH
AND PAUL HODSON

MAINSTREAM
PUBLISHING PROJECTS

For Annie and Jessie

First published in Great Britain in 1997 by
MAINSTREAM PUBLISHING PROJECTS
Edinburgh

ISBN 1 84018 025 0

A catalogue record for this book is available from the British Library

Typeset in Apollo MT
Printed and bound in Great Britain by Butler & Tanner Ltd

Contents

Acknowledgements

Special thanks to the *Evening Argus*, *Albion Almanac*, *Gull's Eye*, Brighton and Hove Albion Supporters Club, Tim Carder, Paul Hayward, Liam Brady, Paul Samrah, Tim Pitt, Sarah Watts, Stewart Weir, John Campbell, Ian Hart, Chris Jones, Tony Burbridge, Jackie Blackwell, Jane Edie and all at Mainstream, particularly Bill Campbell and Judy Diamond.

Also to Brighton Theatre Events, Jackie Alexander and Louise Blackwell, Tessa Burbridge and Chris Hodson.

Also a big thank you to the National Federation of Supporters Clubs, the Football Supporters Association and all the journalists, fanzine editors, programme editors who printed supportive articles explaining Brighton's plight, all the supporters of other clubs from all over the world who came to Fans United, but particularly Rochdale, Wigan, Crewe, Wimbledon, Mansfield, Wycombe Wanderers, Watford, Charlton, Norwich, York, Carlisle, Barnet, Bournemouth, Walsall and Millwall who've all shown their support in different ways over the last two years and football fans everywhere who helped us when we needed it most.

Apologies to those we did not interview due to lack of time, especially Simon Valder and Roy Chuter.

And finally to all who gave up time to be interviewed, and gave up large amounts of their lives over the last two years for the campaign, we salute you: this book is for you.

Other books about Brighton and Hove Albion:
More than Ninety Minutes – photographs by Stewart Weir, text by Paul Hayward (Published by More than Ninety Minutes Publishing)
Seagulls!: The Story of Brighton and Hove Albion – Tim Carder and Roger Harris (Published by Goldstone Books)

Foreword by Liam Brady

I have played professional football for six clubs and been manager of two. Football has been my life and having been involved in the professional game for the last 25 years I believe I know the people who support the game and what it means to them.

For supporters, football and the clubs they follow are part and parcel of their lives, if not in many cases the most important aspect.

In general, supporting a club has less ups than downs but Albion fans have suffered much more than others. In the last five years many of them believe they have been treated cavalierly by directors in control of the club.

I became manager of the Albion in 1993. Then the club had severe financial problems. However, I witnessed at first-hand how a certain style of management at director level could bring a club to the verge of extinction.

Albion supporters have demonstrated unbelievable determination in fighting to save their club. This determination demonstrates that this club will survive and eventually return to happier times.

Authors' Preface

Build a Bonfire is not an accurate, documentary-style account of the struggle to save Brighton and Hove Albion. Rather it tells the story through the accounts and experiences of the people who lived through it. Sometimes it is contradictory, but then as it uses the words of the protagonists who, while united in their aims, come from widely different perspectives and backgrounds, that is how it should be. A 'working-class scummy yob' (his words, not ours), a chartered city accountant and anarchist punk poet will never agree about everything.

Taped interviews with fans, journalists, players, managers, FA representatives and other interested parties formed the starting point for the book. (Only two people declined to take part, or rather ignored our requests for interviews, but then Bill Archer and David Bellotti get their fair share of mentions anyway.) The interviews were recorded in people's houses, pubs and hotels in Sussex and beyond before being transcribed and edited by the authors. We also used television and newspaper accounts and the unbelievably detailed supporters' newsletters and fanzines.

As far as possible we have tried to create the conditions whereby the people who were the story get to tell it.

Introduction by Paul Hayward

Brighton and Hove Albion are as old as the century but have behaved, these past 15 years or so, like a seagull shot with both barrels. Less than a decade ago they were contesting a Wembley play-off for promotion to the old First Division and drawing with Liverpool at Anfield in the FA Cup. Since then, scattered feathers and a violent fall to earth.

The Seagulls were a flat-cap club rooted in a raffish seaside community. 'Brighton,' said Keith Waterhouse, famously, 'is a town that looks as if it's helping police with their inquiries.' There had always been something not quite right with the football club. A lack of transparency, a spivvishness that supplanted the old stiff-collared demeanour created by the club's founders.

The Albion were formed where all proper football clubs are formed. In a pub. They grew, in 1901, from the wreckage of Brighton United and then Brighton and Hove Rangers. The Seven Stars in Ship Street, where the new organisation was created, has changed hands and façades as often as the club itself. Look at pictures from those early days now and you wonder where it all went wrong. Brighton were run by aldermanic figures, civic stalwarts with three-piece suits and wing-tip moustaches. Residents were proud of the fact that Brighton is the only senior club to be named after two towns. Now, you wonder why. The club has brought humiliation on two towns, not just one.

For Brighton supporters – and there is a vast reservoir of potential followers – the past reads much better than the present. They will look nostalgically to the time (1898–99) when Brighton United came into the Southern League and played Spurs, Southampton and Woolwich Arsenal (also New Brompton, Ashford United and Sheppey). Brighton are a Victorian football club who reached the FA Cup final as recently as 1983. Only a lack of top-class management over a long period can have taken it so low. From Gillingham in the east, to Portsmouth in the west, there is no rival football league club south of London. Brighton should have grown into a super power, drawing vast swathes of spectators from Sussex, Kent, Hampshire and Surrey.

Apart from that famous, and infamous, Cup final appearance, the club have been terminal underachievers. They won Division Three (South) in 1958 and picked up a Charity Shield in 1910. But there is plenty to support the theory that Brighton are a club of vast potential. In 1983 they played Real Madrid in a mini-competition. At the turn of the '90s they were meeting clubs like Dynamo Bucharest in friendlies. As recently as 1984 they knocked Liverpool out of the FA Cup (now, Brighton lose to non-league teams). At the end of the 1970s the Goldstone Ground (RIP) was drawing average crowds of 25,000. The record attendance is 36,747 against Fulham in 1958. In 1979 they pulled in 30,859 for a game against Charlton.

In their darkest hours Brighton fans probably have to remind themselves that this is a club where Brian Clough once came as manager (admittedly only for nine months). Good players never stayed too long, but there was enough to set up a pretty decent all-time XI. Mark Lawrenson is the most gifted player Brighton ever had. But there were others – internationals, all of them. Peter Ward, Michael Robinson, Gary Stevens, Gerry Ryan, Micky Thomas, Steve Foster, Steve Penney, Dean Saunders and even Joe Kinnear. How would the club look now if Kinnear had been called back to become manager?

Most supporters trace Brighton's high-speed decline to Gordon Smith's miss against Manchester United in the Cup final. Poor Gordon. I played for an England Media XI against a Scottish equivalent during Euro '96 and had to mark him. People were shouting 'and Smith must score'. I might have taken some terrible revenge on him on behalf of the people of Brighton, had I been able to get anywhere near him. It really was an awful miss, so bad that even now, when you replay it, you think he's going to score. But the Seagull was already falling by then. Brighton were relegated that year and labouring under a huge wage bill. It was an archaic company, going nowhere.

The beginnings of the modern, protracted crisis can be traced to 1993. The club were £3m in debt and, on 28 October 1993, were days away from being wound up in the High Court by the Inland Revenue. An emergency shareholders' meeting was called at the Grand Hotel. Bill Archer from Mellor, near Blackburn, set up a new company, Foray 585, and promised that he would repay by June 1996 the interest-free loans previously made by the directors.

Archer took control of a dying company by parting with £56.25 to buy a controlling stake. At the same time the ancient 'no profit' clause was removed from the club's constitution, enabling the new directors to gain from the sale of the ground. When the change was spotted by the *Evening Argus*, the clause was eventually reinstated, with the club's lawyers calling its removal 'an oversight'.

The club was now controlled by Archer, David Bellotti (the chief executive) and Greg Stanley, who had loaned the club £880,000, at no doubt good rates of interest, but left the running of the club to Archer, his partner in the DIY chain, Focus. What followed was the most acrimonious, life-threatening, turbulent and distressing chapter in the history of English football. The Goldstone Ground was sold to property developers in July 1995 before the club had found an alternative site or the necessary funding.

They lost Liam Brady as manager and plummeted through the leagues to the point where the club's survival in the Football League was secured only on the final day of the 1996–97 season, with a 1–1 draw at Hereford, which followed an heroic sequence of victories under Steve Gritt's managership and sent Hereford down to the Vauxhall Conference. May 3, at Edgar Street, yielded a rare spasm of joy.

Even then, Brighton flirted with extinction. On 22 April 1997, the Football Association convened a press conference to announce details of a takeover of the club by Dick Knight's consortium. Three months later, with the deal still not signed, Archer still as chairman (and Bellotti as chief executive), Brighton faced a motion to expel them from the Football League for not lodging a £500,000 bond on time. The motion was defeated – another great escape. But for the supporters, it seemed they were stuck in *Groundhog Day*, repeating the same demonic cycle of uncertainty and disappointment, with Archer and Bellotti turning the wheel.

A few landmarks from the past four seasons stand out, though they might unsettle the squeamish. The first pitch invasion came on 2 September 1995, after which Bellotti told the fans to 'stop whining'. He also told them the club was £4.7m in debt – a highly flexible figure. One day it was £6m, another day it was £10m. As a detail, it was about as important as the angle at which the *Titanic* went down. But the supporters were entitled to know.

By November of that year Brady, who had been able to spend just £15,000 on players, gave way to Jimmy Case. There was another pitch invasion in April, and after Brighton were relegated, the game against York City erupted into chaos, with supporters wrecking the goal posts and attacking the (mostly empty) directors box. On 30 April, with the club 40 minutes away from being thrown on the street, the board finally paid a £480,000 fee to lease the Goldstone back for another 12 months. It was a familiar pattern of prevarication and brinkmanship.

The following season was even worse. It started with the FA imposing a suspended three-point penalty, plus one match behind closed doors, for the York City 'riot' (as some papers called it). A two-point penalty was eventually invoked after another pitch invasion and almost sent Brighton down. Losses were running at around £1m a year, the club was no nearer to finding a site for a new ground and the team itself was in freefall. A petition bearing 6,500 signatures was delivered to the headquarters of Focus in Crewe and a boycott organised for the Mansfield game on 9 November. Two thousand supporters stood outside.

Later that month, Graham Kelly, the FA's chief executive, invited Archer into mediation talks conducted by the Centre for Dispute Resolution, an offshoot of the CBI. David Davies, the FA's director of public affairs, became closely involved in the Brighton saga and turned out to be a friend. Another petition, this time carrying 5,700 names, was delivered to the FA after a march from Victoria station through Marble Arch. Astonishing, heroic stuff.

In December, Case was sacked. The club was now 11 points adrift at the bottom of Division Three, at the end of football's evolutionary chain. Gritt took the worst job in the game with sniggering all round. It was revealed later that the club had lost £911,000 in the previous year. Archer claimed it had made a profit of £1.5m. The resistance struggle reached a glorious climax on 8 February with the Fans United day in Brighton and Hove. Supporters from across Britain, Europe and even beyond converged on the Goldstone wearing their team's shirts to express their own disgust at the way the club was being run. Brighton today, our club tomorrow. So ran the theory and the fear.

From Fans United we galloped further downhill, with a brief respite at Edgar Street, followed by another tortured summer. Thank you Bill Archer and David Bellotti for disfiguring an ancient and cherished club. History will judge you.

The Cast

(Unless otherwise stated, all the cast are Brighton and Hove Albion supporters)

The A21 club: Initially a travel club for supporters in the East of Sussex, (Hastings, Bexhill etc) but became part of the campaign over the last two years.

Stuart Adams: Chairman of A21 Club.

The *Albion Almanac:* Edited by Tim Carder, a monthly diary of any event about the Albion both on and off the pitch. An invaluable source of information for this book.

Bill Archer: Former Crown Paints salesman from Blackburn. Formed Focus DIY Company with Greg Stanley. Gained the controlling interest in Brighton and Hove Albion for £56.25 in 1993 and became chairman of the club in 1995. It is not known who he supported before he became chairman.

The *Argus:* Brighton's daily paper, generally the first source for most supporters for any news about the club.

Attila The Stockbroker: The self-proclaimed 'Bard of Southwick'. Early 40s. Punk rock poet. Writer for *Gull's Eye*. One of the co-founders of BISA.

David Bellotti: Won Eastbourne by-election for the Liberal Democrats in the wake of Ian Gow's murder by the IRA. Subsequently lost the seat back to the Tories in 1992. Became the Chief Executive of Brighton and Hove Albion in 1993.

BISA: Brighton Independent Supporters Association.

Tim Bohannon: Actor. Early 30s.

Paul Bracchi: Investigative journalist at the *Argus* until 1996. Currently at the *Daily Mail*.

Liam Brady: Manager of Brighton and Hove Albion from December 1993 until November 1995.

Brighton and Hove Albion Supporters Club: The 'official' supporters club, but became a focus of protest against David Bellotti and Bill Archer.

Paul Camillin: Early 20s. Bank clerk. Writer for *Gull's Eye*.

John Campbell: Businessman. Mid-50s. On the board of the club until 1995.

Ivor Caplin: Labour MP for Hove. Early 40s. Ex-leader of Hove Council.

Tim Carder: Member of Supporters Club committee. Co-author of *Seagulls: The Story of Brighton and Hove Albion*. Editor of *Albion Almanac*.

Helen Chamberlain: Presenter of *Sky Sports AM*. Torquay United fan.

13

Warren Chrismas: Journalist specialising in stories from the Internet.

Roy Chuter: Eurostar employee. Writer for *Gull's Eye*.

Liz Costa: Vice-chair of Supporters Club. Mid-40s.

David Davies: The Football Association's director for public affairs. Self-confessed 'cockney red'.

Tony Foster: Surveyor. Chairman of Supporters Club.

Ian Hart: Undertaker. Early 30s. Co-founder of *Gull's Eye* fanzine.

Paul Hayward: Mid-30s. Journalist with the *Daily Telegraph* until September 1997. Currently with the *Guardian*. Sportswriter of the Year 1997. Contributed the text to *More Than Ninety Minutes*.

Tony Hylands: Sign writer. Writer for *Gull's Eye*.

Chris Jones: Partner in Brighton-based PR company, mid-30s.

Jan Merrit: Lettings officer. Mid-40s. Member of Supporters Club committee.

Tony Millard: Sports commentator. Founder of the 'Seagull Line' (telephone service for Albion fans).

Jackie Mooney: Housewife. Late 30s. Took over editorship of *Seaside Saga* for 1996-97 season.

Bob Pinnock: Accountant. Late 50s. Friend and business partner of Dick Knight. Founder member of the consortium which finally gained the controlling interest in Brighton and Hove Albion in September 1997.

Tim Pitt: Writer for *Gull's Eye* under the pseudonym 'Eldrich'.

Paul Samrah: Chartered accountant. Writer for *Gull's Eye*.

Kevin Sherwood: Secretary of the A21 Club.

Stuart Storer: Player for Brighton and Hove Albion.

Nigel Summers: Mid-30s. Royal Mail worker. Writer for fanzine *Gull's Eye*.

Dave Swaffield: Train driver. Mid-30s.

Anna Swallow: Supporter. Graphic designer. Mid-20s. Daughter of Bill and Jan. Writes column on the Albion for the *Argus*.

Bill Swallow: Partner in graphic design business with wife Jan. Early 50s.

Jan Swallow: Partner in graphic design business with her husband. Mid-40s.

Marc Twibill: Late teens. Founder of fanzine *On the Up* (later renamed *Seaside Saga*, for obvious reasons).

Sarah Watts: Secretary of the Supporters Club. Secretary for the southern region of the National Federation of Supporters Clubs.

Stewart Weir: Photo-journalist. Published a pictorial history of Brighton and Hove Albion over the last two years, *More Than Ninety Minutes*.

Paul Whelch: Chartered accountant. Writer for *Gull's Eye*.

1. Little did we know

The timing of the start of it all was so *unfootball*. It was that late June/early July sort of time, when football fans are marooned half way between last season's memories and the twinges of excitement about pre-season friendlies; when Wimbledon means strawberries and cream and 'no British interest left' rather than hoofs up the middle of the park; when the obsessive's hand only dials the teletext football pages *six* times a day to check on things in that parallel universe we inhabit, on Planet Football.

And for Brighton fans, before the news broke, it was a reasonably contented mid-summer slumber. It was 18 months since the dancing in the streets following the sacking of manager Barry Lloyd. Oh, how we had shouted for his dismissal, oh, how we had protested and oh, how we had nodded knowingly about 'fan power' when the man was finally shown the door. 'It was the fans what done it!' we had agreed. Because, after all, the club is the fans and the fans are the club.

So not only had the bad man gone away (the man, who we were later to remember, took us to within 90 minutes of a place in the Premier League at Wembley) but also Liam Brady had been appointed manager. That was *the* Liam Brady, Chippy, who wanted to be *our* manager. And although the days of rising excitement before his first match in charge had inevitably been rewarded by a 1–0 home defeat to Bradford, Brady had turned things around, as they say. From a very dodgy looking-over-our-shoulders-at-relegation-approaching-Christmas sort of position, we finished mid-table and played some fantastic stuff. (Mid-table in the Second Division! Happy days!) And although the next season had not produced the expected promotion and we had instead a relegation battle until the last weeks of the season – we had done OK. Not great, but OK. And Liam Brady was a good man, who always had time for the fans – which was not bad considering his near god-like status as one of the 50 greatest players the world has ever seen.

And so we had all packed up at the end of the 1994 or '95 season, (saying our goodbyes to people we only knew through football, had bought drinks for but weren't quite sure of their names), comforting ourselves with the unnerving, persistent and totally illogical optimism that only football fans possess that next season, next time, more than any other time, when the stripes ran out on to our sacred Goldstone turf, next season – well, it was almost worth putting the champagne on ice and a tenner on at Ladbrokes.

Instrumental in the steps forward the club had taken, particularly the sacking of Lloyd and the appointment of Brady, was a man we had raised our glasses to, one David Bellotti, who seemed a nice enough chap. Everyone knew him as the man who won the Eastbourne by-election, apparently signalling the end of Thatcher. He had lost the seat back to the Tories at the General Election and had somehow found himself chief executive of Brighton and Hove Albion. He seemed to have shaken up the staff at the club causing some upset. (But then what goes on behind the scenes is not of interest to a football fan, is it? We just pay our money and see our team and cheer and moan when appropriate.) So in the summer of '95 the club seemed to be in safe hands and the sun was shining.

But then it happened. Sussex's daily paper, the *Argus*, broke the stunning story that from the season after next the Albion would be ground-sharing with Portsmouth, while the Goldstone Ground, our home for nearly a century, would be sold and demolished and a new stadium built.

This story was a 'leak': there had been no announcement by the club let alone discussion with the fans. We knew Albion had massive debts and some of us had thought that it would be inevitable that we sell the ground one day. And a very tiny number of us knew that on the board of the club was someone called Bill Archer. Because he was the bloke that with Chairman Greg Stanley put millions in when we were going to be wound up in the High Court – wasn't he?

It is astonishing now how little we knew – and how little the average fan knows about the way their club is run or who owns it.

Over the next two years Albion fans – and Albion haters – have become embroiled in the fight to save the club. Whereas before we presumed to know about the merits of 4–4–2 against 4–3–3, the best hot dogs at away grounds and the mathematics of goal difference, we were now plunged into an extraordinary arena where to survive we needed knowledge of Articles of Association, where the procedure for electing local Liberal Democrat councillors is useful and a working knowledge of the laws of libel is an advantage.

We needed staying power and determination, first to unravel the mystery and then to fight the fight; we needed to make huge personal sacrifices, including financial and emotional; we needed to learn the art of compromise; we needed to use a huge amount of imagination to make our case heard; and perhaps most important we needed to learn the importance of solidarity.

And of course there were times when you stopped yourself short – is it really worth waiting at this service station to demonstrate against the chief executive *at three in the morning*? Is it really worth spending another hour making these badges? Is it really worth feeling this sort of depression and helplessness for a football club? Of course there were times when you thought – 'What a berk I am. Does it really matter that much?' But when the answer came back 'yes', you just got on with it again. Because we are football fans and we love our club – it's as simple and as complicated as that – and we won't let anyone take it away from us.

And we didn't let anyone take it away from us. But it was bloody close.

JULY 1995 – DECEMBER 1995

2. Seagulls migrate!

IAN HART (funeral director and co-founder of the Albion fanzine *Gull's Eye*)
Early July '95, I had a phonecall from someone. Said he'd heard Brighton are
going to Portsmouth, they've sold the Goldstone Ground. He gave me the
source. I chased it up.

We'd always had an openness with David Bellotti. We had a good working
relationship with him, if there was anything I had on my chest I could phone
him up and he'd speak to me. He came to a *Gull's Eye* dinner and got a
standing ovation! If he came to one now . . .

When I told him what my mate had said, 'The Goldstone's been sold,
we're going to Portsmouth,' he just smiled wryly. 'I don't know where he's
heard that,' he said. But he knew.

That may have been the significant point where he thought, 'Shit, they've
found out.'

I phoned the *Argus* and they said, 'It's true. We're breaking it tomorrow.'

The Argus – 7 July 1995
Seagulls Migrate – Albion will play home games at Pompey ground.
The Albion are moving to Portsmouth next summer.
The debt-ridden Division Two club will share Pompey's Fratton Park for
   home games in the 1996–97 season.
And it revealed that after that it hopes to move into a 30,000 seater
   multi-purpose stadium at Waterhall playing field in Brighton.
In a statement from the board, Albion said the 'exciting new venture'
   would allow them to sell the Goldstone Ground to meet their debts
   and provide the local community with much needed facilities.
The new stadium would include:
- An ice rink
- A running track
- A 5,000-space car park
The statement says the club's plans will leave it debt-free for the first time
   in 30 years.

PAUL BRACCHI (the *Argus*'s chief reporter during the paper's investigation): It's
the closest thing Brighton's had to investigative journalism, really. It had
everything: the chairman who's a Northern businessman; a politician who'd

lost his shine; a club in decline both on and off the field; and a captive audience who were waiting to read every word that came off your computer. It was a thrilling story to cover.

LIZ COSTA (vice-chair of the Supporters Club): We didn't know what to do. It's as simple as that – you're faced with the biggest crisis that anybody could possibly imagine!

IVOR CAPLIN (Labour MP for Hove and former leader of Hove Council): I think it's well known and on the record that I was not best pleased. There was no approach made to the council beforehand.

TIM PITT ('Eldrich' in *Gull's Eye*): On a Friday night coming home from work, I picked up a copy of the *Argus* at London Bridge station and I was walking down the platform and there it was: 'Seagulls Migrate'. All this about Portsmouth and whatever. I couldn't believe it.

BILL SWALLOW (partner in graphic design business): I know where I was when I heard about it – within 100 yards of this house, on the other side of the road, looking at the *Evening Argus*, outside the newspaper shop here in Hurstpierpoint. That's really been the point at which so much of my knowledge has come from. That little square inch of pavement outside the paper shop.

There was a numbness. I just couldn't believe the goings-on when I read that headline, I just could not believe that they'd done it without any discussion whatsoever. Of course, like many people, I spent a very long time trying to work out exactly what they were up to. I mean . . . why?

MARC TWIBILL (founder of the fanzine *On The Up*): I didn't know how seriously to take it at first. I was just waiting for the club to deny it and say that the *Argus* had got it wrong. It was a talking point. And then as time developed over the next two weeks it slowly sunk in that it was actually true and it was happening.

TONY FOSTER (quantity surveyor, chairman of Brighton and Hove Albion Supporters Club): I had heard that estimates were being done on the demolition of the Goldstone ground. Alarm bells were ringing with me prior to the actual announcement. It was working in the construction industry itself that I'd heard things like that.

STEWART WEIR (photo-journalist, who started a photo history of the club in August 1995): The players, I think, were shocked, even though they were a world within themselves. They do their thing and that's it. They are told what's happening or they are not told what's happening. They concentrate one hundred and five per cent on their job which is training, games, training, games, training. What happens in the outside world they try not to let affect them because it will affect their playing performance — which is pretty much what happened.

Initially they didn't quite believe it, or they may have been told, 'This is not true' because at first the club denied it — Bellotti denied it or Archer said, 'This isn't true, the ground hasn't been sold.'

STUART STORER (Brighton player): You try to draw your own conclusions from it. There were rumours around the club that he was trying to rationalise, and yet the year after they're buying players worth half a million pounds, and you think, why are they putting half a million pounds in? Is that to keep the fans happy or is that just a big smoke screen? You can look at it two ways — they were doing well for the club or they were trying to make a streamlined asset.

KEVIN SHERWOOD (secretary of A21 Supporters Club): Not to be consulted is the ultimate. It really was the ultimate slap in the face.

STUART ADAMS (chairman of A21 Supporters Club): I remember at the time that headline came out I did rather naïvely say 'I don't care where we go as long as we get a new ground.'

ANNA SWALLOW (graphic designer, daughter of Bill and Jan): I don't think anyone realised it was as serious as it was. A lot of people were saying 'these guys are making money out of this' but people liked saying things like that because it sells newspapers.

PAUL BRACCHI: The basis of the OFFSIDE! story, the day after SEAGULLS MIGRATE!, was a press release or statement from Bill Archer that the club were moving and 'don't worry, boys, we've got a new ground to go to', because they'd got permission, apparently, to build at Patcham Court Farm. One of our reporters checked with the council for comment — they never expected the council to say 'Hang on, this is a load of rubbish.' At that stage I think alarm bells started to ring. I was the investigative reporter and the paper asked me to have a look at it. It was something possibly we should have done earlier, but it was probably just about in time to alter the course of events.

21

> The *Argus* – 8 July 1995
> **OFFSIDE!**
> Albion's plans for a new stadium linked to a development at Patcham
>   Court Farm were thrown out by Brighton Council TWO WEEKS AGO.
> Council chiefs were stunned when club chairman Bill Archer yesterday
>   announced an ambitious proposal to develop two council-owned sites.
> The shock news that the Albion will be moving to Portsmouth next
>   summer was followed yesterday with details about the club's plans to
>   buy Patcham Court Farm for £8 million.
> The club said it would develop a large shopping centre there and then
>   use the profits to build a 30,000 seat stadium at Waterhall near the
>   Brighton bypass.
> But a council spokesman said, 'We met with their finance chief and
>   Albion chief executive David Bellotti two weeks ago to discuss their
>   proposal and told them then it wasn't a runner, so they have known
>   it since then. Their plans for Patcham Court Farm were not what we
>   wanted at all.'
> Brighton's director of business services, Steve Rayson said, 'The council is
>   surprised Albion call this an exciting new venture as we have already
>   informed them the council could not accept such a proposal.'

TIM CARDER (co-author of book *Seagulls!: A History of Brighton and Hove Albion FC*, editor of *Albion Almanac*): You start thinking, 'What the hell is going on? Have they got any plans?' And that's really when it started going off.

LIAM BRADY (Albion manager 1993–95): Archer asked me what would my reaction be to going to Portsmouth. 'From the playing point of view – we are professionals,' I said. 'If it is going to save the club we'll have to do it. But,' I said, 'the only way you're going to sell it to the fans is to actually start building whilst you're down there – if they see the first brick going down in a new stadium here in Brighton or in Sussex then you can do it.'

LIZ COSTA: We demanded a meeting with Bellotti and to give him his due he was quite open and said, 'Yes, I welcome the opportunity to discuss frankly and fully with you.' We demanded to see Archer and we were told, 'He's very shy and reserved and doesn't like meeting people. I am the appointed spokesman. I am the Chief Executive. I'm local. I've got my finger on the pulse. I know what's going on.' So we said to him, 'Has the ground been sold?' And he said, 'I categorically deny that the club has been sold.' Now people were hearing, 'Oh he hasn't sold it! What's everyone worried about?' It was only later we realised the question was 'Have you sold the ground?'

KEVIN SHERWOOD: The first few meetings we walked out thinking, 'This is fantastic.' They were telling us what we wanted to hear and we were suckers for it. Football is a business, but it is a unique business, because your customer base will always come back for the product no matter how bad the product is and this guy knew he had us.

Bill Archer was the shadowy character on the periphery of all this. We said, 'Okay, Dave, we'd like to speak to him.' That wasn't unreasonable. He said he was up in Blackburn and his statement was that he was not one for the limelight and he's not much of a face in the Press – he's a very quiet man.

SARAH WATTS (bank registrar, secretary for Brighton and Hove Albion Supporters Club and the Southern Division of The National Federation of Supporters Clubs): We'd taken along what we thought were fairly smart members of the Supporters Club at that time, and we had the A21 representatives there, people who were associated with us and quite a few of the members. We asked him about the debt and he said that we were in debt for four and a half million. So when a few weeks later he announced on Radio 5 Live that we were going to be six million in debt we thought we're not losing that much on the bank – I think the bank interest was half a million – so where's this extra million come from?

LIZ COSTA: All the supporters agreed that, if we went to Portsmouth, within two years, the club would disintegrate because people wouldn't go: (a) it's your arch enemy, (b) trains are abysmal. So there would have to be coaches, which the club wouldn't subsidise, so who's going to be able to afford them? Evening games were going to be a nightmare to get to. The traffic would be horrendous. There's no parking. The police down there are horrible – they wouldn't want us. And the residents in the area sure as hell wouldn't want us.

PAUL SAMRAH (chartered accountant, writer for *Gull's Eye*): I started to get involved around the time of the winding-up orders in 1992. I started looking at the accounts and the more I dug the more I felt there was a lot more that we weren't being told by the board.

I went along to the High Court hearings and started to create a name for myself as a troublemaker with the board because I was asking awkward questions.

After the announcement of the club moving and the selling of the ground in July 1995, I wrote a letter to the *Argus* listing six or seven points that I felt the board hadn't considered: how the proposed new development was going to be funded, why didn't they consider refinancing the mortgage and all the other debts of the club and so on.

23

Mr Bellotti had claimed that the club was now breaking even. Therefore the losses were stabilised. Half of the debt was owed to the directors and these directors had gone on public record saying they didn't want their money out of the club. So why couldn't it then be refinanced given that the debt was probably in the region of about one and a half to two million at that point in time?

The *Argus* printed my letter and it started to get people thinking about what the club's motives were: why aren't they picking up on some of these options that have been suggested – for instance, the sale and lease back of the ground? Or some kind of share issue? I was trying to be constructive.

PAUL BRACCHI: The key thing in the whole two-year campaign which the whole story hinged on was whether the ground had been sold or not. The answer was lying there in the Land Registry but no one had thought to look. Paul Samrah and I decided to.

And there it was, in legalistic language: they'd got involved in a deal with a company called Chartwell. I didn't know what that actually meant when I looked at it, I just suspected and so did Paul. It was only when we looked a bit closer it was apparent – the deal had already been done.

What we decided to do then was have a look at who might benefit from the sale of the ground.

PAUL SAMRAH: I looked at the accounts in more detail and I then looked at the club's Memorandum and the Articles of Association which show the rules by which the company operate. It became patently clear that Archer had invested only £56.25 in the club to gain control and then reorganised the structure of the club by creating a holding company called Foray 585.

Before Archer came on the scene, the football club was a limited company, Brighton and Hove Albion Football Club Ltd (and two or three other companies which weren't really trading any more). When Archer arrived as a shareholder to save the club from the winding up, he introduced a holding company which controls Brighton and Hove Football Club (and all the other subsidiary companies). The shareholdings in this company called Foray 585, are 56.25 per cent Archer and 43.75 per cent Stanley.

With that established he was able to secure additional loan finance to see it through its High Court winding-up petition. It was put across in the media by Stanley and Archer that funds had been invested by Stanley and Archer themselves, but that wasn't the case: a loan was financed by the Co-op Bank. At the time a number of us asked the question, how is the club going to fund the repayment of any loans? – but we were specifically told it's the directors putting money in themselves. Well, that wasn't the case, it was a question of a loan being arranged. It comes back to the old question that I kept on raising: why couldn't they have refinanced the whole loan package, especially as at that time the ground value was going up.

So, we found out, all Archer had done was pay for the shares, they were one penny shares and there were 5,625 of them costing £56.25. Archer had invested £56.25 and everything else was loaned finance.

I turned my attention to the club's Articles of Association. I remember distinctly, it was a Wednesday evening, late July, the last week in July 1995. And I remember looking at the microfiche which I got from Companies House. Suddenly, there on the screen, was the fact that the club had changed the Articles of Association, originally dated 1904. Around November 1993, when the restructuring took place and Foray 585 was introduced, the club decided to change its Articles . . .

There was a notice of the minutes of an Extraordinary General Meeting of the club on 23 November 1993, when the new Articles of Association were adopted.

JOHN CAMPBELL (ex-director): Stanley signed the changes to the Articles of Association at the extraordinary general meeting, when we were all still shareholders, that was signed on 23 November 1993 and the takeover documents were not dated until the 30 November 1993, so technically everyone of the shareholders should have been advised about that change of Article. It stinks; the whole thing stinks.

PAUL BRACCHI: Of all the thousands of words of meaningless legal jargon in the original version, only one paragraph in the Articles of Association had been changed — and that was the one that allowed Archer and the other share-holders to profit from the sale of the ground.

PAUL SAMRAH: This was in the original Articles of Association: 'On the dissolution of the company any surplus assets shall be applied first in repaying the members the amount they paid on their shares respectively and then any surplus assets shall be given to some other club or institute in the county having objects similar to those contained in the memorandum of the association or to any local charity or charitable or benevolent institution situated within the same county. Such club, institution or charity to be decided upon and such property apportioned among all or any of such clubs, institutions or charities by the members of the club.'

So what that meant was, under the old Articles, that on any winding up where there was a surplus of assets, having repaid all the debts, that surplus money should be paid to another sporting institution in Sussex, i.e. a non-league club or distributed or shared across sporting institutions.

In other words it was not to go to members as their profit on their investment. If you invest in a private company or public company, you hope for an increase in your value of your shares, but that was not permitted in the old Articles and that remained from 1904 to 1993.

In the new Memorandum and Articles of Association of the club that was totally dropped. If there were going to be surplus assets after the winding up of the club, the board, the shareholders, could take the profit and go.

I felt absolutely horrified, I mean both professionally I felt it just wasn't right and as a football fan of the Albion I felt sick. I was desperately trying to find a reason, that maybe I had misread it or that they had been changed back subsequent to that, and it hadn't hit the microfiche. I couldn't believe that it was there, in front of me – and they had been found out.

Archer says it was 'an oversight' and we have to accept that.

They had the upper hand on the sale of the ground without it being leaked out, now suddenly I had something that looked as though it was less than open behaviour, and we knew, Paul Bracchi and I, that that was going to be something that a lot of people could pick up on: the fact that the founding fathers of the club had thought long-term about the future and shareholders not making a profit – and suddenly the Articles had been changed.

PAUL BRACCHI: They say it was a mistake. I have to say I still don't know the answer. It's very, very curious that the only change in the club's constitution was that one paragraph basically saying if it wound up the shareholders can profit, and I think that was really the start of the two-year campaign. We broke the story on a front page with a two-page inside story and that really was just the beginning of possibly one of the most high-profile, successful campaigns the *Argus* has ever run.

DAVID BELLOTTI (reported in the *Evening Argus*): The ground has not been sold and I can say that categorically. I'm afraid the *Evening Argus* has rather jumped the gun.

PAUL BRACCHI: And that was the irony – that there were 20-30 words which proved that Archer and Bellotti had been hiding probably the most important fact in the club's history from the other directors.

TONY HYLANDS (sign writer): Once that announcement came out that the Goldstone had been sold everyone just went ape shit! It's our sacrosanct home, isn't it? You expect your aunty or your uncle or your gran or granddad to die but you don't ever expect the football club to. I personally have been through a divorce, the solicitors demanding money and maintenance pay, but good old Albion's always there for sanctuary, so for two hours you can forget all about it – suddenly that was being taken away

Argus a.m.

D READ · FRIDAY, AUGUST 4, 1995 · 28p

Fun in the sun!
Have a great day out at Butlin's Southcoast World for just £2! (normally £6.50)

PLUS £31,500
(It's still there. Are you still interested?)

TOMORROW

GOING, GOING GOLDSTONE

Chairman Bill Archer

Chief executive David Bellotti

THE ALBION is involved in a deal to sell the Goldstone Ground.

The Argus can reveal that the debt-ridden club has already signed a contract with a property development company.

Details of the agreement are contained in documents filed at the Land Registry.

The buyer is named as Chartwell Development Properties Ltd.

The firm is part of the giant Kingfisher Group which owns Woolworths, Comet, B&Q and Superdrug.

Chief Reporter PAUL BRACCHI

Chartwell has developed retail parks, superstores and shopping malls all over Britain and is now in line to buy the Goldstone, which is believed to be worth at least £7 million.

The conditional contract to acquire the land was drawn up three weeks ago on July 14. The conditions are not listed.

Today's revelation follows an Argus investigation into the troubled Division

Two club, which has been at the ground for nearly a century.

The Seagulls have to move out by next Summer to meet crippling £4 million debts and interest payments.

Chief executive David Bellotti and chairman Bill Archer say profits will go towards a new stadium, but today the reality is that the Albion is no nearer finding a new home than it was 20 years ago.

● How the rules were changed, Pages 4 and 5

Today we publish our special report on the growing crisis at the Albion. Now have your say by phoning the Argus hotline on 0891 789029. Clearly state your name and address, spelling any unusual words, before leaving your brief message.
If possible, please leave a phone number in case we need to contact you.
A selection of your messages will be printed in the paper. Calls cost 39p a minute cheap rate and 49p a minute at all other times.

What the Argus says

TODAY we have a simple message to David Bellotti: Tell us the score.

Turn to Page 4

Betty Barclay

27

Evening Argus

MORE THAN 220,000 READERS EVERY DAY   WEDNESDAY, AUGUST 16.

THE £7m DEAL

 PAUL BRACCHI, CHIEF REPORTER

THE ALBION has sold its Goldstone ground for more than £7 million.

The deal was first revealed exclusively in the Argus on August 4.

Albion chief executive David Bellotti then went on radio and television to deny our story, telling one news programme: "The ground has not been sold and I can say that categorically. I'm afraid the Evening Argus has rather jumped the gun."

We had evidence the deal was under way and we have now obtained details of a statement drawn up by the club, which confirms our front page story.

ALBION SELLS GOLDSTONE

Did you see it? How the Argus revealed the Goldstone had been sold

Your verdict, Page 5

The sale price is not listed but the figure is £7.4 million.

The statement reads:

"Chartwell Land PLC, one of the country's leading retail property companies, has exchanged contracts to acquire the site of the Goldstone Ground football stadium from Brighton and Hove Albion Football Club.

"The 4.9-acre site has planning permission for 70,000 sq ft of non-food retail warehousing. The football club will lease back the stadium for its use during the 1995-96 season. Work will begin on the site to develop the retail scheme in June 1996.

"Both Chartwell Land and the football club believe this is an excellent opportunity to secure the club's future whilst providing some much needed retail facilities in the area."

So hot, that it's lift off!

EIGHT people stripped off after they were stranded in a sweltering broken-down lift for more than an hour.

They took off shirts and blouses in a desperate bid to keep cool as they waited for firefighters to free them after the lift in Churchill Court, Stonehouse Drive, St Leonards, shuddered to a halt just above the ninth floor.

One firefighter said: "When we did finally get the doors open, there was steam coming out. It had got really hot in there."

544544 Advertising (01273) 544300   Save Our Surgery   **The Argus backs the Hurstwood Park campaign**

from you. It's like part of your life is being taken away from you with no control over that event and it hurt. There was a lot of confusion because of the double statements, statements being made perhaps to reassure.

I can put my hand on my heart and say that I could understand it: we got debts, we've got to square the debts and the only asset you've got is your ground. But in an ideal world, your board sit down with your supporters and the council round a table and say, 'Look, we've got to sell the ground to pay these debts. We're going to need somewhere else to play.' And two years ago if they'd got round a table and sorted it out, we wouldn't have this now.

JAN MERRITT (lettings officer, member of Supporters Club commitee): I just couldn't believe that they had actually sold the ground without making any plans for where we'd be playing in the future – it just seemed an absolutely ridiculous thing to do.

The Articles of Association: it didn't seem right that they hadn't checked what they were doing, I just didn't believe it. It seemed to me that it was a deliberate omission. And knowing also that Bill Archer really is a business-man and perhaps isn't interested in the football side of it seemed to make it even worse and one was suspicious that his motives were purely financial and for his own ends.

NIGEL SUMMERS (Royal Mail, writer for *Gull's Eye*): Archer blamed his lawyer for the mistake over the Articles of Association – if a lawyer had made that much trouble for me I would have a go at them and get compensation and tell the people that I've offended that I've had a go at the lawyers. That is when possibly we started understanding something was seriously eerie and you could see that perhaps they hadn't got the best will of the club at heart.

BILL SWALLOW: They didn't understand that football is entirely about place. I think somebody once pointed out that there are only three or four football clubs in this country that don't have a place in their name. It is all about place and identity and location and for somebody to simply, and very insensitively, sell a football ground in these circumstances is selling part of the birthright of the football club. That is not to say that no one should never sell football grounds. We've got to be practical and realistic – 20 clubs have moved in the last four or five years. That's always going to be sad. But this was something beyond that. They were simply kicking the soul of the football club into touch. And that's what made it dreadful.

TIM CARDER: The fact that the club had nowhere to play or nowhere locally to play was actually not of much importance to Archer, as far as I'm concerned. Bellotti probably thought that sharing Portsmouth was a good idea in the interim but he was presumably told we were selling the ground; that it would be vacated in May/June '96. So Bellotti was probably behind the Portsmouth ground share because he realised that the club did need to have somewhere to play but Archer, I'm sure, was fairly indifferent. Something that really filled me with trepidation was when they revealed about the Articles of Association. We thought that Archer and Stanley could just pocket that lot.

29

HELEN CHAMBERLAIN (football TV presenter and Torquay United fan): I thought this has got to be wrong; surely this can't happen.

IAN HART: We were doomed because we should have smelt a rat. The problem is: with women, if you look back on relationships you've had, you've known that a woman probably hasn't wanted to go out with you for about three months, but you haven't realised it – and I think by the same token we were trying to tell ourselves that everything was going to be all right because no one would want to do that to our club, so it can't be true.

STEWART WEIR: I've said right from the very beginning that had the club sat down with fans' representatives and said, 'Right, we're going to sell up the Goldstone, pay the debts, please help us. These are the accounts, okay we made a cock-up with the Articles of Association "no profit" clause, that was a mistake by us, etc. etc.' – none of this would have happened – full stop.

ATTILA THE STOCKBROKER (alternative poet/musician, co-founder of Brighton Independent Supporters Association): I think Archer subscribed to this Northern stereotype that we were a bunch of Southerners, that we wouldn't get that angry and that we'd forget about it. He wasn't even sufficiently aware of the number of people that go to Albion games, that we are potentially one of the best supported clubs in the country. I think he genuinely thought that he could do what he wanted and that nobody was really going to say much about it.

PAUL HAYWARD (sports journalist with the *Telegraph* during the two years, now with the *Guardian*): It all goes back to that day when we had an outsider walking in, forming a shelf company (which you or I or any of the fans could do), with a very significant name, Foray, which means sudden attack or raid. You buy the club for £100, sell the ground, which a cub scout could do – it's not very difficult. Having done that, you could sit there and wait for the thing to atrophy. And all you've invested is £100. The £7.4 million of the ground sale is always going to cover the debts of the club.

What the motivation was, we've all yet to determine.

I don't believe, looking at the evidence, that they ever had a credible scheme for building a new stadium. If they did, why did they still keep submitting plans that had been ruled out of bounds by the environmental authorities and by the local council? I don't think there was ever a serious will to build a new stadium and suddenly Archer was in charge of a fund of £7.4 million and the debts were much less than that. So you have to ask yourself what happened to the difference between the debts and the £7.4

million? The 'no profit' clause was removed from the club's constitution and was only put back when it was pointed out that it had been removed in the first place. So it was put back under duress and I think for a period of about a month the 'no profit' clause wasn't there. Nobody can really say for sure what happened and it may remain, unless we can unearth the truth, one of the great financial and footballing mysteries. We can all wonder.

TONY HYLANDS: It was no going back then, the adventure had started.

3. 'This isn't about football, this is about right and wrong' *(former player at the Albion)*

Match programme – home to Notts County, 2 September 1995:

From the boardroom – David Bellotti

It is not surprising that supporters are very concerned about the future of the club. Our local paper the *Evening Argus* has presented little factual information about the club, while fuelling controversy and generating bad feelings. It may sell newspapers but it certainly does nothing to help the Albion.

At the end of this season we have to repay more than 6 million pounds of debt.

The only way we can be sure of survival within our own resources is to sell our asset (the Goldstone Ground) repaying our debt and finding somewhere else to play. There are now conditional contracts to sell the ground in place, although the sale has not yet been completed. To guarantee our survival we have a provisional agreement to play at Portsmouth.

Bill Archer and Greg Stanley will invest money into the club, provided we have the council's support to build a new stadium. The Goldstone Ground cannot be developed as a football stadium. The Taylor Report has rightfully dictated comfort and safety standards. All-seater modern stadia facility will be available to the Albion. Whatever the obstacles!

Stop whining and listening to *Argus*-backed speculation.

They want to sell newspapers. The more they whip up frenzied inaccurate comments, the more they assume will be the sales of the newspaper.

If you want to help ensure a successful future for the Albion you could write to the leader of Brighton Council and the leader of Hove Council at their Town Halls. Tell them you want them to help the club both in the short term with a move to Coral's and in the longer term with a move to a permanent stadium. These two Councils will merge into one Council in 1997 and after all we are Brighton and Hove Albion Football Club.

Finally, let me try to reassure everyone again – this club which we all support is not going out of business. Our hopes for the future are get to the Premier League and play in a stadium fit for it.

To do that the club requires the understanding and support of everyone.

ANNA SWALLOW: When Bellotti told us in the programme 'stop whining' I just thought, he's insane, the man is mad.

TONY FOSTER: I've never been involved in any of the pitch invasions, I am conscious that it is an illegal act. But having said that, with everything going on, I fully understood why these people went on. We weren't appearing to get help or answers from anywhere else, the Football League and the FA. People starting to write letters, make phone calls. Are you interested in Brighton? Are you making enquiries? Are you investigating how this club is being run? People weren't getting satisfactory answers and so people took action through other means. So I understand why they did it.

STEWART WEIR: Really the initial vocal stuff came from the North Stand and from what you might call a minority – probably about a couple of hundred. In the early days no one really knew what to make of it or how to react or decide which way they were going to go.

TIM CARDER: It was all 'Bellotti out' at that time, there was no 'Archer out.'

TONY HYLANDS: We were in the Hove Park Tavern before the Notts County game and the word has gone round, everybody go to North West Terrace, don't go in the North Stand, so me and my mate put the word round that we're going on the pitch and everyone was up for it and said, 'You know we're not going to take this any more, the papers, the board, they're not going to get anything done, we need some direct action now. We can only get kicked off the pitch and banned from the Goldstone but at least we can say that we tried to do something.'

So just before half-time we get the nod and as the half-time whistle went we went on the pitch and we said, 'It's a sit-down, quiet, peaceful protest with no excuses for getting arrested; just voice your concern about what is going on' and that is what happened. At that point Liam Brady came walking out and he spoke to us. People started singing, I said, 'Shut the fuck up, let the bloke speak.'

LIAM BRADY: I said, 'Look lads, come on we've got a chance here. I know there's problems at the club but this is not going to solve anything, do me a favour, we're struggling at the moment, we need a bit of backing.'

TONY HYLANDS: And Brady come up to each and every one of us and said, 'Come on lads, get off the pitch.' We said, 'But, Liam, what the fuck is going on?' He said, 'I don't know as much as you don't, but I promise you if you get off the pitch we'll win the game for you.' So we all quietly got up for Liam Brady – not for David Bellotti or Bill Archer or Greg Stanley – for Liam Brady; we had the utmost respect for the guy.

LIAM BRADY: They just all got up and walked off. And they didn't like that, Archer and Bellotti, because at the press conference I think I might have said how I can understand why they feel this way, and they wanted me to say they shouldn't be on the pitch.

STUART STORER: The referee popped his head in the dressing-room, 'There's been a delay lads, some people have gone on the pitch. We'll have them off soon and we'll be able to get on with the game.' I remember seeing it on telly the Monday afterwards. Liam plodding out in his usual style and asking everyone to go back to the seats, which they did in the end. It's a bit frustrating sometimes. Your concentration's there, you're all ready to go out for the second half and it sort of throws you.

BILL SWALLOW: I was sitting in the West Stand, right at the back – we'd bought season tickets about six or seven years ago and only stopped last year because we wouldn't give Bill Archer any large cheques – and sitting up there of course the atmosphere is slightly different. There's traditionally been a sort of 'town and gown' and a 'them and us.' My feeling, though, continually grew that the North Stand were the salt of this club. And I tended, and I believe those around me, tended to become more and more warm towards what the North Stand did. Having said that, let's be honest, going on the pitch is a bit like winking at a nun – it's something you don't actually do. If you ask me for my first reaction, I think it probably was 'they shouldn't be doing this.' I must be honest.

JACKIE MOONEY (editor of *Seaside Saga* fanzine): I remember thinking that that wasn't going to change anything, that there wasn't much point in doing that other than out of sheer frustration. I wouldn't have done that myself because I couldn't see how things like that would change anything.

JAN MERRITT: I think they had a point and I didn't really see too much wrong in what they were doing. I know one isn't supposed to invade the pitch but I thought it was handled very well and when Liam Brady came out and talked to them they quietly went back, so I didn't really see that there was too much wrong with that.

TIM CARDER: I saw nothing wrong in the pitch invasions, I don't approve of fighting, but this was something different, this was a peaceful sit-down protest at half-time and I could see nothing wrong with that at all. It's against the law to go onto the pitch but I think throughout the whole thing the police have acted very sensibly at the Goldstone, they just allowed it and let everyone get back off the pitch. I've never been brave enough to go on the pitch in a demo, I'm the sort of background character. I really approved basically of what they were doing.

STEWART WEIR: Here was a beginning that would really become the norm. The fans wanted answers and they were not getting them.

4. 'There's only one Ivor Caplin'

TIM CARDER: Ivor Caplin was the first real fan that had been on Hove Council. If you trace it back we can probably thank Margaret Thatcher for making the Tory government so unpopular that Hove got a Labour Council in May 1995.

IVOR CAPLIN: I used to follow the movements of the boardroom just out of curiosity, as a supporter, that's all I was really. I first met Bill Archer in 1993, in relation to the club's Inland Revenue debt, by the fact that they were trying to clear up the financial situation of the club.

The then board (Bill Archer wasn't, of course chairman) had always given assurances to the Council and others that they would never sell the Gold-stone Ground without a replacement having been built. A sensible way to do things and how most other clubs have dealt with that issue.

I think there were six Labour councillors out of 30 on the Hove Council in 1991–95, but I think it's fair to say that we were all football fans. It became a cause for us. If there's only six out of 30 you need a few causes! It was a political campaign – I don't want to pretend here – I'm driven by being a supporter, but of course there was a political campaign behind it.

PAUL SAMRAH: In the programme for the Notts County game Bellotti suddenly said the debt was £6 million! To arrive at £6 million, the loss for the 15 months from 1 June 1994 to mid-1995 would have to be £1.3 million – which would be absolutely unheard of and conflicted with Bellotti's own comments that the club was breaking even: if the club was breaking even there could be no loss.

Gates were rising in 1994–95; interest rates were low and the redundancy programme was virtually complete. We were over the worst; we were in the Brady years and things were looking good.

TIM CARDER: Brighton and Hove Councils both got involved in meetings with the club. The Councils commissioned a quick report into the future of the club if it moves away. Basically it said that the club would die if it moved away from the area and that's what we all believed as well.

PAUL SAMRAH: There were figures coming every which way, and of course people who aren't figure-oriented were getting so confused, it was driving fans crazy! Simply, in August of 1995, my analysis of the situation based on the latest available accounts was:

SUMMARY	LONG DEBT	DUE TO 10.6.96	ON GOING
Greg Stanley (1)	600,000		
Co-op	880,166		
Barclays/Lloyds			1,583,591
Directors	725,000		
Greg Stanley (2)		200,000	
Mortgage		715,612	
	£2,205,166	£915,612	£1,583,594
			£4,704,372

Only £915,000 appeared to be really due on 10 June 1996, the date Bellotti had said £6 million was due. Yet the club still said that refinancing was not an option. In my opinion at that time, selling the ground and leasing it back over five years was still possible.

In the August '95 edition of *Gull's Eye* I challenged the board to confirm or deny the above debt position. I went on to say:

'Anyone can sell the ground to pay off debts – that could have been done years ago. You don't need to be a businessman to do that. The Greg Stanley money is hardly at risk – all loans are secured on the ground, so all will be repaid – with interest too! A pretty safe investment really! What is not safe is having a company with no firm place of business and that is exactly what we will face in June 1996. The confusion, apparent lies, and false promises show no sign of abating. It is therefore vital that we keep the issue in the public eye – nationally too – I for one do not want to look back and say I did nothing to try and salvage the situation.'

IVOR CAPLIN: The Council approached the football club with an offer to consider purchasing the free hold of the Goldstone, in relation to paying off the institutional debts. We weren't prepared to consider paying any of the directors – we felt that they had made this deal and it had gone bad, that's tough, that's business for you. But we did feel that there was a case for saying that the club would be better off not having the institutional debts and for us to secure the future of the Goldstone site. And to that end some of our work had already started on looking at whether we could relocate businesses to a place in the south end of the ground in order to give a bigger site for the Goldstone in the longer term.

When we started these discussions with the board, they were very, very anti. The discussions were very much on the basis of they'd made their decision, they'd sold the ground for £7.4 million and they were going to Portsmouth and nothing was going to change their minds. It was very much along those lines and they weren't prepared to listen to reason.

Through our contacts we were able to talk to the three banks involved in the loans – it was clear that no one, none of the three banks, was pressing for closure of the club. They didn't need to be repaid their debt in that time.

Of course in the end we didn't pursue our option. Unless we were going to get some indication that it was worth talking, there was no point in spending what is taxpayers' time before you even get around to spending taxpayers' money, on developing a scheme for the Goldstone site and looking to relocate other businesses.

But I think in the light of events, that would have been a visionary way to have dealt with the problem.

The *Argus* – 19 September 1995:

Towns throw down gauntlet to the Albion

LET'S PLAY BALL!

by Paul Bracchi & Adrian Monti

Councillors have thrown down the gauntlet to the men who run the Albion. They want to form a new partnership with the Seagulls, who are facing the biggest crisis in their 93-year history. But they will not enter into talks to safeguard the club's future or help it find a new ground unless the board agrees to certain conditions. These include:

- Reinstating the 'no profit' clause in the club's constitution. The *Argus* revealed how this clause was changed after the current regime took over the Albion, allowing chairman Bill Archer and co-owner Greg Stanley to legally keep money from the £7.4 million sale of the Goldstone Ground.
- Dealing with Hove and Brighton Councils in an 'open and transparent manner.'
- Withdrawing from the sale of the Goldstone.
- Giving up ground-share plans with Portsmouth.

The challenge from the two authorities was issued at Hove Town Hall last night, but there was no offer of financial help, and no one from the Albion was present.

Hove Council leader Ivor Caplin said: 'Now the ball is in the Albion's court. If they do not agree to our proposals we will have a clearer picture of what the club's motives are.'

He added: 'We expect clear, open discussions with the club. That has not always been the case in the last six weeks.'

Councillor Caplin also criticised the club for banning the *Argus* from the Goldstone by saying: 'This is not the way forward.'

The challenge was issued to coincide with publication of an independent report into the club's future, commissioned by the Councils.

TONY MILLARD (commentator and founder of the Seagull Line, the telephone information service for Brighton and Hove Albion): I got hauled over the coals by David Bellotti for putting on the *Seagull Line* an interview with Councillor Ivor Caplin stating the Council's position with regard to the future for Brighton and Hove Albion Football Club. I received notice that my line would no longer be the club's official line from David Bellotti just before 1 January 1996.

PAUL SAMRAH: Greg Stanley said, 22 September 1995 in the *Telegraph*, 'I'm resigning as chairman.'

I did have certain questions that never got answered: Stanley said that he was not seeking repayment of his personal monies loaned to the club – did this include the Trust monies (£600,000) that was in there?

Mr Stanley quoted a figure of £2 million personal investment. The May 1994 accounts only attributed £800,000 to him. The £6 million debt due in June 1996 – we now had a date being attributed to it, June 1996 – did not include the Stanley money presumably because he wasn't seeking repayment, so were we therefore to assume that the debt was £6.8 million?

I mean, nothing seemed to add up.

LIZ COSTA: Paul Samrah and Paul Whelch went marching off to the Football Association and said, 'Look, this is what's happening – you've got to do something to help us because we are powerless. You have the power to deal with these people or actually stop them in their tracks.' And the FA did nothing.

PAUL SAMRAH: The national press were picking up on it and I think the first big article was the *Telegraph* and then *The Times* in September and we had started the process. There was starting to be significant chanting at games.

Then Paul Whelch decided to try and make contact with the FA and this was the start of something. He's an accountant as well and it was a two-pronged attack. He made an appointment for us to go to the FA. It was the famous meeting of the three Pauls. There was Paul Bracchi, Paul Whelch and myself.

We met John Ryder and Mike Appleby of the FA. We presented them with the information that we had so far: the change of the Articles of Association, the sale of the ground, nothing in place for where we're going to play in the future, Portsmouth, etc. – this was September 1995.

PAUL WHELCH (accountant, chairman of Seagulls Over London and writer for *Gull's Eye*): The first issue was these are the Articles – do you accept these as *bona fide* rules of the Football Association? They said, 'No we don't.' So clearly, the first issue was that they were unaware that the Articles had been lodged.

PAUL SAMRAH: To our amazement it actually transpired that not only did changes of Articles of Association need to be registered with the FA before they're permitted, and that hadn't happened, but also all football clubs (other than the ones listed on the Stock Exchange) are required to have the 'no profits' clause in!

So that clause wasn't just unique to Brighton, it was a clause that was meant to mean that football clubs were charitable, ultimately, and any surplus must be distributed to other sporting institutions!

The men from the FA looked quite appalled. They said the FA had got wide-ranging powers and they told us that if they were satisfied somthing was seriously wrong they could suspend the directors, they could call in external auditors; they wanted answers to the questions. Why was the 'no profits' clause changed? Why wasn't the FA told about it? A clear breach of FA regulations we were told. They said they would definitely study the *Argus* dossier and our own dossier. They were going to investigate and demand answers to the questions.

We came out of the meeting thinking, 'Yes, we've got something, we've got something against the board.'

PAUL WHELCH: They immediately, the following day, wrote to David Bellotti and said that they wanted to see a copy of the latest Articles of the club. And they took a hell of a long time to do it, about a month to actually formally lodge the Articles, which was a scandal. Once they'd done it, it was clear that they'd changed the wording and we got them to get all three – Stanley, Bellotti, Archer – to Lancaster Gate to explain their conduct with a solicitor and to change the Articles, which they subsequently did.

PAUL BRACCHI: I certainly think the FA should have acted sooner. They said later they didn't have powers, but I remember someone saying, 'Don't worry, we have got powers and they are going to get rapped for changing the Articles of Association, and we're going to stop this and the courts will back us up.' In the end they couldn't even bring themselves to publicly criticise Archer for actually changing the Articles of Association; they couldn't even publicly make a statement saying they were wrong to do it. They didn't do anything, so I think that they were culpable.

The *Argus* – 29 September 1995:

An *Argus* dossier on the Albion is being studied by the Football Association.

Soccer's governing body asked for copies of our exclusive revelations after meeting worried fans this week.

The move could lead to an official investigation of the club.

FA officials will want answers to two key questions: Why was the 'no profit' clause in the club's original 1904 constitution changed? And why wasn't the Association told about it?

The new clause would allow chairman Bill Archer and co-owner Greg Stanley to legally keep the money from the £7.4 million sale of the Goldstone.

This is a clear breach of FA regulations. Every other club in the country

---

> has a 'no profit' clause written into its Articles of Association. Any changes have to be sanctioned by the FA.
>
> But we can reveal the fact that the Albion failed to submit the amended constitution for approval.
>
> The papers lodged at Lancaster Gate still contain the 'no profit' clause. Football's ruling body has now given the Albion a week to submit the new Articles.
>
> The FA has already had a number of letters from dismayed fans.
>
> The FA has wide-ranging powers. It can ban directors from taking part in football management; can call in external auditors and can even expel clubs, which effectively stops them playing league football.

LIZ COSTA: The FA did nothing. And I think the reason for that was that those Articles of Association had been submitted to the FA and their own people hadn't picked it up. So they could hardly penalise our board for one of their own omissions.

The FA felt that it was something which was an internal problem, which they shouldn't be getting involved in, because it was a private company and as such they couldn't interfere in the dealings of a private company. They hadn't, on paper, contravened any footballing regulations.

Everybody took us for granted and nobody realised that we were going to go on and on and on fighting until somebody gave us some answers, or we got a result of some sort, and whatever that result was going to be.

We'd got to the point where the roller-coaster had started.

5. 'Oh I do like to be beside the seaside'

LIAM BRADY: The results were terrible and where the fans had been with me all the time I began to feel they were getting restless. And what happened with Archer and Bellotti and me was I wouldn't sing from their hymn sheet as regards the plans for the club. They wanted me to pacify this restlessness among the fans by saying, 'The club's in good hands, everything's all right, I trust the people I'm working with — let's stick together.' But all I said was, 'The results are what they are because we've had no investment, nobody knows what's happening, there's been no communication.'

Bellotti phoned me one day and said he didn't want me doing interviews with TV — I'd done an interview with Sky after one of the pitch protests and said, 'You can't blame the fans, they want to know what's happening at the football club and no one's yet told them.' I knew what I was doing, I was saying, 'Well, I'm on this side with the fans, no way am I going over there, with Archer and Bellotti.' At the same time I tried to say to the players, 'Look, it's your careers and your profession, don't go out and lose games — let's go out and do ourselves proud.' I didn't want people saying, 'Liam Brady's side lost again, Liam Brady's side lost again.'

STUART ADAMS (A21): The Bournemouth trip, when we knew it was going to be televised was an opportunity far too good to be missed.

KEVIN SHERWOOD (A21): Paul Samrah had asked everybody to bring banners along so it was an opportunity for us to get some ideas, get some banners, get them ready, go to the game, go up there, fantastic, everybody enjoyed it.

TONY FOSTER: I was unable to attend the Bournemouth away game. There were a lot of things being said before it about encouraging people to go on the pitch. People thought, 'Here's an opportunity: we're live on the television; Brighton are very rarely on the television; here's an opportunity to protest and have our problems aired and voiced.'

KEVIN SHERWOOD: I think we did ourselves proud that day. When these things start you're all a bit sheepish about doing it, so it was like, well, we've got a banner but shall I put it up and then once you've done it once, you take your banner with you everywhere. I just want to watch the football but I can see the sense in fighting for it and you're a bit backward in coming forward until someone organises it and says, 'No, get them banners up, this'll be great.' It really worked. Now we are hardened to the things we have had to do.

LIZ COSTA: We got to that match and someone came up to me and said, 'Guess what? Bournemouth's chairman says he quite happy for us to demonstrate.' This was as the red cards for the red-card protest were being handed out and I thought: 'This isn't on!' We'd already been told by Meridian that if there was any pitch invasion, they would cut from the game immediately and they would take the Millwall match.

We were very much against it, I've been against pitch invasions right from the start because it's illegal, it's non-productive. Okay, it gets headlines, but what does it achieve?

STUART ADAMS: It was so clearly building up to a pitch invasion, the fans were gathering just to the right of the goal — it was right in front of us. We'd stood slightly to the right 'cause we wanted our banners to be seen. It was gathering up and people were standing on the fence and not one copper made any attempt to get anyone down, they knew what was going to happen and they were ready for it and they enjoyed it, I'm sure they loved it. A bit of training for them, a bit of real-life action instead of just a demo.

> The *Argus* – 26 September 1995:
> The Football Association today called for reports on yesterday's pitch invasion by Albion fans at Bournemouth. Sixteen Brighton supporters were arrested as police with dogs and truncheons dragged invaders from the field. Police were seen clubbing some fans and wrestling other fans to the ground to handcuff them.
> Albion manager Liam Brady said, 'We had a feeling something was going to happen because of the uncertainty surrounding the club and because going three goals behind probably tempted a few of the unintelligent lads.'

TONY HYLANDS: Months before the Bournemouth game the word had gone round, 'We're going on the pitch, it's live on telly, this is how it's happening, this is how it's going to be, this is the minute it's going to happen.'

So me and my mate Chris, who'd been going 30 years together home and away, got the train from Eastbourne. We drink all the way: Eastbourne to Brighton, Brighton to Southampton, Southampton to Bournemouth. Between Southampton and Bournemouth hoards get on so there's a mob on the train. We get a taxi from Bournemouth station to the pub nearest the ground, we get tanked up further, not drunk and disorderly, we've consumed a lot of alcohol, but we are still in charge of our faculties but your inhibitions are loosened.

So we walk with the hoards, it's ten minutes before kick-off, we walk past the main entrance, there's a guy with a cap and a sash and Chris went, 'Here, watch this.' He walked up to the door and they opened the door of the main entrance so we just walked straight in, we had shirts on and trousers, you know, dressed nicely.

'In there, gentleman, sponsors down that way, sir.' Walked down this corridor, up these steps, right into the top – into the executive boxes.

'Drink sir?'

'Lager please.'

'Yes, sir.'

'Free drinks. This is good, isn't it, come to Bournemouth, thanks Bournemouth, nice little place.'

A guy comes into the bar, 'The game's about to kick off, please take your seats in the stand.'

'We've, um, we don't know what seats we've got.'

So he said, 'Follow me to the glass-fronted executive box.'

Television in the corner, sitting in this box thinking, 'Can't believe this, free day out, free executive box, free drink, lovely, thank you Bournemouth' – such a shame they're in the state they're in now! Perhaps if more people paid for their drinks they wouldn't be in the state they're in!

So the game kicked off and I said, 'I can't stand this executive box, I'm a terrace man, I've got to be down there amongst the people.' So we come out of the executive box and were ushered into two seats adjacent to the directors box in the big stand. Half-time in the bar, free drinks, more free drinks, second half seats in the box again.

At this point in the second half, Jones, Bournemouth striker races into the box, appears to drop his left hand, apparently brings the ball under control with his hand, slots it in the net. I said, 'I ain't having that, that's handball, how comes the referee hadn't seen that!' So I'm up down the aisle, over the wall, on the pitch, I got Jones round the throat, 'You bastard, that was handball!' He's going, 'Fuck off, Brighton.' I've got him round the neck and next thing I've got stewards all over me carting me off the pitch.

Of course, reality sets in very quickly, doesn't it, and you think, 'Shit, what have I done? I'm going to get banned for life now from all football grounds, invading the pitch, attacking a player, shit, what a prat.'

Of course, I'm ushered out of the ground, over the wall, through the stand and they're all going, 'Piss off, you Brighton scum, get him out of here, you bastard' and I was just grinning and thinking, 'Yeah, you ain't seen nothing yet, mate.'

So the steward's taken me out, he was a really nice guy, I said, 'If you let me go I ain't going to run off, fair cop, I've done wrong.' He said, 'Why did you do that mate?' I said, 'Look, the club, we're in shit – last year you were in the same position, you're going bust and got nowhere to play. It's frustration, I'm so angry, our bloody board don't want to know.' He said, 'Oh I do agree with you, mate, but you're a bloody prat, I've got to hand you over to the police – nothing personal.' I said, 'No, it's all right' and we shook each other's hands. 'Good luck to you, mate, I hope you do well.'

And I was just going up the steps to the police wagon and they're all in there banging like caged animals and I'm thinking, 'Shit, this is it, fine, ban' – and then the steward comes running out shouting, 'They're on the pitch, they're on the pitch, Brighton are on the pitch.' The next steward goes, 'Go on, release yourself – fuck off, mate.'

So I just walked straight back into the Brighton end and said, 'What are these bastards on the pitch? What are they doing?'

43

6. One Liam Brady!

The *Argus* – 20 November 1995:
BRADY GOES!
Manager Liam Brady sensationally left the Albion today.
He parted company with the football club by mutual consent.
Brady finally conceded defeat to the club's off-field crisis this morning and made a thinly veiled attack on the Albion hierarchy.
Reading from a prepared statement, Brady said, 'After speaking to the chairman, Bill Archer, yesterday afternoon, it was mutually agreed that I should stand down as manager of the club. I firmly believe if a manager and team are to achieve good results with limited resources the club must have a stable and harmonious environment. This has not been possible this season for reasons beyond my control. I wish to thank the supporters, staff and the players for the support they have given me during my time at the club.'
Albion Chief Executive David Bellotti said, 'On behalf of the club and directors, I want to place on record our appreciation of the two years' service Liam Brady's given to the Seagulls and I want to wish him well for the future.'

BILL SWALLOW: I remember the moment when I discovered that he was going to come to the club – I couldn't believe it. I'm afraid I could believe it when I heard that he was going. It was desperately sad because it was the moment when all the troubles behind seemed to be coming out in front. And Liam Brady – one of the jewels in Brighton's history – was here for such a short time, I mean it was a colossal appointment, it was almost unbelievable.

And it seemed to me that if that sort of person could be sacrificed, then what was going on behind the scenes was clearly appalling and it was just such a lamentable waste – it really was.

NIGEL SUMMERS: I didn't blame him for resigning. Because I couldn't work for them people and I think he had come to the end of his tether and fair enough, fair play to him. I wasn't convinced how much of a good manager he was anyway. I think that he was a big name figurehead which was good for attracting young players, he was obviously keen on the youth set-up, but

44

I didn't see him do a great deal to affect the performance of the players on the pitch, in my opinion.

IAN HART: The real wrong turning for me was when they got rid of Liam Brady because he was the finest manager this club has ever had and probably will ever have.

JAN MERRITT: It was very sad, but I can understand what was behind it. He felt he couldn't carry on under those conditions.

LIAM BRADY: To be fair to Archer, when I took the job I was told it was going to be 18 months to two years before I saw any money to buy players, but it would be forthcoming as long as I could keep the thing fairly stable and on track. So I was happy enough with that and I always tried to relay that to the fans, you know, it wasn't going to happen overnight – but I think we all got a feeling that it might happen after my first season.

But it started to go sadly wrong, we got knocked out of the Cup by Kingstonian, right bang smack in the middle of a poor run when we were struggling to get a result and we were tumbling down the table. I was always searching around for players, always on loan. I never had any money to buy, and we finished half way again. You know, as far as I was concerned that was a good result for the resources that were at our disposal.

DAVID BELLOTTI (in an interview in the fanzine *On The Up*): 'There was money available for players. Liam Brady knew he had money to spend.'
'How much?'
'I can't tell you that for political reasons.'

LIAM BRADY: At the end of that season, '94–95, that was where the rifts started with me and Archer. We were playing up north somewhere and I'd been told by Bellotti that Archer was going to tell me I'd have money to spend next season. I went to that meeting and Archer said, 'There is no money, in fact, you're going to have to trim your budget.' And I looked at Bellotti and he didn't know what to say to me because only a couple of days before he's told me at the meeting I'd be told I'd have a few hundred thousand pounds to spend – and Archer told me I'd got to cut the budget. In fact, Archer told me I'd have to trim a member of my staff. 'But it'll all come good in the end, when everything falls into place.' He said to me, 'You'll do well to stop the team from going down next season, I know you will.' Those were his words.

GERRY RYAN (ex-Brighton player and Brady's assistant manager, from a *Gull's Eye* interview January '96): There was no way we were going to survive the

'95–96 season with 19 players, a lot of them first-year pros. The way we did it, which really galls me now – Liam, Jimmy and myself took a cut in wages to get one player.

LIAM BRADY: I came away from that meeting with Archer, I didn't say anything publicly, but after a week or so I said to Gerry Ryan, 'I'm going now. I've gone as far as I can go here and we're only going to go under – a manager lives or dies by results – because we're going to be worse off next season. The team needs improving, the Fosters and John Byrnes are getting older, we need to buy some players.' And Gerry and George talked me out of it. I was on for resigning after the home game against Wycombe at the end of that season and explain to the fans that I'd enjoyed my time here but the way it was I wasn't going to be able to give them what they wanted. And I wish I had done that now, I regret that I didn't do it.

When we came back for pre-season, we had been told this was to be our last season at the Goldstone, I asked Archer to come down from Crewe, or wherever he is, to speak to the players, because the players are reading in the *Argus* day in and day out what's going to happen. And he came down with Stanley and Bellotti and it didn't satisfy anyone, he just waffled his way through. He said to them they definitely wouldn't be at the Goldstone at the end of that season, they would be leaving. But he didn't convince anybody, gee anyone up.

And we started the season off very badly – which I anticipated.

STUART STORER: We did have one meeting when Liam was here to try and settle the players but what was said in that meeting everyone just took tongue in cheek, because they didn't really trust what was going on, what we were being told. It was a pointless meeting to me. They seemed to have a reasonable excuse for everything that was going on. At the end of the day you can either take it or leave it and I was one of them that left it.

LIAM BRADY: Bellotti started coming up with all these rules – he tried to stop the players parking in the carpark. He told the little gate man Jock to keep the gates locked and not let anyone in and I'd come along and say, 'Open the gate Jock' and he'd open the gate and all the players would come in and when Bellotti would come in he'd go absolutely potty!

TIM CARDER: I remember Brady coming to a meeting at Southwick. He had to be quite careful about what he said but there was no misconstruing that he was anti the board. It all came to focus over a minibus the youth club were given which Bellotti refused to pay the insurance for. This absolutely disgusted Liam and in the end the Supporters Club paid the insurance for it.

He really lambasted into Archer and Bellotti that night. I think that was only about two or three weeks before he resigned.

LIAM BRADY: Many people thought that David Bellotti as chief executive was an absolute joke — I had to persuade the coach company to take us up north one time because they hadn't paid their bill. The driver said, 'I've come today, Liam, but I'm not taking the team up to wherever we were going.' I said, 'What do you mean?' We were all standing waiting to get on the bus on a Friday afternoon. He said, 'Well, I haven't been paid for three months.' So I rang Archer and said the coach driver is saying he's not going to take us because he hasn't had his money and he said, 'I told Bellotti to look after the priorities.'

ATTILA THE STOCKBROKER: Brady realised that his hands were tied behind his back and whatever possibilities he had envisaged were being denied to him. There he was with a proven track record, one of the great players in football history — respected throughout the game, intelligent, articulate, being treated basically as some little office boy.

LIZ COSTA: The team started losing and morale started getting worse and Liam couldn't seem to instil any confidence into anybody — least of all into himself.

LIAM BRADY: I remember away to Canvey Island, on a Sunday, we very nearly lost the match. I was quite pleased with the result because I knew the atmosphere at the club at the time was diabolical and I knew we'd beat them back at the Goldstone. The following week we lost 3–0 at home, Archer rang me and said, 'What's going on?' I said, 'What do you mean "what's going on", you tell me what's going on.' Archer said, 'What's going on on the field — the players are playing rubbish and I've heard that you're not putting in the time on the training ground.' I said, 'You're never here, who's told you that?' And he said, 'Well, that's what I've heard.' So I said, 'Well, tell me who's told you that?' And he said, 'No, I don't want to tell you who's told me.' He said, 'Well, you've got to fight it out. Are you tough enough to fight it out?' And I said, 'Quite honestly, Bill, I don't know whether I want to fight it out because of all the stuff that's going on. Didn't you tell me up at Crewe that I'd do well to keep this team up next year?' And he said, 'No, no I never said that, this team is obviously good enough to stay up.' And I said, 'Well, I'll think about it, Bill,' and I rang back and said, 'I resign. I don't want to work with you any more. I didn't want to work with you a few months ago and I wish I'd resigned then.' That was it.

I went in the next morning and I called a meeting with George Petchey and Jimmy Case and Gerry Ryan, and I said I thought I'd been forced into the situation where I had to resign, and I don't know what's going to happen, but this is what they will do – Gerry, you'll be sacked, because Gerry and I were like that. I said they'll offer you the job, Jim, and I said George, I don't quite honestly know. So Jimmy said, 'What shall I do?' And I said, 'Jim, I can't answer that but you know the people you are working for, the problems I've had with Bellotti and you know the lies I've been told by Archer. It's not the circumstances that you really should take a job in, but you have your mortgage to pay, you have your family to look after, so you do what you want to do.' And that was it. And Greg Stanley appeared at the ground for the first time in months with his arm around Jimmy and he became manager.

TIM BOHANNON (actor): Liam Brady's left foot was like the Hermitage in Saint Petersburg, that's how cultured he was.

IAN HART: I think if you've got people within the club like Bellotti, as I said to Brady when we sponsored a game, 'Alex Ferguson would struggle at this club.'

LIAM BRADY: Archer told me at that very first meeting when I went for the job interview that Bellotti was a nonentity; he told me several times, try not to let him get up your nose because he doesn't mean anything. But in the end he did mean a lot. He meant that Archer was going to be protected from the flak that was going to come his way, so he was a very important player as far as Archer was concerned.

7. 'What the fuck is going on?' *(Chant on the North Stand 1995–96)*

DAVID BELLOTTI (programme notes, 14 October 1995): 'The club could not be in safer hands, please trust us.'

PAUL SAMRAH: When the May 1995 accounts were filed we looked at the £600,000 loan that Greg Stanley had made to the club. It had clocked up £381,000 of interest in three years – which included a £250,000 penalty because the club had been unable to meet its interest payments.

Forget who the loan was from – I think it was ineptitude. If you have got a loan you do everything in your power to meet the payment terms of that loan, especially when you are going to be hit with a £250,000 penalty! If you don't meet the interest charge – £45,000 a year or a little over £10,000 a quarter – you're going to get stung with the £250,000 penalty charge. Wouldn't you make every effort to pay that £10,000 interest on a quarterly basis?

The *Argus* – 7 October 1995:

WHAT A RESULT!

The Albion has backed down following a series of recent exposures.

The move comes just one week after the Football Association asked for a dossier on the crisis-hit Seagulls. We revealed how rules preventing directors making money from the sale of the Goldstone Ground had been removed from the club's original constitution.

The news outraged fans and councillors. But yesterday the club announced that the crucial 'no profit' clause had been reinstated.

The Albion has also agreed to:

- Allow council accountants to inspect the club's books.
- Lift its ban on the *Argus* entering the Goldstone.
- Reveal more details of the £7.4 million deal to sell the ground to a property development company.

Mr Archer told the *Argus*, 'I'm hopeful that by the end of November you will be printing in your newspaper a complete drawing of where we are going to play football in the future.'

The *Argus* – 20 October 1995:

Two pledges made to fans by Albion chairman Bill Archer are falling by the wayside.

Archer was hopeful of revealing the site and a drawing of the Seagulls proposed new stadium by next month.

WRONG

Hove Council leader Ivor Caplin said, 'It is not possible. We have agreed that the first stage of relocation is a consultant's study and we cannot have a planning application until we consider the impact of that study.'

Archer also told the *Argus* everything possible will be done to make sure Albion's temporary home is in Sussex.

WRONG

Half-hearted plans to ground-share with Crawley appear doomed, a bid for Hove greyhound stadium has been rejected and the club have no other alternative to Portsmouth.

A consultant's study into potential stadium sites follows a two-hour meeting between Caplin and Archer yesterday.

The report financed by Brighton and Hove Councils rather than the club will examine half a dozen possibilities.

Caplin says the findings will be published by Christmas.

IVOR CAPLIN: It's a very interesting document.

At the time it did give us an overview of the sites available and what we were trying to show was our commitment to trying working together and that was never shown by the then board.

I suppose we kept the report under fairly close lock and key – it looks now to have been the right decision. At the time it was a very difficult decision to make: I'm a believer in freedom of information, I'm a believer in open government; so is Steve Bassam, leader of Brighton Council and there was the two of us saying we can't actually publish this report. It was a very difficult decision for both of us in terms of our individual political beliefs and for Labour's political beliefs, but I think with the benefit of hindsight we took the right decision.

The report is now available to Dick Knight and McAlpine's.

The *Argus* – 7 December 1995

CLEAR OFF!

Hove Council leader Ivor Caplin has called for the men who run the Albion to quit.

He urged them to go after announcing that the Seagulls can stay at the Goldstone for another year.

> At yesterday's press conference, the Council revealed it has negotiated a
> new deal with Chartwell plc, the property developers who bought
> the Goldstone for £7.4 million.
> This will delay building on the site until June 1997 on condition that
> Chartwell can build a food store.
> Councillor Caplin believes the club's owners should step down and let
> fresh blood take over.

IVOR CAPLIN: At a press conference I inferred that I would like to see local people running the football club, which I have to say is something that I agree with — I don't think you can be part of the local community if you live 300 miles away. And my good friends at the *Evening Argus* managed to turn this into 'Clear Off' as a headline which raged all the next day. Mr Archer took exception to this and the outcome of it was that the next week I received a writ.

I think from the board's point of view it was a low point — if you start suing local Council leaders for representing public opinion, which is what it was, I think it just shows how out of touch with that public opinion they were. It didn't involve Bellotti I have to say, it just involved Bill Archer and Greg Stanley and Greg Stanley has since had his name withdrawn from the writ and denied that he knew anything about it. I have to say that I fully and unreservedly believe what Greg Stanley has told me, I don't think he did know anything about it.

I think Archer's aim was to stop me speaking out and I'm afraid that as an elected representative I have more right to speak out on the issue, as the leader of the Council, than other people who want to speak out such as Mr Bellotti who is unelected to the post of chief executive.

What it showed was that the tactic was to try and bully rather than to work together. I think their concept of partnership working was 'let's work as partners if you do what I say'.

> The *Argus* — 22 December 1995:
> Albion have unveiled ambitious plans for a £32 million stadium and
> sports complex at Toad's Hole Valley in Hove.
> What are Albion playing at in putting a fanciful planning application for
> Toad's Hole Valley?
> The club does not own the land. The scheme will not be passed by
> Hove Council as it contravenes all planning rules for the area.
> And where will the money come from?
> To succeed and stay in business, Albion needs the support of the two
> Councils in Brighton and Hove.
> Yet Hove's leader Ivor Caplin has been served with a writ which if

> intended to shut him up certainly will not succeed.
>
> The club has also not waited for the study commissioned by the Councils at their expense into the siting for a future ground.
>
> It is inexplicable, as is so much about the Albion these days. Co-operation not confrontation is the key to success.
>
> Yet Albion seem to alienate almost everyone, most of all their long-suffering fans who will know that this scheme is pie in the sky rather than toad in the hole.

GERRY RYAN: You're looking around and asking why? All the way down the line you're asking why? All the way along the line you're hoping something good is going to come out of it.

Everything I'd seen worried me.

The plans changed so many times it probably means there wasn't a plan in the beginning.

DECEMBER 1995 – OCTOBER 1996

8. Toad in the Hole

> *Brighton and Hove Leader* – 28 December 1995
>
> Brighton and Hove Albion Football Club have announced plans for a new 30,000-seater football stadium on the 90-acre Toad's Hole Valley site in Hove.
>
> David Bellotti, the club's deputy chairman and chief executive, unveiled the controversial multi-million pound scheme 'to take the club into the 21st century.'
>
> He declared, 'It has the tremendous advantage that, given planning permission, it can be fully funded without financial help from the local authorities.'
>
> Both Brighton and Hove Council leaders said they would immediately refer the scheme to the Department of the Environment to nip it in the bud.
>
> 'The club needs something like £50 million for the scheme,' said Hove leader Ivor Caplin. 'A large slice of this must come from retail shopping. Offices simply do not command the premium required.'
>
> Mr Bellotti said the scheme was the culmination of two years' work by the club to identify a site which can host a Premier League team.
>
> 'It is up to Hove Council to decide whether they can support our vision for the future,' he added.

PAUL WHELCH (article in *Gull's Eye*, February 1996): The lame duck planning proposal to develop Toad's Hole Valley depended crucially on trust. The club were asking Hove Council, in particular, to trust the board that finance would be provided to develop a stadium and sustain the club at the stadium. However, the decision of the Highways Agency to oppose the application will, almost certainly, mean that the planning application will be rejected locally and at any subsequent public inquiry.

Where would the money come from? This was among a number of issues raised by members of the Supporters Club committee with David Bellotti at the Goldstone on 30 January 1996.

Supporters were reassured that the club planned to take good care of the badgers currently nesting in the north-west corner of the valley by building an elaborate web of tunnels leading away from the 30,000 all-seater stadium. The financial plans for the project were somewhat more disguised.

Essentially, the club's plan was for the owners to buy Toad's Hole Valley, recreate the San Siro south of the A27, together with an on-site sports complex and a 'commercial' development, lease the commercial site and win the FA Premiership.

The main source of funds would be a cash injection from the owners. By my reckoning the site will cost £10 million, the development of the stadium a further £20 million and the peripheral developments another £5 million or so. Even if £15 million were to be recovered through sponsorship, commercial franchising and soft/lottery monies, this would require a cash injection from Greg Stanley of around £20 million. The cornerstone of Bellotti's case is that he trusts the owners to come up with the cash.

Bellotti is asking us to trust him that a bankrupt club will be born again in the new stadium. Money will be invested in the team not because other costs would fall nor because the club would start trading at a profit. No, the money would be found simply because it would be a real shame to have a Third Division club playing in such a magnificent stadium – according to Mr Bellotti, the owners would have to buy a team to fill the stadium.

Of one thing I have no doubt, David Bellotti trusts his employers.

9. 'We'll never go to Pompey!' *(Chant on the North Stand 1995–96)*

TIM CARDER: Ivor Caplin negotiated a deal with Chartwell, who had bought the Goldstone, for the Albion to stay at the ground for an extra season. He negotiated deals on planning permission: if permission was given for the land to be used as a food warehouse or supermarket they would let the Albion stay rent free for a year; if no food permission was given – which was by far the most likely – they would agree to lease the ground back to the club for the following season for £480,000. Why Archer, Stanley and Bellotti had never actually negotiated to start with is one of the big questions. There was no response from the club.

IVOR CAPLIN: It is absolutely ludicrous that the Council negotiated an extension of the ground with Chartwell – we did that – we had to circulate 5,000 leaflets ourselves to get the message across directly to the supporters.

PAUL SAMRAH: Chartwell made the offer and it was something like £480,000 a year as a charge, but Bellotti's argument was that we're going to lose money if we take up that offer – he said we had to go to Portsmouth because we'll make more money that way. That was totally untrue. Regardless of how much it was to hire Portsmouth, the fact is the fans would not go there to make it economically worth while. By staying at the Goldstone ground, by getting the marketing going for one year, you could boost the numbers.

LIZ COSTA: We had a game against Hull which was just after Chartwell had worked out a lease-back figure of £480,000. The Council had worked out how much it was going to cost for that year if we went to Portsmouth, taking into account the cost of transporting everybody down there, the lost revenue in terms of no season tickets being sold, and no money coming through the turnstile, and the extra policing that it was going to cost. It was going to be £1 million.

   The Council said would I get people to hand out leaflets to try to explain to people why Portsmouth was not a good idea and why we must put pressure on Bellotti to stay at the Goldstone for another year.

TIM CARDER: I was round the East Terrace in my usual spot handing out these leaflets. Now there was a lady pensioner, Peggy Thick, she's a member of the Supporters Club, handing them out outside the West Stand and some blokes started trying to wrench the leaflets off her. I think this lady is in her seventies and eventually people started gathering round and told them to lay off her and Liz Costa was amongst them. Bellotti summoned Liz into his office and basically gave her a dressing down.

LIZ COSTA: I was outside the West Stand handing out leaflets. I was actually in the middle of the road and at the time I had three policemen looking over my shoulder reading it. They wouldn't actually physically take one from me but they were reading it. And all of a sudden, John Back, the security officer, came along and he dragged me inside. I didn't have to go but I thought, 'I'm playing this absolutely by the book. I'm not going to cause a scene' and for twenty minutes there was a shrieking match with Bellotti. It wasn't just a shouting match – he completely lost his rag. He was totally out of control.

   In the end he said, 'Where do you watch the game from?' I said, 'I beg your pardon?' He said, 'Where do you watch the game?' And I said, 'Well, it just shows how bloody observant you are because I stand approximately 25 feet from where you sit. And I have stood there for the last 20 years – unlike you who's been here five minutes.' And he said, 'Well, from now on, you're going to have to pay to get in.' I said, 'I've got a season ticket.' And he said, 'That will be withdrawn.' And I said, 'I get that for selling lottery tickets.' He said, 'It's only a concession.'

Eventually I went out and there was the biggest cheer.

TIM CARDER: This really summed up the paranoia of the man at the time. He took her season ticket from her, saying it cost them more in administration for Liz's ticket than she brought into the club. Liz did loads and loads of selling of lottery tickets and brought in loads of money for the club. What sort of encouragement is that for anyone who goes out selling tickets on behalf of the club?

LIZ COSTA: That was the day I completely turned. That completely changed my whole attitude as to how I was going to conduct myself and whatever I did. Okay, I wasn't going to run on the pitch but I determined from then on to destroy him, because that just showed the calibre of the man.

DAVID BELLOTTI – matchday programme, 16 March 1996: Our business is football and we have two objectives, the first to build a team and the second to obtain a new stadium; paying half a million pounds for one season would undermine both those objectives.

NORTH STAND: 'One Ivor Caplin, there's only one Ivor Caplin!'

> The *Argus* telephone poll, 21 March 1996:
> 1,730 against attending games regularly at Fratton Park
> 41 for.

TIM CARDER: As far as we knew from programme notes and everything we'd heard, the club would not be signing a deal with Chartwell, they were still relying on the Council to give food permission.

10. 'Bellotti Out!'

The *Argus* – 16 April 1996:
FA GET TOUGH
The Football Association are turning the heat up on the men who run
  relegation-bound Albion. They are writing to chief executive David
  Bellotti demanding answers to three key questions.

WHY have the club rejected an offer from Chartwell which would allow
  them to stay at the Goldstone next season?

HOW can they justify, in terms of cost, their alternative to ground-share
  with Portsmouth?

WHY have they repeatedly ignored the FA's suggestion that the profit
  from the £8 million sale of the Goldstone to Chartwell should be
  placed in an independent trust fund?

Bellotti says £480,000 for the season is too much and the club have
  offered £200,000 instead.

This was instantly rejected by Chartwell.

They say their figure is non-negotiable and they have given Albion a
  deadline of April 30 to accept, which is three days after the final
  home fixture against York and just four days before the Seagulls' last
  game of the season at Walsall.

Otherwise the bulldozers will be moving in.

FA spokesman Steve Double said, 'It is a worrying situation which is
  causing us increasing concern with each passing day.'

ARGUS OPINION
A frightening game of brinkmanship is being acted out by the men who
  run the Albion. In 15 days, the bulldozers could move in and
  demolish the Goldstone unless a rent can be agreed with Chartwell
  that will allow the Albion one more season. A proud club does not
  deserve to be treated like this. It is a situation that should never have
  been allowed to develop. Those involved should be ashamed of
  themselves.

Albion Almanac – match report, 20 April 1996:
Albion 1 Carlisle 0
There is continual barracking of David Bellotti and the board in general
  throughout what was quite an entertaining match. In fact, when the

> chant goes up 'If you all hate Bellotti clap your hands', there is prolonged applause from all corners of the ground. In the first half Jimmy Case restrains two supporters and persuades them not to run on the pitch.
>
> At the final whistle there is a brief lull before angry fans run on to the pitch from the North Stand and North West Terrace. The police and stewards adopt a low profile during the demonstration by an estimated 600–1,000 people.
>
> However, some fans climb into the directors box, hurl cushions around and pull down fittings.
>
> They then attempt to storm the boardroom but the confrontation is ended 35 minutes after the match finishes by police reinforcements.
>
> It is rumoured that Bellotti, who inflamed passions by appearing in his regular seat a few minutes after the second half had started, was rushed out of the ground rapidly after the final whistle.

LIZ COSTA: That was when we first realised that we were getting through to other supporters because the Carlisle fans came down on to the pitch with us and they were shirt-swapping – and that was when we realised that in fact we weren't alone, that we had got friends out there.

But having said that, that was when people did try to break into the boardroom and there was quite a lot of damage. It was obvious it could get out of hand if it wasn't kept under some sort of control.

STEWART WEIR: I was outside overlooking. I was quite shocked at what was going on – certainly no one was expecting that – but it was the game before what we thought was the very last ever game at the ground and still there were no answers. There was just this silence and this regurgitating of rubbish from the club. You should have seen the police's faces – doors, windows smashed. I'm sure they were scared because there were probably 50 or 75-odd fans storming in there with one person on their minds. A very scary moment but nothing compared with what was going to happen.

11. Everybody's friend

GREG STANLEY – BISA public meeting at the Concorde bar, Brighton, 22 April 1996: We will go to Portsmouth over my dead body. I love this club through and through. My word is my honour.

HECKLER – BISA public meeting at the Concorde bar, Brighton, 22 April 1996: You'd better not be lying or we're taking the place apart on Saturday.

PAUL SAMRAH: Of course, on Monday of that week we had the infamous meeting at the Concorde bar with Greg Stanley, where he made a total fool of himself saying that he had resigned as director and I was able to totally refute that and said, 'You haven't, you are still director of the board.'

JOHN CAMPBELL: Stanley's got no courage. The minute problems start to arrive he runs for the first bunker. I think that he's always wanted to be loved by the supporters, he goes to the big meetings down in Brighton and he knew that if he was tainted by any of this, it's right on his doorstep and Archer was 300 miles away, big difference. I think underneath the table he still had control, I don't see any reason why Archer should have officially had the controlling interest apart from the fact that he needed to say it was him calling the tune, I'm convinced of it.

ATTILA THE STOCKBROKER: I genuinely think that Greg didn't know. I don't ever underestimate Greg's ability to not know things. I want to see Greg separated from Brighton and Hove Albion FC in terms of any involvement. I think it's fair enough of him to leave his money in the club as long as Archer has got nothing to do with it but he doesn't want the kind of day-to-day involvement which is commensurate with having that kind of financial involvement. If he's going to be one of the major investors, he's got to have a hands-on attitude and Greg doesn't want a hands-on attitude. The irony of Greg's position is this – his position is, 'Yes, I've got this money but I'm a socialist and I love football and it's a fans' game, so I don't want to be the big boss man. I don't want that.' But the logic of that position turned into, sadly, 'So I will allow other people to run my control and represent me – people who do not love this club and are not part of it.' And that's what happened. So, ironically, by taking up a position of non-aggressive, non-macho, non-posturing business-

60

man-football-club-owner type, he allowed Archer to do it. As I've said before many times, the legal position is that Archer gained control through his negotiations with the other directors but that was as a result of the fact that Greg Stanley was never prepared to have a shareholding commensurate with his investment, which again is because of the political attitude that he's got. So, ironically, it was his kind of socialistic attitude towards football which meant that these people that we hate so much were able to gain control.

12. 'We've sold the ground, and now we're going down' *(Chant from the North Stand, 1996)*

> *Albion Almanac* – Tuesday, 23 April 1996
> **Notts County 2 Albion 1**
> Albion's relegation to the League's basement was confirmed by defeat at promotion chasing Notts County.

NIGEL SUMMERS: There was only two issues, one was saving the ground and the other was kicking out Archer and Bellotti. We could have gone down two divisions that year and I don't think we'd have noticed. The penalty for going down this year was big. The penalty going down last year – I mean what's the difference between the Third and Fourth Division? Sod all.

> *Albion Almanac* – Thursday, 25 April 1996:
> On BBC Southern Counties Radio, Chartwell's development director, Nick Light, confirms that the deadline of midday on 30 April is absolute. Once that time passes without Albion signing the lease, 'pretty irreversible processes' will be started and the club will have to vacate the Goldstone by the end of May.

TIM CARDER: Bellotti in his programme notes at the Carlisle game said that if food permission was granted for the site then the club would stay rent-free. But Chartwell actually said that there is a deadline on the 30 April and if you do not sign by then, regardless of whether you get food permission or not, we will start all the necessary things to get the ground demolished and the retail warehouses built. So again that was a distortion of the truth – it was wrong.

13. Bill Archer

JOHN CAMPBELL: I phoned Bill Archer at his home in frustration on the morning of the York City game as I was genuinely concerned about crowd reaction. I appealed to him to realise that while he controlled the club he would never get the support of the fans, the Council, potential sponsors or the media.

He replied, 'That's tough fucking luck because I own it lock, stock and barrel and there's nothing you or any of those fuckers with half a brain can do about it.'

I asked to whom he was referring and he said, 'The supporters – or the so-called supporters, like you, they've only got half a brain and all they are doing is trying to destroy the club – you and them are not proper supporters, just troublemakers.'

He got really excited and angry (the first time I had heard him in this mode) and slammed the phone down on me.

14. 'A different kind of riot'

BRIGHTON AND HOVE ALBION v YORK CITY, 27 APRIL 1996

TIM CARDER: There was a carnival atmosphere; I was on the East Terrace, as I had been for the previous 30-odd years; people were singing 'We love you, Goldstone – we do'. There were cries for Peter Ward, Kit Napier and Tug Wilson – who was around in the 1920s! It was a happy atmosphere to start with.

BILL SWALLOW: From my eyrie in the West Stand I knew, like everybody else knew, that there was going to be a pitch invasion. I didn't know when it was going to happen – I gather others did. But it was clearly going to happen.

ATTILA THE STOCKBROKER: I knew it was going to happen and I wasn't surprised. We knew that game was not going to finish. How quickly it happened and what did happen – that was quite surprising in that sense.

TONY HYLANDS: We were all saying, 'Fuck it, last game of the season, let's go on the pitch. What can they do – kick us out of the league. We're bottom of the league anyway.' We must admit it was planned for the 55th minute and not the 15th so I think there was a breakdown in communications.

STUART ADAMS: The rumour was that it was going to happen at 3.16 pm and it did.

TONY HYLANDS: We all said in the pub that we were going to go on the pitch and I'd been saying the whole season, each week it was a joke, 'What you having, Tone?' 'I'm having that net – Christ, 30 years of investment financially and emotionally, I'm going to have my souvenir.'
As soon as I see them come on I went down the front, got on the pitch, hung on the crossbar on the North Stand goal – you can see me, any news clip, yellow tee-shirt, jeans, hanging on the North Stand crossbar. It's a joke and the next thing there's eight guys on the crossbar and it snapped.
The aim was just to go on the pitch. There was a lot of people larking about on the goals, having a laugh. There was too many people on the bar, with the sheer weight it broke it and then it was too late. The game was never going to kick off again. If the goals hadn't have broken the pitch would have cleared and that game would have carried on.

STUART ADAMS: I think it had to be done and if it hadn't been done on that scale – and let's face it, it was destructive but it wasn't violent – then nobody would have given a monkey's what we done. It had to be done and I don't think we did enough. We did it too late – that should have been done in January of that year, January '96 rather than April.

TIM CARDER: I remember seeing people come on from the South West Terrace and then the North Stand basically emptied on to the pitch. Police let them on which I think was the right thing to do, everyone knew there was going to be some sort of action. But it was quite traumatic, actually, watching the crossbars being destroyed. I thought that was a very potent symbol of the football club, the crossbars and the goals, seeing them destroyed. It brought tears to my eyes and I remember standing there for at least 45 minutes just leaning against the barrier just watching everything that was going on in front of me. I didn't go on the pitch, not because I didn't want to, but I just felt a bit numb, really, not knowing what to do and thinking how could it have got to this where our own fans were wrecking our ground. I think it was pretty unprecedented, there had been match abandonments but not really for any reason like that. There was no violence towards anyone – it was all directed at the board, who weren't there. In Tottenham in '78 there was pure thuggery – this was a desperate cry of 'help' from Albion fans.

STEWART WEIR: Everyone came on the pitch and there was certainly an element there that were interested in trouble. There were certainly faces there that I've never seen at the ground before. It was as if there was a very small minority of probably 20 out of the 10,000 that were there.

TONY HYLANDS: There were faces I didn't know but there was a lot of Moulscombe boys there and there was a lot of old firm. People who had not been there since the '70s were there to say this is the last game at the Goldstone. There may have been infiltration but I personally don't believe there was because it was planned by Brighton supporters, two-fold: one, it was a souvenir hunt and two, it was 'well, if that isn't going to get the media and the FA involved, nothing will'.

PAUL CAMILLIN (bank clerk, writer for *Gull's Eye, Scars and Stripes* fanzine): Everyone said there was a hooligan element there, but that was bollocks! There was a lot of Brighton fans that hadn't been there in a long time, sort of got the call, as it was. We also gained one hell of a lot of respect with what happened at the York game. I think a lot of people, regardless of what the media said, saw what was going on and read between the lines. Most people could say it was a riot, and troublemakers, and people still come up to me and say, 'That big riot at Brighton.' I just say it wasn't a riot, we stood up and said, 'You are not taking the fucking piss. Sort it out.'

JAN MERRITT: I felt sorry for the York City supporters to have come down for the game and to have it come to a premature end like that. That must have been dreadful. And the worst thing was seeing the destruction – seeing the goal posts being broken. I felt like crying at the time because at that point we knew that the game was never going to restart and to have come down to watch a match and for it to finish like that was very sad, although I can understand what was behind it and why it happened.

TIM BOHANNON: The York supporters at the so-called riot were absolutely brilliant – the solidarity. I always thought that if enough people kept these protests going we could make a difference.

PAUL SAMRAH: We went over to Tony Millard, who was having an argument with one of the spectators who leant over and said, 'Oh you're supporting the board.' And Millard was saying, 'No I'm not, I'm not' and then he grabbed hold of the microphone and said, 'And on Wednesday there will be the Steve Foster testimonial game' which made everyone just burst out laughing and probably in an ironic way helped diffuse the situation.

TONY MILLARD: I upset a few supporters by saying on the radio at the time that I felt the scenes were disgraceful. I do accept that the supporters reckoned they had a point to prove and reckoned that they were being totally shafted and one has to appreciate the strength of feeling and understand that. It got Brighton the wrong type of publicity, but it did get the efforts of supporters publicity for their cause. Perhaps I shouldn't have said on the air at the time 'these scenes were absolutely disgraceful', the scenes were no credit to football but I believe that they were premeditated and brought upon the club entirely by the lack of foresight.

JAN SWALLOW: I thought something was going to happen and it was a question of when it was going to happen. I thought people would just get the game stopped but I didn't think people would be breaking goalposts and that kind of thing, I mean, that just made me cry, you know, it was so upsetting. But actually, it really did bring things to a head, didn't it?

TIM PITT: I actually think, from the way things turned out, wrecking the goalposts enabled the police to diffuse the situation quite easily – there wasn't any pressure to get the game restarted after that happened so they could actually let the riot run its course.

LIAM BRADY: I think the fans conducted themselves with a lot of dignity and control. I think the scenes on television of York City were not scenes of people intent on mayhem and bloodshed, it was a different kind of riot. Okay, so the goalposts got pulled down but it was out of frustration. It was really fans saying, 'There's nothing more we can do, let's go on to the pitch and let people know what's going on at our club', but you know that should be to their credit.

STEWART WEIR: It was an incredible day. It was an incredible sight – you know, people were sitting on the floor and the only thing they were missing was the strawberries, cream and bottle of champagne. It was surreal. I remember the York fans – I went over to the York side and they were clapping and yelling 'Archer Out.' And I remember thinking, 'Are they shouting because they don't want an invasion of a few hundred fans into their end or are they saying this because they understand and they really don't mind the game being abandoned because here is something that goes far beyond just an average-sized club having troubles?' This was about fans saying to football club owners, 'We're not going to take this any more; we are the people that inherit this club when you've done what you want to do with the club. We have to pick up the shit when you leave.'

SARAH WATTS: The TV was going on about the riots – and you looked at it and there were people walking around with their kids – it wasn't a riot. I think one goalpost would have been enough. All of a sudden it was on Sky news, it was a big thing. I remember interviews on *Match of the Day* and they said about the terrible scenes at the Goldstone.

TIM CARDER: It was headline news on the BBC national news and went all round the world. Of course it got branded as a riot by some papers, which technically it probably was, but not a riot in the way we normally associate the word. It was a peaceful destruction, if you can have such a thing, of the goals and a cry for help.

PAUL CAMILLIN: At the time I did not agree with it. I agreed with the pitch invasion but was on my way down to go on to the pitch and I saw the crossbars being pulled down and I thought, 'No, that is wrong' at the time, and with hindsight, all respect to the people who did it. Perhaps they had a little more of an inkling what it would achieve. The thing that really turned me – I saw the news at nine o'clock that night and I couldn't bloody believe it. Brighton had never been on the national news and, fucking hell, it really brought it to a head, really.

PAUL HAYWARD: There obviously is an element in my profession who go to an event or a place hoping that a fire's going to break out, and a fire certainly did break out that day. I remember people connecting it with the start of Euro '96 because it was just before that and some newspapers actually said, 'Football hooliganism is back. Euro '96 is going to be a catastrophe', which was a preposterous connection to make.

TONY FOSTER: I was in the pub that evening when it was the third item on the main news and you thought, 'For God's sake, someone do something now!' The whole place emotionally and physically being pulled apart from within. It was bad.

PAUL SAMRAH: I felt, 'Well, we've done it, what more can we do, for God's sake?' – and of course it hit the nine o'clock news! I remember I went to see a play in the West End that night and all the radio was non-stop all about it.

STEWART WEIR: The media of course reported it in many different ways. The *News of the World* was probably the worst, and of course there were big concerns about Euro '96. I think it was a very successful method of trying to get the message across.

It's the same for any club, you cannot treat a football fan in the way that they have treated them.

TONY FOSTER: Then there was Archer's announcement of infiltration by fascists! Amazing! People said there were infiltrators that day – there appeared to be some supporters from other teams, probably because people realised that something was going to go off. But it was a peaceful protest, there were people sitting on the pitch playing with beach balls and having picnics.

PAUL CAMILLIN: There weren't Combat 18 there. They were Brighton fans. And if the Supporters Club didn't accept it then or wouldn't condone it, they do now.

MARC TWIBILL: I think measures could have been taken by the club to stop the riot. Surely some deal with Chartwell could have and should have been struck before the York City game.

ATTILA THE STOCKBROKER: The most aggravating of all the things that they did was to delay the announcement that we were going to be sharing the Goldstone for another season until after the York City match.

TONY HYLANDS: It seemed to the fans that Archer and Bellotti were trying to hold the Councils to ransom and trying to hold the FA to ransom, and were trying to hold the supporters to ransom and everyone knew that was going down.

BILL SWALLOW: I spent a long time trying to work out what these guys' game was. Clearly, it's very simple. They want to build a lucrative property development on the South Downs. Nothing wrong with that. Hundreds of property developers would like to do the same. They've come to the view that owning a Football League club will help to get that planning permission. And everything that happened, including most certainly the situation at the York game, reinforces that theory.

PAUL WHELCH: I think there are two explanations. They either believed that Chartwell would change their conditions if taken to the wire the following week – clearly that didn't happen and in my view there was no reason to believe that it would have happened. The alternative, which I think is possibly understandable, is that they kept it quiet in the hope of getting a 10,000 crowd.

And quite scurrilously, and even ignoring the advice of the police, they deliberately allowed that situation to develop for financial reasons. You could look at either of those and say they just simply didn't know what they were doing, which is probably the truth although it's the less flattering to say they had no idea.

But clearly the circumstances surrounding the York City game could have been avoided and, in my own personal view, if the FA had taken firm action at that point and said the situation is now out of control and we will impose a commissioner on the football club – not in an executive capacity but with the powers of the FA to impose direct action, almost acting in loco of Graham Kelly, to actually issue sanctions and charges and sitting on Bellotti's shoulder and saying, 'No, you will not be permitted to do that' – I think the situation might well have changed. Because Bellotti probably would have found the circumstances unworkable and would have resigned . . . or he might have done.

TONY FOSTER: It was only the third or fourth time in league history that a game had been abandoned by supporters. Was it that that got the FA involved? If it did, it was certainly still on the quiet side. That's when, of course, we got the suspended sentence and the possible three-point deduction. But no action taken against what could be seen as the board. Action then could have at least shown the FA's position on it, and they didn't act! I've no idea why not.

IAN HART: The FA copped out 'cause they could have had them after that game. They could have said, 'You can't control your fans, we're going to charge you.'

CHRIS JONES: My view of it is that Archer played a game of brinkmanship by leaving the deal to the last minute and I think before everyone knew that York City was going to be an awful game, a terrible time.

TONY HYLANDS: That agreement could have been announced on the Friday and saved all that trouble, but for two years we have concrete proof that the board don't want to work with anybody, they don't want to work with the supporter.

It's too easy in this day and age, isn't it, too easy to sit round a table like this with the council of the FA, the football club and the consortium and sort it out and work together. Am I being naïve? Can't we do that nowadays?

TONY FOSTER: This was when Archer started to really get the flak and people began to realise that Bellotti was comparatively lacking in influence, that the board delayed announcing it to us. No one, absolutely no one can, forgive them for that. If they build a stadium and if Archer has a major input in that stadium, people will not thank him for their new stadium, they will not, because they remember what happened to the Goldstone.

NIGEL SUMMERS: I remembered that we definitely turned the focus from Bellotti to Archer because it was fairly clear that if we got rid of Bellotti we wouldn't get rid of Archer. If you get rid of Archer, Bellotti is going to be gone as well because Bellotti was like Archer's PR man, he was taking all the stick and taking all the flak for what Archer was doing and Archer was the real enemy.

STEWART WEIR: After the York game, I looked back at the ground and there were no goalposts left and turf ripped up and it looked a little bit like a war zone. Well, obviously things happened the next season that kind of put that game into the shade. However big that event was, it was nothing compared to what was going to come.

PAUL SAMRAH: The average fan was on that pitch saying, 'What have you done to our club?' and they had a perfect right to ask that question on that day. At the end of the season they had seen the club relegated, not only through poor performances by the players, but through poor performances by the board.

In a way it was a Brighton's Fans United day that day because it said we are not going to be pushed around, we've had enough. None of us are thugs, none of us are hooligans, none of us have got criminal records, we just want to know what the hell is going on. You can't push us about like this.

STEWART WEIR: I think 'watershed' is a good term but since then there have been a lot more. But that was the point when a lot of people realised that they have the power, if only they can get organised, to make things happen, to force people to look at what's happening.

IAN HART: You can't bore people with the words 'I cannot condone' – we're fighting for our football club.

CHRIS JONES: I think that part of the story of Brighton and Hove Albion and the message to other clubs is that you have got to have a bit of direct action.

LIZ COSTA: I have to grudgingly admit that the York City pitch invasion probably saved us in a roundabout way because it got the interest of the world. The only time that the law was broken was the time when it actually paid dividends.

15. The only way is up

> Press statement from Liam Brady, read out in Hove Park opposite the Goldstone Ground, Sunday, 28 April 1996:
> We believe that with good administration and public relations, the club can attract sponsorship and work with the Council to get a new stadium. As a gesture of goodwill I am prepared to pay the £40,000 deposit required by Chartwell for the lease on the ground myself. It is my opinion that the club will die if it moves to Portsmouth. If it does it won't be the fault of the supporters, the Council or this consortium.

TIM CARDER: At the BISA meeting on the Monday on the week before the York game, Stanley had confirmed that there was a consortium in the background, there'd been a few rumours, and he was in touch with people. So this, at last, sort of gave us a little bit of hope that there were people there willing to take the club forward.

LIZ COSTA: There had always been rumours that there were consortia in the background and nobody ever knew really who was involved. Suddenly Liam Brady turns up on a Sunday morning, going public on behalf of Dick Knight and the consortium.

> The *Argus* – Monday, 29 April 1996:
> **Brady's Bunch**
> Albion chairman Bill Archer was under intense pressure today to keep the club at the Goldstone.
> Former manager Liam Brady has turned the heat on the beleaguered Seagulls' supremo.

> Yesterday, Brady was revealed as the prime mover behind a bid to stop the club moving to Portsmouth. He is willing to pay the £40,000 deposit demanded by Goldstone owners Chartwell by noon tomorrow to keep Albion at the ground next season.

LIZ COSTA: It was quite interesting because we still didn't know who this Dick Knight was, although probably everyone in the North Stand had stood next to him at some stage or another because he used to watch every game from there.

BOB PINNOCK (accountant and member of Dick Knight's consortium): As far as the Albion is concerned, Dick had actually known one or two of the previous directors, in particular Ray Bloom and Dennis Sullivan. Ray had spoken to Dick on more than one occasion from the early '90s, about, you know, why don't you join the Albion, come and join the board, we need people like you who've got some marketing flair, and probably a bit of money as well. And at the time Dick had thought it's not really something he'd had time to do.

Sadly, shortly after the time, Dick's wife developed cancer and unfortunately died. And I think it was at that point that Dick felt he wanted to tackle something serious in his life and it was at that particular time that he was introduced to Liam Brady.

I attended Dick's second meeting with Liam. My role is the finance man, the money-man, which is what I always did in Dick's advertising business, he was the front man, and I was the chap who kept things ticking over, the admin. man if you like.

LIAM BRADY: I rang Dick a couple of days previous to the York City game and said, 'Dick, are we going to try and do something about this place or otherwise it's going to go under?' And he said, 'Yes, I'll be with you.'

So I went in and said, 'There are people with me who have money and are willing to invest in the club, but these people must go – get their money back and go – and leave us to pick up the pieces.' I'd been talking to Ivor Caplin all through that season saying, 'Yes, I'm interested, because I know the club has potential, but I won't have anything to do with these people – let's get them out.'

TIM CARDER: It was what every Albion fan wanted to hear, here was a man that they trusted and knew he was a genuine football man and there he was saying that he, with others behind him, were ready to invest in the club.

TONY FOSTER: They had the fans' favourite and he got a great reception at Hove Park as he got out of his car and walked over to the fans.

LIZ COSTA: The offer that was made that day, by Liam, for us to remain at the Goldstone for another year, was rejected out of hand by Bill Archer, totally discounting any word of a consortium and, even at that point, still not admitting that they had planned to renegotiate a year's extension.

> Press statement from Bill Archer, issued by David Bellotti:
> The offer is totally irrelevant and will not be accepted.

16. The Goldstone gamble

> 11.03 am, Tuesday, 30 April 1996 – Statement from the board of Brighton and Hove Albion Football Club:
> After very careful consideration of all the relevant facts the board has unanimously voted to stay at the Goldstone for another year. The club will now vacate the site by 31st May 1997.

LIZ COSTA: The statement was read out quite cleverly, I have to say – the guy should have got an Oscar for the way he did it. Bellotti had people waiting outside his house! It was all done from his house, which was totally bizarre because he should have been at the club. He should be on the stage. He seems to be on a high whenever this sort of crisis happens. I mean, he was part of the problem and then felt he was doing the big thing by getting us out of it!

11.55 a.m. – Legal papers signed with Chartwell.

12.00 p.m. – Deadline passes.

TIM CARDER: I was at work at the time, listening on the radio at ten o'clock, when they said there would be an announcement. I stood outside too nervous to do anything really, for about an hour. I think it was about five past eleven when the news was actually broken that they would stay at the ground. I felt absolute relief but tempered with absolute astonishment at how the board could continue to treat the supporters in such a cavalier fashion – basically leaving it till 55 minutes before the deadline to make the announcement that they were going to stay.

STEWART WEIR: Standing in Hove Park, opposite the ground, overshadowed by the floodlights from the North Stand – just waiting there. There must have been 30-35 fans and everybody was glued to the radio. As every single radio report came through it was 'Shhh, be quiet.' And of course it came over that we'd be staying at the ground for one last season.

The reaction was 'YES.' We're staying for a season and we're not going to have to go to Portsmouth – I think those were the two immediate reactions.

PAUL SAMRAH: We hung around at the ground – another day off work – the Tuesday, we hung around and we hung around, delayed, delayed and eventually we got the announcement.

It was the decision we wanted to hear.

LIZ COSTA: They didn't actually sign the document leasing the thing back until five minutes before the deadline, which really is brinkmanship of the most extraordinary behaviour. It sowed the seeds for distrust to absolutely everybody. They had held everybody to ransom, including the Football League and the Football Association.

PAUL SAMRAH: Having seen the Carlisle trouble, they should have known then that they had to make the decision before the York game. There was no excuse for leaving it until Tuesday morning.

NIGEL SUMMERS: Bellotti seemed to us to be just playing silly buggers.

JAN MERRITT: I remember being in the park at the meeting when the news came out, it must have been an hour and a half before it was due to come out and the waiting was agony, it was really horrific. And the way it was timed was just unbelievable.

ATTILA THE STOCKBROKER: My considered view is that Archer partially took the decision to withhold that statement till the following week because I believe that Archer liked the idea of the media being able to portray us as unruly or hooliganistic – which he no doubt regarded us as. The tendency of the media always is that any form of protest connected with football is hooliganism. He'd referred to us as half-brains and troublemakers. I certainly cannot think of any other reason to delay that statement, other than that.

73

Albion Almanac – April 1996:

David Bellotti holds a lunchtime press conference at the Goldstone at which he allegedly implies that *Evening Argus* and Andy Naylor are more culpable for the riot than he is. Laughing at suggestions that he might resign, the chief executive says the delay in announcing the club's decision on the Goldstone was because of delicate negotiations with Chartwell, and that it was better to come away with the right result even if it took longer than hoped. He hopes he's offered an olive branch to the Council and asks for some credit in keeping the club at the Goldstone for another year.

STEWART WEIR: Was the York incident really necessary? Because Greg Stanley said the week before at the Concorde bar, 'Over my dead body will we go to Portsmouth.' Did he know something that only Archer or Bellotti knew? I personally think that they had considered staying at the ground for another season, just by the comments of Greg Stanley. Whether the abandoned game had an effect on their decision I doubt very much for one simple reason – they would have been intent on taking Chartwell to the brink.

SARAH WATTS: The next time I saw Bellotti was outside Walsall's ground – he knew fully that he had been asked to stay away by Walsall, and there were 60-odd Brighton fans outside – this was after the York City game, the last game of the season and we'd been relegated, and he turned up. I remember the stunned silence as all the Brighton fans looked and their mouths were falling open – and every other word I said was 'fuck'. I'd never done it before – to his face. I said something like, 'What the fucking hell are you doing here after what happened last week?' Things like that, but it was totally uncontrolled. Other people might have been controlled but I went completely – completely flipped. I gave him hell.

LIZ COSTA: And then all of a sudden, out of the blue, we had a letter from Archer inviting selected members of the Supporters groups to a meeting on 29 July in the Goldstone.

17. 'Dick Knight's Barmy Army'

> Brighton and Hove Albion news release, 1 July 1996:
>
> The chairman and directors of Brighton and Hove Albion have today kicked off a new plan to involve supporters and take new steps for a football club in working with the fans. They have invited representatives of all the supporter groups to meet regularly with them. The first meeting will be pre-season.
>
> Chairman Bill Archer commented, 'Following the events of last season we are making genuine attempts to keep supporters informed about what we are doing and giving them an opportunity to question us. We are doing everything possible to make next season successful both on and off the pitch. Working with supporters should help.'
>
> Deputy chairman and chief executive David Bellotti commented, 'After the disastrous period of High Court hearings in 1993 we rebuilt the trust of supporters and had a good rapport. Unfortunately last season we lost it. Everyone who works at the club wants a good relationship and will be working hard to achieve it. There are so many benefits from directors and supporters working for the same goals.'

MARC TWIBILL: In July 1996, the seven main Supporters groups were all summoned to the boardroom by Archer and Bellotti to talk it out. They were saying that they thought we were all very negative and they wanted us to be more positive. They were blaming us for the demise of the club, saying we were stirring up the supporters and we should take more responsibility.

TIM CARDER: It is difficult to get a proper representative body and these were the bodies that were in existence and they just sort of continued as the only groups of Albion supporters.

IAN HART: It was like something out of *The Godfather*. Liz Costa got really upset because Archer mistook her for Jackie Mooney from *On The Up!* Archer was trying to shoot the consortium down, and it was just basically 'wait and see'. With a lot of fans that may have worked. I mean, the Supporters Club was going on about catering and things like that, Liz Costa was going on about the away strip – I was thinking, 'Fucking hell, the club's on its bloody arse, the club won't even be playing next year so why worry about the colour of the shirts?'

PAUL SAMRAH: I didn't get an invitation to the meeting on Monday, 29 July, which was the 'start of a new era in relations between Bill Archer and the Brighton fans' – but I turned up. I saw Ray Bloom go in and I said, 'I haven't been invited, I think I should be in' and I was invited in.

It was good to have a face-to-face meeting and I felt that maybe there were grounds for some sort of way forward, thinking that it might be hopeful. He promised to keep us in touch with everything but I think, as Ian Hart said, which was absolutely excellent, 'It's not just a case of locking the stable door after the horse has bolted, the horse has bolted down the road and been run over.'

LIZ COSTA: We turned up to find Archer, Bellotti, Ray Bloom and Jimmy Case sitting at one end of the table and there were, I think, 12 of us. We were handed vast quantities of paper which had been copied by Archer to indicate the dealings which he had been having, not just recently with the incoming board but over the years. But of course the whole picture was incomplete. Most of it we knew about and the bits we didn't, shouldn't have been given anyway because it was highly confidential information about the financial background of the people that we were led to believe were the backers of the new consortium, which really wasn't our business. These were highly confidential documents which, if they got into the wrong hands, could have been misused.

TONY FOSTER: The first thing I said to Bill Archer was, 'Thanks very much for this meeting, but it should have happened at least a year and a half ago.' In front of David Bellotti I said, 'But, of course, as Mr Bellotti said at the time, you're far too shy a gentleman to come and see us when you weren't ready.' Well – Bill Archer is not a shy gentleman.

LIZ COSTA: A lot of ideas were thrashed out. Bellotti put on a really good act, I have to say, but he had been instructed by Archer to stay completely silent throughout this meeting – he was not allowed to speak. In fact, Archer, when questioned, said 'Mr Bellotti is a defunct voice piece' which was a classic quote. The man sat there staring at the floor like a naughty boy who had been berated in front of the class by his teacher. It wasn't until a question was specifically put to him, he chose not to answer it and Archer rounded on him and said, 'Answer the question, it surely isn't too difficult'. As a double-act, Laurel and Hardy have got nothing on these two.

IAN HART: I was actually wavering. At one point, he had me believing him, then I pinched my leg and came back to the land of the living.

ATTILA THE STOCKBROKER: I refused to go. Paul Samrah went and the others went. I didn't go. After everything that had gone on with Archer I wanted him out and I felt that it would give the wrong signal for everybody chumming-up. So I didn't have any objection to the meeting taking place but I regarded myself as someone who should keep away. I said, 'You go and do that, I'll reserve my judgement and you tell me what you think.'

Of course, some of them were won over by Archer for a short period of time because he came up with all these enthusiastic statements, and I saw some of the stuff he wrote to Paul Samrah and it was garbage. But a few of them thought, 'Oh well, he really does care about the club.' He talked about not wanting 'to push water uphill', and then he signed these things 'Bill Archer – Chairman Presently', 'I will relinquish my chairmanship and my interest in Brighton and Hove Albion Football Club if this is what the fans want.' And they're only chanting 'Archer Out' for the rest of that season and going to his house and everything and it's like, 'Yes, Mr Archer, this is what the fans want. Now fuck off.' And he says, 'No.'

JACKIE MOONEY: It's embarrassing, isn't it? People can put a face on, can't they, and he seemed quite nice enough, he just looked like an ordinary person, people don't have horns sticking out of their head or anything, do they? My only problem was – would he do what he said afterwards?

PAUL SAMRAH: Archer said to us at our meeting on 29 July, 'I will give up my majority shareholding if the consortium can show that they have got the expertise to build a new stadium, can show what funds they have to replace the loan monies in the club and that they can deliver the future' (whatever that means). 'I will go if they can do that, I will step aside.'

We knew the terms and it was clear that the consortium could meet all those demands.

MARC TWIBILL: They promised us several things – they would, from now on, ask the fans rather than tell us, consult us all the way; they said they would give the accounts to Paul Samrah; they would make concerted efforts with Dick Knight and the consortium.

Evening Argus – Friday, 15 August 1996:

An FA commission at the Goldstone Ground finds the Albion guilty of breaking Rule 24 by failing to control fans during the York City game on 27 April. The punishment is to play one match behind closed doors and to have three League points docked, but is suspended pending good behaviour by fans. Spokeswoman Claire Tomlinson says that 'both penalties are to be suspended until the end of the current season and to be invoked, in full or in part, in the event of any serious misconduct involving Albion supporters, either at home or away matches'.

PAUL SAMRAH: Now this was an interesting time, of course, because I said I wanted to look at the books and I was promised: yes, you can, Bellotti will be in touch and we should be able to have a meeting in September time.

I then had discussions with Liam and Dick Knight and obviously I was keen for the consortium to take over the club because I feel, and have always felt, that they are the best solution.

TIM CARDER: The consortium actually got back into talks with him around the beginning of September and this was when it was all supposed to be confidential. Archer started releasing all the correspondence to the relevant Supporters groups and this is when we first heard of the involvement of McAlpine's for instance. I remember hearing that on the TV news that night and I thought McAlpine's had built Huddersfield stadium and a few others, maybe this club has got a future after all if a company like McAlpine's is actually interested in investing in a stadium for us, and that was a real boost.

---

6 September 1996 – letter to Bill Archer from Dick Knight

At our meeting on 22 August your strongly expressed wish was that all present at the meeting – the consortium, Ray Bloom, yourself – should not make our discussions public at this stage, and the consortium readily agreed to this. Until we have something tangible to say concerning the Albion, I believed it would be wrong to raise people's hopes prematurely.

On this and all other matters tabled at the meeting, the consortium has met your stated requirements. Your further requirement introduced and agreed in the meeting, we fulfilled in my letter of 28 August. This provided substantiated evidence of the consortium's progress to date towards delivering a new stadium for the club. You have yet to respond to this letter.

The ball is now firmly in your court to honour your side of the agreement – to immediately make available to the consortium the club's

---

financial information for our necessary assessment prior to active negotiations. I would remind you that you have publicly announced, and confirmed at our meeting, that you are prepared to sell your controlling interest in the club for the exact value paid for the shares, provided the consortium can meet your stated financial and stadium expertise criteria, which we have.

The overwhelming body of public opinion clearly supports the need for change. If not my consortium, then another committed group would suffice.

But our patience is running out. We have met all of your conditions with more than sufficient evidence of our credentials. I now expect you to respond in the manner agreed at our meeting, by providing the club's financial information so that we can take things forward.

9 September 1996 – letter to Dick Knight from Bill Archer

Thank you for your letter dated 28 August 1996 with enclosures.

You will recall, I am sure, that the ingredients missing are:

1. How are you going to fund the new development?
2. Where is the development?

I personally do not know you from 'Adam', therefore it is only due diligence to want to know a little more about your finances. Until you do come up with some tangible answers, all your comments on financial status are very shallow to me.

Why can't you give me the information?

Until you do, I will not be furnishing you with any figures. Although very shortly the accounts will be in the public domain, as statutory accounts.

I look forward to hearing from you in the format we agreed. Otherwise your comments, through the press, are at worst upsetting the fans! But, I must say, the fans who start to think what is going on, will ask the same questions as me.

9 September 1996 – letter to Martin Perry (McAlpine's) from Bill Archer

To enable me to distribute possible contract tender documents, should Dick Knight's consortium not be able to satisfy the club's request, are Alfred McAlpine plc interested in having a discussion on new stadia/ enablings, etc.? You certainly gave me the impression when I met you over a year ago in Blackpool, that you wanted to meet.

If it is not your domain because you are a consortium member, which senior director would I write to, to see whether McAlpine plc are interested in tendering?

10 September 1996 – fax to Bill Archer from Ivor Caplin

It is important that I make clear to you in writing, as I did at the time, of the irretrievable breakdown in relationships between the club and the local authorities, supporters, business sector and the community in general. No stadium development can take place without the support of the local Council and the other key stakeholders of a football club which must at the very least include all of the above.

The consortium (including McAlpine's) have clearly shown their desire to work with everyone involved and have the record of joint working with those communities and the local authorities to be able to bring this matter to a successful conclusion.

At the present time that is the ONLY hope if Brighton and Hove Albion Football club is to have a future. Bill, you said to me and to the supporters that you would step aside if the consortium could properly demonstrate their commitment to the club and its future. That has now happened. I urge you to be a man of your word and bring this issue to a speedy and rapid conclusion.

12 September 1996 – letter to Bill Archer from Dick Knight:

Your letter of 9 September totally ignores my letter to you of 6 September. So I will repeat once again. The consortium has met all the conditions – original, plus the further one introduced at our meeting – you have set.

Now honour your side of the agreement by giving us the financial information we require. It is obviously readily available. The deadline date of Friday 13 September still stands.

You cannot keep moving the goalposts to suit yourself. We reject your attempts to obtain further information concerning the new development as a cynical move to benefit from the hard work and progress the consortium has already made in this respect.

And your attempt to divide McAlpine's and the consortium in your letter to Martin Perry of 9 September will come to nothing. The consortium under my leadership is united, as one, on this.

We have met all your conditions with more than sufficient evidence of our credentials. Now do what you promised, and provide the club's financial information so that we can take things forward.

Please indicate to me by Friday 13 September your willingness or otherwise to do this. To ensure your prompt receipt of this letter, I am also faxing it to your office today. Your previous responses, seemingly unaware of my letters sent earlier, indicate that postal delays may be the inevitable consequence of you living so far from the South of England.

PAUL SAMRAH: Suddenly it transpired that talks between Knight and Archer were floundering – Knight had been promised the books but had never actually got anywhere near them. Suddenly I got a phone call from Bellotti saying, 'Oh, we'd like you to make an appointment to look at the accounts at our accountants' – and I suddenly thought why on earth am I being offered a look at the accounts when the consortium wants to have a look at the accounts and you're depriving them? I'm not going to be put in the middle, thank you very much. Having made the appointment, I then rang up Bellotti and said that, in view of what had happened in the last week with the consortium, I was not prepared to go ahead and look at the books, it wasn't relevant – I don't need to be involved.

MARC TWIBILL: And the promises they made at the time never really came to fruition. We were supposed to meet each other every month from then on, but within three weeks of our first meeting with them it was already clear that they were not likely to keep the promises that they had made. So we all took a joint decision not to speak to them.

TIM CARDER: I argued that we should hold Archer to his word, he'd said in correspondence that the supporters would decide the issue and I argued that we should hold him to that – turn up to this meeting and say 'are you going to let the supporters decide the issues?', and if not, walk out. The Supporters Club argued that point of view but other factions argued against it and called off the talks anyway.

Faxed statement issued to the media, 16 September 1996:
Issued on behalf of:

A21 Supporters Club
Brighton and Hove Albion Supporters Club
Brighton Independent Supporters Association
Gull's Eye
Horsham Blue & Whites Supporters Club
On The Up
Seagulls Over London
By: Paul Samrah

BRIGHTON & HOVE ALBION FC
We have unanimously agreed to cease all further dialogue and communication with the present board of directors. This follows the continued stalling and prevarication by Mr Bill Archer and his failure to honour his word in his dealings with the consortium. The

---

81

> consortium have proved that they have the resource to deliver a new
> stadium and secure the club's immediate future.
>
> Archer must open the books to the consortium and agree to stand aside
> in the interests of the club's future. Until this happens, the supporters
> are united in their condemnation of Archer and his continued
> intransigence.
>
> There can be no benefit in an empty dialogue with the board. Now is
> the time for action, rather than false promises.
>
> As an immediate consequence of our decision, we will not be attending
> the next scheduled meeting with Bill Archer planned for Monday 30
> September.

TIM CARDER: I think what really sparked it off was on 30 September there was
a meeting arranged at Lancaster Gate by Graham Kelly, which brought
together the FA, Archer and Bellotti and the consortium and by then we
knew Dick Knight was the man behind the consortium. Liam had actually
got a job at Arsenal by that time. There was a group of about a dozen of us
outside this hotel just along from the FA. We all had our hopes pinned on
this meeting and that something was going to come out of it. I remember Ray
Bloom – he was director at the time, and he had the guts to walk past us and
say 'good morning' to us, while Archer and Bellotti went in the back door.

NIGEL SUMMERS: Archer and Bellotti turned up late and everybody including
the Football Association just shook their heads at this type of behaviour.

TIM CARDER: We stood out there all day. There were talks from about 10.30 to
about 3.30 and I remember Graham Kelly at the end of it came out and he
was very grim-faced. He stood in the doorway of the hotel to give a press
statement and I remember thinking, 'Whilst he's standing in the doorway,
Archer and Bellotti will be sneaking out the back while everyone's at the
front.' And I was right.

NIGEL SUMMERS: Graham Kelly comes out and announces that you've got one
party who doesn't want to sell 100 per cent and one party who doesn't want
to buy anything less than 100 per cent, it's completely intractable, they've
talked about it all day, they're not getting anywhere and there's no plans for
any further meetings. End of story.

I was absolutely furious. That's when Archer had the chance to hand over
to someone who could give the club a better future.

LIZ COSTA: We had Graham Kelly coming up and saying that nothing had been
resolved and they didn't see that there was a way forward, which was 24

hours before the home match against Lincoln City and I remember thinking at the time, 'God, this is going to be bedlam tomorrow.'

TONY HYLANDS: They should have called that game off, I still say that. And Archer and Bellotti should have been charged with bringing the game into disrepute. Twice – York City, Lincoln – people have got to be held responsible for their actions.

The rest is history, isn't it?

18. 'On the pitch, on the pitch, on the pitch'

BRIGHTON AT HOME TO LINCOLN CITY, 1 OCTOBER 1996

TIM CARDER: The day following the FA meeting was the day of the home game against Lincoln, and the Supporters Club – Liz Costa, mainly – tried to get that game postponed because we could sense that there was going to be a lot of trouble.

LIZ COSTA: I phoned up the Football League and I said, 'Look, I'm trying somehow to get this game called off – I'm doing this off my own back but I've spoken to a lot of supporters and they all say yes, we think it might be a good idea.' This was more than 24 hours before the game was due to take place and we all know they can call a game off at five minutes' notice if they really want to – you know, if there's bad weather or the floodlights fail or something happens, and with 24 hours for an evening game there really was no reason why they couldn't have postponed it.

On the Tuesday morning I did a broadcast on Radio 4, my colleagues did one on Radio 5 and I did Southern Counties, where we were begging them somehow to call the game off, because we really feared for somebody's safety. And of course nothing happened and they said 'No, the game's got to go ahead.'

NIGEL SUMMERS: I sent a fax to the FA that day saying, 'Thanks for doing what you tried to do, there's bound to be trouble at the football tonight – just because there's bound to be – and in the next few days you are going to have to "not condone" it and apologise for it.'

LIZ COSTA: At six o'clock Bill Archer issued a press release, which was the most ridiculous thing he could possibly have done. He said, 'Talks have broken down, we are going to Portsmouth, don't take any notice of any consortium because we are not even going to enter into any more discussions with them. I am in charge and we are going to Portsmouth and that's the end of it.' The timing was abysmal. Bellotti had actually been escorted from the ground at six o'clock by stewards who refused to allow the game to go ahead if he was there.

TONY HYLANDS: I couldn't get to that Lincoln game but I knew what was going down, they were going on the pitch. Every Brighton supporter knew there was going to be a pitch invasion. We'd been led up the garden path again, we were led to believe that there was going to be this mega-deal sorted out by the FA and the day before a home game Archer and Bellotti do their usual act and walk away from it. All the supporters' hopes have been built up, the emotion and everything else, only to be totally let down.

So my wife said, 'What about the football?' and I said, 'I'm not going, you're at work and so I can't go. And I'm not going to get a babysitter because I know I'll end up getting arrested' − because I was so angry myself − and I thought I'll sit home here and listen to it on Southern FM without getting involved. And at 6.30 Meridian or BBC said we've got a statement from Bill Archer, and I snapped. I picked up the phone and dialled the police and said, 'I would like to report someone for inciting a riot.'

Press release − 1 October 1996:

Following a full and frank discussion yesterday with the Football Association and Football League, the board of Brighton and Hove Albion placed on record their gratitude to them for their involvement and to the Council leaders, Councillor Steve Bassam and Councillor Ivor Caplin, as well as the Knight consortium.

Chairman Bill Archer said, 'Our way forward now has to be with the local Councils. The Knight consortium only want to be involved if they have 100 per cent of the shares and that scenario is not acceptable to the board. So there is no way forward with the consortium.

The club will be pursuing its planning application at Toad's Hole Valley and will be playing games next season at Portsmouth. Brighton and Hove Albion will not be going out of business.'

It is important for everyone to understand that there is an area of land in Brighton and Hove which the Council have put forward, where they will give planning permission for a multi-purpose stadium. We remain willing to work with the local Council on their site. We believe they should now tell everyone where that site is.

> If the Council is willing to work with the club, the board is prepared to consider how the club can have a key role in the future decision-making at the club. We are therefore inviting the Councils to another meeting to discuss how they could participate in the club's future.

STEWART WEIR: One thing that comes out of all this is that Archer would say the wrong thing, at the wrong time, in the wrong way. If he wasn't going to talk to the consortium, why say it?

TIM CARDER: I went to that Lincoln game in total trepidation of what was going to happen. It just inflamed the crowd and the inevitable happened, which was that when Lincoln scored about 100 people from the North Stand went on the pitch, sat in the middle. Again it was a peaceful demonstration that held up the game for about 13 minutes and that was it.

PAUL SAMRAH: Lincoln scored and they walked on – it was totally peaceful, it didn't need police to take them off. After about three or four minutes they walked off to applause from everyone.

BILL SWALLOW: The timing was deplorable, because we came on immediately after Lincoln scored a goal. That was exactly the wrong time to do it because it suggested that we were protesting about the fact that we were losing.

SARAH WATTS: Every time you understand what the reasoning and the emotions behind it were, even though you thought it wasn't the way to do it. And we, the Supporters Club, wanted the game postponed and we said that on the radio.

STUART ADAMS: That night, the pitch invasion started when the goal went in. Only a handful out there. That was the only game that season I didn't take my son and I wore totally different clothes so I wouldn't be recognised because I knew damn well I was going to do whatever I felt needed doing. I went on the pitch; sat there for ten minutes.

KEVIN SHERWOOD: We stood there as one. If we'd sat in our seats or stood on the terrace and written nice polite letters – I mean, I'm not a militant and that sounds like the statement of a militant, but direct action was what did . . . I've no guilt about that, no qualms at all about what we did and I'd do the same again.

PAUL CAMILLIN: I was down the front trying to get on. A few of my mates got on, and I was well behind that. At the end of the season if we had gone down by two points I wouldn't have had any queries or quibbles with anyone that went on that night because it had to be done.

STUART ADAMS: It was quite a sort of buzzy feeling and at the same time a fear of 'God, what am I doing and why am I doing it?' You don't want to be doing it – it's not natural to be down there. And after a while there was me and this other bloke saying we'll have to get off because there's not enough of us to call the game off, and we were saying, 'If we go off now we look like an organised unit and we know what we're doing and we've made our point.'

When you're out there and you're sitting there it's a real low, it's a weird feeling. I felt ashamed of what I was doing at the time, although looking back I'm not. I think it had to be done and I felt as though I'd done my bit – and I also think that the biggest thing of all with that was although the FA wouldn't admit it, they wouldn't have got involved at all if we hadn't done that. That pitch invasion and the disruption of the game for eight minutes was broadcast all over the world. My parents were in Spain and they said they saw me on telly on satellite – sitting in a villa in Spain.

NIGEL SUMMERS: That's what they call trouble, is it, a few people running on the pitch and players running off?

MARC TWIBILL: At the time I was praying that the other fans wouldn't follow. I felt that that could have been the end of Brighton and Hove Albion. There were two perspectives at the club, you had half the people condemning what the people on the pitch were doing and deciding that it wasn't the way forward, while you had the people on the pitch thinking that the people still in the North Stand didn't care.

STEWART WEIR: Lincoln was when I got banned. There were probably about 75 fans on the pitch. I was doing some shots of this guy having his arm twisted up and around his head – but, anyway, an excuse for a ban. I think it was the Sky camera crew that went all the way on to the centre circle. A few days later I get a letter from John Back saying I've been banned from the ground for infringing ground safety regulations.

BILL SWALLOW: I also have to say, and maybe this puts me in a minority of one, I wasn't terribly happy with the Lincoln City protest. I didn't think it was wise. If they'd opened fire on David Bellotti I wouldn't have a problem with that, no difficulty at all. I thought the strategy went off the rails.

TIM CARDER: Everyone supported it – I mean there were about two cries of 'get off the pitch' because we were under suspended sentence at that point.

We knew that anyone going on the pitch and holding the game up was going to cost us points, but we were in such a desperate state at that time that the vast majority of the crowd applauded them. I clapped them. It was all very orderly and the crowd was fully in support. We had to show that, even with the threat of losing points – and we were very near the bottom at this stage.

LIZ COSTA: I don't know whether I agreed with it or not. My heart sank because I thought, 'What is going to happen? They could close us down tomorrow.' That was my worry. But it was well orchestrated and I felt in the back of my mind that we'd done everything we could to stop this happening and the League had got it on record that we'd tried to stop it happening and the BBC could produce taped evidence that we'd begged them to stop it and they hadn't. So in some respects they had been responsible for this happening.

STUART ADAMS: The next game after Lincoln, I think it was Cambridge, I was just walking near to the ground and I was being told so-and-so has been nicked because he was on the pitch and so I immediately tried to cover myself up. There were people coming up saying they'd got nicked an hour ago and were banned from the ground for 12 months. I went in multiple disguises – one week I'm wearing my cap and one week I'm wearing my glasses.

PAUL CAMILLIN: It was what we saw as the only way out. The Supporters Club have got a lot to answer for, if they are turning round saying you should never have gone on, because they whipped it up a fucking treat. By going on the national news and saying, 'We will get the game abandoned, there is going to be trouble' – that's just sending people onto the pitch, double negative.

TONY FOSTER: It wasn't dramatic, it was peaceful. I say it wasn't dramatic, of course we had the three-points deduction hanging over us.

TIM BOHANNON: The pitch invasion cost us two points, which I think was awful – the FA didn't fully appreciate the reasons for it. At Lincoln there weren't that many people involved. I didn't go on to the pitch to protest because I didn't think it would do any good.

LIZ COSTA: It should never have been points deducted against the team. But of course you appeal against a suspended sentence, you don't appeal after the offence has been committed. You appeal as soon as you get your first sentencing, any Court of Appeal will tell you that. Of course, Bellotti appealed, I believe, in February and it was turned down.

TONY MILLARD: The way they handled the appeal was completely wrong in terms of football protocol. What should actually have happened was that they should have appealed against the York City penalty in the first place and then the other one would not have had to be imposed. To announce that they were taking legal advice was again completely wrong.

ATTILA THE STOCKBROKER: from the 'Archer Out' Rap

> So now I want to talk about the sweet FA
> Footballers' governing authority? Hey –
> I've seen more authority in an anarchist squat
> than in that sad floppy lot
> They couldn't govern a WI cookery class.
> It's just a farce.
> It must be hard to talk with your tongue up Murdoch's arse –
> hey give 'em a buck to pass.
> FA policy: government story
> Every stricture sells a Tory
> Riches for the rich, nothing for the rest –
> everything done at Premier League behest.
> Corporate sponsors – all hail the Big five
> but it's the fans that keep this game alive
> and most of us aren't supporters of the chosen few.
> Check the stats: it's true.
> We're the grass roots and hey we're coming through
> so what does the FA do?
> Nothing. Zilch. They live up to their name.
> Archer scot-free, Brighton gets the blame
> North Stand on the pitch in peace to have our say –
> they take two points away.
> But Fans United are with us all the way
> and hey, we'll win the day.

I mean that was the point with the FA – it was like a regurgitated mantra, wasn't it? 'We can't do anything because it's a private limited company and we can't do anything because it's outside our powers.' So, you're the Football Association and it's a football matter. Why have you allowed this situation to arise, where somebody can just grab hold of a football club and do to it what they will? Why don't you tear up your rule book and start again?

STEWART WEIR: Pitch invasions are never justified. But when the FA and the club don't do what they're meant to do or don't do things that are in the best interests of the fans, it's not a question of the FA patrolling 42,000-odd football clubs, it's also their responsibility to safeguard the interests of the football fans of which there are millions. So the responsibility goes far beyond what they want to get involved in and it seems to me that all they're interested in is World Cups and things like that.

PAUL SAMRAH: It became clear then that we were going to have to start a campaign. Virtually every home game after Lincoln something was happening.

SEPTEMBER 1996 – APRIL 1997

19. Protest and survive

BILL SWALLOW: I just felt a growing sense of solidarity. I have never protested about anything before because I've never had the need to. It's the suburban spirit of Thatcherite England that if you've got a problem, you work out a way personally of getting round it. I'd suggest that 95 per cent of all the people down there who protested, including me and certainly including my wife . . . had never protested about anything before.

In Sussex we have never had miners' lodges and protests through the streets. This was when it came to us for the very first time. In Lancashire, or wherever, it happened a hundred years ago. But for the first time ever in this county, there has been widespread community spirit and protest. I'm not talking about students going off the rails with some particular agenda of their own, but it was a general feeling of absolute solidarity from all sorts of different people. There's the most extraordinary range of people from every flash country enclave in Sussex to every council estate and no one is superior to anyone else.

STEWART WEIR: When you use the assets of the ground, you sell the ground, you change the Articles of Association, you remove the 'no profits' clause, you issue libel writs on Ivor Caplin, who was the very person who was really essential to get any kind of planning permission, it's no wonder that the fans reacted and organised themselves in the way that they did. In fact, when you look back on things it's actually a miracle that nothing catastrophic happened. And one of the reasons was that there was a very strong under-current of organisation where things were planned and people's energies were focused on one thing, whether it was a march, whether it was a boycott, whether it was petitions, letting off balloons, blowing whistles, whatever.

BILL SWALLOW: It's the first time the ersatz spirit of socialism has arrived in Sussex. And I actually think it's far more strongly based than that.

20. If one Liberal Democrat can ruin a football club, what can a Lib Dem government do for your country?

LIBERAL DEMOCRAT CONFERENCE OPENS IN BRIGHTON –
22 SEPTEMBER 1996

STEWART WEIR: The Liberal Democrat Party conference in Brighton was an outstanding achievement by the Supporters Club. There were about 15 to 20 of them planted outside the conference on the Sunday with banners and all sorts and the next day they knocked the Liberal Party off the front page, of which I heard the next day from one of their press people because I was covering the conference during that week.

LIZ COSTA: We decided to actually come up with a real protest to show at least one group of people that Bellotti was bringing the Liberal Democrats into disrepute by the way he was behaving because his actions were neither liberal nor democratic. They had, in their wisdom, chosen to have their conference in Brighton and I, together with two ladies who were well into their seventies, one in her sixties and two other women plus two or three children, stood on the seafront opposite the entrance to the party conference totally silently – just with a large banner which said, 'If one Lib Dem can ruin a football club, what can a Lib Dem government do for your country?'

SARAH WATTS: There were about 30 of us very quietly standing outside the Brighton Centre with a banner and placards. We weren't shouting, we weren't harassing, we were on the seafront.

TONY FOSTER: I have to say that the majority of the people holding those banners were Liberal Democrats. They weren't Conservative, they weren't Labour, contrary to the accusations. It wasn't a party thing.

SARAH WATTS: Some people didn't read it and just saw it as an anti-Lib-Dem/pro-Tory demonstration. So we said, 'Read the banner – this is about one man who has destroyed a football club and it's our football club and our club colours are blue and white.'

JAN MERRITT: I had to be a little bit careful because, being a Liberal Democrat, I couldn't really be holding up any sort of banner that was against the party. We got a lot of people who were delegates actually coming over and speaking to us.

SARAH WATTS: I was talking to a sergeant who came over for a chat, and the police took it very well – Brighton and Hove police have been pretty good. We were trying to get people to hoot as they went past in their cars. As we were talking I said, 'Isn't that David?' I yelled out – my voice carries when I want it to – he turned round and I don't think he could believe what he was seeing. Predominantly women of four generations, standing outside a national party conference.

TONY FOSTER: We made the front page of the *Argus*. Paddy Ashdown made page five, doesn't that speak volumes? We had people inside, not to demonstrate but to keep us up to date on what was being said. There was a scurry of activity, people asking questions like, 'What's going on? Why are people demonstrating? Is this all for David Bellotti? What's he done? What hasn't he done?' It was an embarrassment to the Lib Dems.

STEWART WEIR: Apparently Paddy Ashdown was not impressed whatsoever at losing that front page – they got relegated to page five. But Bellotti turned up there and a couple of prospective parliamentary candidates who had been spoken to by the supporters who gave them a run-down on what had been happening at the club.

LIZ COSTA: We felt that that protest had achieved quite a lot. It got national publicity and we had, to a degree, disrupted a party political conference and the point that was made was that we weren't your stereotyped football supporters – we weren't the lads who had just come out of the pub with their tattoos and football shirts.

21. 'We're here in your village, angry as hell'

MARCH IN MELLOR AFTER WIGAN AWAY – 5 OCTOBER 1996

TIM CARDER: In the past BISA and the Supporters Club had been a little bit wary of each other, especially during the Barry Lloyd days when BISA were really anti-Barry Lloyd – and the Supporters Club adopted a bit less of a stance on that, but everyone knew now that there was only one enemy, and we all had to join in this fight to save the club. I think the first real joint activity was the invasion of Mellor.

ATTILA THE STOCKBROKER: The big thing for me this season was as early as possible to really focus on Archer, which was why the whole thing in Mellor came about. When I saw the fixture list I thought, 'Right, this is the next one, we've got to go to Mellor, we've got to bring it literally to Archer's doorstep.'

TIM CARDER: It was publicised three or four days beforehand and I remember Archer was interviewed all over the place – on TV and radio. I actually went up on the Friday beforehand to help leaflet the Mellor area with Paul Whelch. I was listening to Radio 5 and there was an interview with Bill Archer – this was on the Friday – and the trouble is, to anyone who doesn't know the situation he comes over as quite plausible. There's an element of truth about a lot of what he says but a lot of it doesn't convey the whole message. He just got away with murder in these interviews, which didn't do our campaign much good with people outside of the club.

ATTILA THE STOCKBROKER: If you want to have a go at Archer you've got to travel 260 miles – that's why I made such a thing about going up there and saying to Archer, 'We will come back and we will come back again and we will come back again. Yes it's a bloody long way to come, yes it's a pain in the arse, no we don't want to do it but we will if we have to because we do not like you and we hate what you're doing to our football club.' That was the point.

TIM CARDER: We went to the Wigan game which we lost 1–0. It was actually our best away performance of that season but that sent us to the bottom of

94

the League for the first time in virtually 50 years and we got a lot of support from Wigan fans. Wigan was quite an eventful game because it started off with Bellotti appearing in the directors box – they'd got one very small but very tall stand there and there were a lot of Albion fans in there. When Bellotti arrived there was just uproar in the seats and he had to beat a really quick retreat, but I remember them singing 'One-nil to the Albion' once he had vacated his seat. There was initially a 'One Billy Archer'-type taunting song but I think a lot of the Wigan fans knew what it was about and quickly shut up those who were singing that sort of thing. From then on they were very supportive.

PAUL CAMILLIN: The Wigan fans came out with an 'Archer Out' chant and they sang it throughout the game.

TIM CARDER: The Traders Arms in Mellor was the sort of focal point of the demonstration and there were police everywhere when we got to the house.

STEWART WEIR: The pub was absolutely jam-packed and I'm thinking, 'My God, here are 150 fans packed into this pub and there's loads outside. We are miles from anywhere going to visit this guy Archer' and there was the beginning of an organisation.

NIGEL SUMMERS: There was loads of police up there, a police helicopter, I couldn't believe it. I said to one policeman, 'What you expecting, the IRA?' It was just so orderly.

PAUL CAMILLIN: The fact that we lost 1–0 and went bottom of the League, I mean, 200 Brighton fans, you probably would never see anything like it. Marching through the quaintest, quietest Lancashire village you could probably find and we totally took the village over. We got a brilliant reception from all the people there, absolutely superb, and standing outside Archer's house, that was quite emotional when Attila played on his violin, 'Sussex by the Sea'. That was gut-wrenching.

> Good old Sussex by the sea
> Good old Sussex by the sea
> and we're going up
> to win the Cup
> for Sussex by the sea
> (famous Albion song)

TIM CARDER: I thought Attila handled it absolutely fantastically. He had his fiddle and his recorder with him and he was allowed to stand up on the low wall, gave a little speech, sang a few songs and we had quite a few anti-Archer chants and the bonfire song.

ATTILA THE STOCKBROKER: What is the opposite extreme of the conventional concept of football hooliganism? Poetry. So I did the poem and in spite of the fact that a few people said to me, 'Leave it out, John, it makes us look like a bunch of pansies.' I thought, 'Well, you can say what you want.' I play the fiddle and the recorder and I'm a poet. There was a piece of propaganda going round the village with it on a leaflet. The villagers really took to it and it became immediately apparent that very few of them had much time for the bloke.

TO THE GOOD PEOPLE OF MELLOR, LANCS
Saturday, 5 October 1996

We're here in your Village, as angry as hell
(If it happened to you, you'd be angry as well)
To call for the Prompt and Immediate Departure
From all our lives of a certain Bill Archer
Who lives in your midst – Vinehouse Farm, Whinney Lane -
And causes unlimited Anguish and Pain......
So what has he done, perchance? Why are we here?
It's because of the Football Club we all hold dear.
He's the 'chairman' of Brighton. At wondrous expense
(All of Fifty-six Pounds on, and Twenty-five Pence)
In a deal we can only describe as grotesque
(If it wasn't so wrong, it would be Pythonesque)
This Archer got hold of the Shares of our Club
For the price of a happy weekend in the Pub
Then he sold off our ground, so we'd nowhere to go
Tried to groundshare with Portsmouth – until we said NO!
Now we're right at rock bottom, with nowhere to play
But things will improve – if he'll just GO AWAY!
The Seagulls soared high once; we've thousands of Fans
A consortium waiting, with loads of new Plans
And one man from Mellor, of whom we want Rid
Is holding things up with his Fifty-six Quid.
All of Sussex can't stand him. The Councils, Police.
Even Tory M.P.'s tell him 'Leave us in peace!'
Our Local Newspaper's petition is clear:

'That's really been where so much of my knowledge has come from. That little square inch of pavement outside the paper shop' (© Stewart Weir)

'It was a political campaign – I don't want to pretend here – I'm driven by being a supporter, but of course there was a political campaign behind it': Ivor Caplin talks to the press (© Stewart Weir)

Liam Brady with Bill Archer and David Bellotti (© Stewart Weir)

'The Bournemouth trip, when we knew it was going to be televised, was far too good an opportunity to be missed' (© Stewart Weir)

'We will go to Portsmouth over my dead body': Greg Stanley (seated) faces angry Albion fans at the Concorde Bar days before the York City game. Three hundred fans are locked out (© Stewart Weir)

'You should have seen the police's faces: doors, windows smashed, fans storming in there with one person on their minds': home to Carlisle, 20 April 1996 (© Stewart Weir)

'A different kind of riot': home to York City, 26 April 1996 (© Evening Argus)

Liam Brady announces the arrival of the consortium the day after the York game; Ivor Caplin and Paul Samrah (right) are amongst the onlookers (© Stewart Weir)

'The board has unanimously decided to stay at the Goldstone for one more year': Paul Samrah (centre) and Nigel Summers (right) react to the news as it comes over the radio (© Stewart Weir)

'Not the first of, but the latest in, the series of football fan love-ins':
Walsall fans salute Brighton fans (© Stewart Weir)

Dave and Sam Swaffield away at Walsall (© Stewart Weir)

'When you're out there, it's real low – it's a weird feeling': pitch invasion at home to Lincoln City, 1 October 1996 (© Stewart Weir)

Tim Carder and Sarah Watts on the pitch at Rochdale, November 1996 (© Stewart Weir)

'We're here in your village as angry as hell . . .': Attila The Stockbroker addresses fans outside Archer's house, 5 October 1995 (© Stewart Weir)

Outside David Bellotti's house (© Stewart Weir)

SEPTEMBER 1996 – APRIL 1997

'You're no Robin Hood, Archer – you're not wanted here!'
From Hastings to Chichester, one thing is plain:
If Archer's got Fans, so has Saddam Hussein!
If you like him in Mellor, well that's up to you.
(I suppose it's conceivable three of you do)
But he's nothing to do with our Club, or our Town,
And he's outstayed his Welcome, and getting us down!
So we've come here, in peace, to your Village and Pub
To tell you what Archer has done to our Club
And now that you know what this Visit's about
Come, Mellor, and join us: WE WANT ARCHER OUT!

6 p.m. The Traders Arms, Mellor Lane, Mellor (off the motorway near Blackburn – it's on the map and in the Good Beer Guide). Politeness and Diplomacy Essential. Leaflets for the Neighbours (it's obviously a very select area – I'm sure they like Poetry!) and then a Short Orderly Stroll – or if necessary, Car Convoy – to the Archers' Residence for Carol Singing (now that Archer's gagged him, Bellotti may provide a Mulled Whine).

By going up there and not doing anything out of order but by being amusing and having a poet and a fiddle, some of them didn't like it particularly because there's still this element of our supporters who are young and testosterone-filled, who want to be seen as being hard. It's not something that's of the slightest interest to me. What I want is to get the media attention and for people to see us as being different and this is how it's worked.

STEWART WEIR: You think, 'Is this going to come to anything? What is the point of us being here?' And I think the point of it came out the next day in the papers when it got a lot of media attention. As soon as people realised that by coming up with clever stunts the media would take an interest, and it would prove to Archer that we are very determined in what we are going to do and quite simply were not going to give up.

NIGEL SUMMERS: That was the first time that there was an imaginative protest which the media could latch on to if they wanted to; it wasn't a pitch invasion or people writing letters to the Football League, it was something quite different and people had to make a bit of effort to go all the way up there.

LIZ COSTA: It was extremely well supported, extremely well behaved and orchestrated by Attila, to give him his due. He may be a bit of a militant but he got that organised down to a fine art and, again, gained a lot of respect, even a very sort of sycophantic statement from Archer saying thank you very much for being so well-behaved.

ATTILA THE STOCKBROKER: The next thing that I found actually surprising and disappointing was the realisation that most people, if they are loathed publicly by lots of people, go 'Oh God, I hate this, I can't stand this, I'll get out of the way', but Archer's the opposite. The more you have a go at him, the more he responds to it. It is bizarre. It is definitely a fact that Archer is more likely to behave in a reasonable manner, or do something which is less unacceptable than anything else which he does – I don't want to be too complimentary to the guy – if you basically relax and don't really hammer him, because the more you hammer him, the more his back goes up and he digs his heels in. It's a kind of Mr Nasty and Mr Nice approach.

What was the first thing he did after we'd been to Mellor? He issued a press statement thanking us for being well-behaved.

Press release issued by the club – 7 October 1996:

Following the peaceful and lawful demonstration on Saturday at the home and village of the chairman. The board want to put on record their gratitude in the way the protest was conducted. The fans who made the journey did not let down Sussex or Brighton and Hove. It is a credit to each of them for the way they behaved.

Because of the latest attempt by the supporters to bring about a solution, the BHAFC board are determined to bring about a change to everyone's satisfaction.

The BHAFC board believe that the Council have a key role to play in bringing about an agreeable share-restructuring process. To this end the board have extended an offer to the Council, to consider a meeting to discuss an offer of receiving shares of the ultimate holding company, without any monetary consideration. If the Council accept this process they would play a pivotal role in ensuring that in the future the Council would always have shares and balancing the role of play.

The owners have the funds to develop the stadium. These funds must not be lost in a 'sea of emotion'. They will do everything in their power to bring about a solution.

Everyone on the board very much hope that this will bring about a meeting to discuss the detail and, therefore, move forward to develop a stadium for the 21st century.

PAUL SAMRAH: Archer started revealing his face far more. Bellotti was no longer in the media spotlight, it was Archer who was now putting himself forward in October.

ATTILA THE STOCKBROKER: The crucial stage in consciousness was reached when people realised that Archer should be the main target.

SECOND VISIT TO MELLOR – 7 DECEMBER 1996

PAUL SAMRAH: At that time, 7 December, we were managerless. They had sacked Jimmy Case, the club was not playing on Saturday because it had been knocked out of the FA Cup by Sudbury and feelings were running very high. We had talked about approaching the team for a players' strike but at the end of the day the players have their wages to earn and they've got mortgages to pay for, it was just a non-starter.

STUART STORER: It's not as if we could stop playing. If we'd stopped playing we'd have got our money docked. We've all got families to feed and mortgages to pay; we're not like superstars in the Premier League who don't have a mortgage or repayments on a car – it's just a job. But really we were stuck in the middle of the fans and the club itself and the way it's being run. We've got to do well for ourselves and our own careers and we want to do well for the fans, but the way it was going the fans weren't really interested in what was going on on the pitch as much as off the pitch and I can understand that. People have been watching this club 30-40 years and there's some very big emotional strings attached.

PAUL SAMRAH: At the Fulham march, Paul Whelch had circulated this little bit of paper which was a sort of coded message to fans that, given we had a blank Saturday the week later on the 7 December, maybe some people might like to go on a little 'day trip'. That day trip was obviously to Mellor but we didn't want to attract the publicity in the media or indeed to attract the police's attention. As it turned out there were probably about five car-loads. I set off with Paul Whelch, Attila and Stewart Weir. We arrived at about three o'clock and we went into the pub in the village of Mellor. We were just having a drink and as I walked past the front doors of the pub to go to the loo I happened to glance out and in the carpark were three vanloads of police and it was as though we had been rumbled. I really felt like I was a bank-robber who had been tipped off. We went out and met them and they said, 'Well, we just didn't know how many you'd be. We had no idea. We'd heard – we'd got wind of you coming up on the Monday. Mr Archer isn't there, he has gone away.' But I mean, there were only about 12 of us.

We walked down to his house and Attila delivered a note through the door which attracted an incredible response from Bill Archer. That letter was not signed 'Chairman Presently' as was previously signed, it was just signed

'Bill Archer, Chairman' and copied to the Supporters Club executives.

He was obviously under a lot of pressure. The FA had then arranged the CEDR talks a couple of weeks before and he was being forced into a negotiation situation by a third party, the very third party that he didn't really respect. It was obvious that he didn't really have a lot of love for the FA because of the way the Articles had been treated and the way he'd responded when he was summoned to the FA to explain the situation.

Brighton & Hove Albion Football Club
Goldstone Ground Hove East Sussex BN3 7DE
Telephone: (01273) 778855 Fax: (01273) 321095
Albion Clubline 0891 440066

WEA/VSP
10 December 1996

Mr J Baine
6 Colebrook Road
Southwick
West Sussex
BN42 4AL
Without Prejudice

Dear Mr Baine

Thank you for your undated letter, left at my home on Saturday 7 December 1996.

Inspector Coate informs me that you planned your visit to my home because I keep refusing to speak to you and the other supporters' club members. I am astonished by this comment, because I arranged a meeting with the supporters' club executives for 30 September 1996, at the Goldstone. I received a polite letter from Paul Samrah informing me that the supporters' club members did not wish to discuss the plans.

The door is always open for you and the supporters' club executives, to get around a table and discuss the future.

I have been accused of many misdemeanours, all of which have proven to be untrue. The 'Argus' has been non stop. The select band of supporters have been totally destructive in undermining the manager and players at 'home games'. Fireworks, walk-outs, boycotts, riots, pitch invasions, criminal damage, little wonder we are adrift at the bottom of the third division.

When was the last time you and your select band of 'supporters' actually went to a match to support the team against the playing opposition? I can guess that you and the disruptors do not feel a 'jot' of responsibility for the team's predicament. It is always me and the board. When is the penny going

---

to drop? You are destroying the very club you love!

I have to say, Mr Baine, that your name did not come up when the club was in and out of the High Court. Where were all the vociferous supporters then?

The Council have used the unrest to keep the criticism away from them. The club hasn't asked for one penny of Council money. Kirklees put in £2m, Stoke Council £2.5m, all to support the clubs' new stadiums.

Brighton and Hove Albion actually offered £8m to Brighton Council for their land at Patcham.

Only to be told after 18 months that 'we are not selling to the club, but we will sell it to Waitrese Supermarkets!'

If you and your colleagues had not been 'hoodwinked' by the propaganda, I believe we would be a long way now towards a stadium being built.

I have agreed with Graham Kelly at the F.A. that I will discuss any consortium's proposals to assist the Club. I will not be 'black mailed' into a total abdication.

I would welcome your views on a local temporary playing surface, whilst the new stadium is being built. I have looked at the obvious local stadium, the dog track. I have offered to purchase this, but the owners turned several offers down. I have tried to rent the dog track, to convert it in to a temporary football stadium, which would cost in excess of £1m. The board and I will always listen to offers of help. If you know of a stadium which is more convenient then let's discuss it.

I would welcome your help. I want to work with you, not against you. Every time I read your correspondence, I know it's from a loyal supporter of the club. I know you and your colleague supporters love Brighton and Hove Albion Football Club. So do I. Otherwise, I wouldn't be taking this awful stress you are putting me under.

I have offered the council a partnership using the same model Kirklees has with Huddersfield Town F.C.

I said in 1993 that the debts would be paid and a new stadium built.

I have told everybody my plans, Toads Hole Valley. That's where the Council advised me to go in 1992. If any consortium has got a better site, then they must discuss it rationally and openly.

I have been accused of 'moving the goalposts'. I have not. Please read the first paragraph of my letter to Dick Knight. It is self explanatory. Paul Samrah will have a copy.

I am not asking you to like me, but I am asking you to support the team you love.

Yours sincerely

W.B. ARCHER
CHAIRMAN

c.c. Supporters Club Executives

22. Fifteen minutes of football, against the rest of our lives, is a small sacrifice – THINK ABOUT IT!

WALK-OUT – HOME TO HEREFORD (EVENING GAME) – 15 OCTOBER 1996

LIZ COSTA: The thing that we discovered was that pitch invasions gained no friends so it was a case of trying to come up with anything that was innovative that nobody had tried before. I don't even know where that idea came from but everybody got to know about it so it happened, and if you supported the club you had to do it.

BILL SWALLOW: I always remember when the firework went off and everybody walked out. Paul McDonald was in the north-west corner and I remember him looking round in total astonishment at what was happening in front of his very eyes.

LIZ COSTA: I suppose the players were a little bit worried because they knew it was going to happen. It had been well publicised that it was going to happen a quarter of an hour before the end so they were constantly looking around wondering how was it going to happen. It could have been absolutely anything.

SARAH WATTS: I wondered whether I would do it – I have never left a game early except the Tottenham game 15 April 1978, when the North Stand ended up on the pitch. Then the firework went off and I just walked.

NIGEL SUMMERS: I again had my little radio on and I was listening to Tony Millard while we were walking out and it was fantastic. 'I just can't believe what has happened here, a firework has just gone off, everyone is just walking out and the ground is empty.'

STEWART WEIR: I was in the garden when they went off. These things were cabbage-sized, like bazooka-shaped tubes, and I knew when I saw them that this was going to be a good firework.

I was going to do some snaps of them as they went up. One of them was on a short fuse and literally exploded about 20 feet off the ground and my ears

WALK OUT . . .

Tuesday 15th October

If you've followed the Albion for 1, 10 or 40 years, make no mistake this could be your last.

Whether you agree or disagree with the form the protests have taken, you cannot deny that our plight has gone national; and that is because we have **NOT** sat on our backsides and allowed ourselves to be ridden roughshod over by the current owners (read cohorts).

It's up to every one of us left to heap the pressure on and squeeze the board to submission.

Approximately 15 mins before the end of the match an unmistakeable signal will be given to say that its time for everyone who cares to desert the ground
(a good 95% should create a stir).

Should you wish to, you can join us behind the grandstand to make as much noise as possible and prick the consciences of those who choose to remain in the ground to watch the countdown to extinction.

Alternatively you could just leave the ground to show unified loyalty to achieve a common result, either way, it's peaceful (not quiet!). It's legal (not illegal) and it's time (not too late . . . yet).

Don't sit back . . . make some noise . . . or Saturday afternoon's may never be the same again!

15 minutes of football, against the rest of our lives, is a small sacrifice . . . **THINK ABOUT IT!**

rang. I did a few snaps of people looking from the overlooking garden and I thought, 'Bloody hell, they're all leaving.' And I can't remember what the gate was there but there must have only been 500 left.

TONY FOSTER: Where I sat is the front row in the West Stand, and by the time I got to an exit it had been locked and I couldn't get out. God forbid if something had happened like a fire, it could have been dramatic. I couldn't get out of the West Stand, the doors had been locked because people were already milling about in the Newtown Road and coming round behind the main stand. They didn't want people coming in there. I was actually locked in the ground, whether I liked it or not.

JACKIE MOONEY: That was quite hard to do. It's almost harder to walk out than to not go in in the first place, but that was only ever going to work if a lot of people did it. It felt like that you'd walked out on the team, I found that hard.

CHRIS JONES: I mean, after the Hereford game. It was an awful game. We lost 1–0. I just felt the nearest I had come to either jacking it in or crying. I felt really, really depressed after that.

JAN MERRITT: It was very hard to walk out of a match before the end. I had to force myself to do it and I thought it needed as many people as possible to actually do it to make a point. I remember at the end of the match seeing people come out who hadn't joined in and feeling rather angry, perhaps, that they had stayed to the end. Because I am so passionate about the club, I find it very difficult to understand people not wanting to get involved and not joining in.

TONY FOSTER: Seeing everyone leaving the North Stand *en masse* was quite dramatic! There were just a few people stood there at the back but, again, everyone left at the same time, just like at the end of a game.

MARC TWIBILL: I felt all our protests were successful to some extent. Perhaps the walkout was the most successful because it was then, after the fireworks went off, you saw that 90 per cent of the crowd did completely support what the fans were fighting for.

STEWART WEIR: I ran around to the West Stand and there were flares going off. Attila was on the microphone and it was another example of fans realising they had the power and the overwhelming support to actually carry on these actions. But it was another small piece of the fans' story that added to the feeling that 'here we are, we're all in the same boat together'.

TIM CARDER: There were people of all ages, all sorts of shapes and sizes all there outside the West Stand, all really genuine Albion fans.

NIGEL SUMMERS: The protests have gone on and on and on, but at the end of the day they've pretty much been peaceful. I wonder sometimes how we have managed to keep them as peaceful as we have because at the end of the day people are pretty level-headed.

LIZ COSTA: The way that was done was brilliant and, in fact, two games later Hull City copied it for their own protest. This was the point, we were becoming stereotyped demonstrators for other clubs to copy, which they found was much more innovative than pitch invasions and the usual sort of protest. They always say imitation is the best form of flattery.

STEWART WEIR: It was strange the connection between Attila The Stockbroker and Paul Samrah: here we have a kind of punk rock anarchist poet standing side by side with a City accountant and football is the only thing that can do that. Everyone was in the same boat – there were no ifs and buts. At that point it was do-or-die stuff and I got the feeling that everyone, or the vast majority of fans, would do whatever it needed to prove the point and to get the result that the fans wanted which was the board resigning and handing over to the consortium.

23. 'We are Brighton, we are Brighton, super Brighton from the South' (to the tune of 'Sailing')

MARCH THROUGH BRIGHTON BEFORE HOME GAME TO FULHAM – BELLOTTI LEAVES DIRECTORS BOX – 26 OCTOBER 1996

PAUL SAMRAH: It could have been dreadful; it was brilliant. I have never walked so far in all my life. From Brighton station right through across the streets of Brighton and we were blessed with good weather, as with all our demonstrations.

I think it was fair to say the response from Brighton people was disappointing. We weren't cheered as we went, which was disappointing. I think they thought that we were just loud-mouthed football people who didn't know what we wanted, which was actually wrong.

CHRIS JONES: A lot of people were beeping their horns and waving out of windows, you know, non-football people. You felt you weren't on your own either, that you weren't a marginal group.

PAUL SAMRAH: We were reasonable people who had had enough and that was quite significant. We didn't need the football that day to bring us together. We were doing something outside of three o'clock till twenty-to-five.

CHRIS JONES: Inside the ground we were faced with a choice of: do we chant at the board all the way through the game, or do we get behind the team? Difficult – it is very difficult.

DAVE SWAFFIELD (train driver): That was one of the best days, huge crowd, sell-out that day. Bellotti comes out and he starts getting hounded and sworn at, people are jumping down in the West Stand and having a go at him, and he decides to leave the ground.

TIM CARDER: I remember he was driven out with about 20 minutes to go and whereas before it had all been chants to get rid of Bellotti, the atmosphere just completely changed, everyone got behind the team. I think Fulham were top of the table at the time and we put in a good performance that day. The atmosphere completely changed as soon as he went.

LIZ COSTA: There was that photograph, in the *Independent*, it shows the anger and the relief.

PAUL CAMILLIN: He is completely hunched-out. You can see the anger captured in the faces, it's a superb picture.

CHRIS JONES: The picture in the *Independent* which went back and back with people like normal people, old people, young people, men, women, children, it was like a bus queue of people all just really happy that he had gone and been chased out.

DAVE SWAFFIELD: We haven't had many good moments this season and that was one of the best ones, seeing that git and his wife walk out, hunched up walking out the ground. There's a great photograph in the *Independent* on the following Monday of all these people around him, everyone applauding him going, it was a really good moment.

TIM CARDER: His mere presence provoked people and I cannot understand how he can possibly think that turning up at matches was at all in the interests of the club. He went match after match, he used to creep out of the directors box a few minutes in and there'd be an uproar in the West Stand and throughout the ground.

LIZ COSTA: That was the first one where he actually had to leave and never came back, but then he started this exclusion zone extending to the bit in front of him so that no one stood in front of him. He then decided to exclude non-season ticket holders from the West Stand and from the West Terrace.

JAN MERRITT: To take the crash barriers away and then put them around where he was sitting just seems to me the behaviour of someone who's keeping his power.

BILL SWALLOW: Bellotti – what's his role? He is unfathomable. I cannot work him out. His continually coming to the club – I don't know why he was doing it. I don't like barracking away supporters or virtually anyone, but quite honestly it got to such a stage that I would have been pleased if I'd heard somebody had shot him. He didn't appear to me to be human.

TIM CARDER: Quite honestly, in my opinion, he should have been dismissed for persisting with what he did. How could the team play when the crowd was spending its whole time just trying to drive Bellotti out of the stadium? And the fact is, once he did leave the atmosphere improved.

DAVE SWAFFIELD: The roar that went up when he left the stand was absolutely incredible, it was like winning the game. Amazing – one of my best moments.

24. The only glimmer of hope that we had

FANS' FORUM, HOVE TOWN HALL – 28 OCTOBER 1996

TIM BOHANNON: If Dick Knight hadn't taken over then there would have been serious trouble; someone might have died – not necessarily Bellotti or Archer but something very, very serious would have happened. That's how deeply people felt about it.

ATTILA THE STOCKBROKER: There were loads of different initiatives coming from all sides. It was brilliant. There were people phoning me up saying, 'Shall we do this, shall we do that?' My attitude was that if it's inventive, if it will get good publicity and it's witty – do it. The only thing is we don't want anyone to get hurt and we don't want anything stupid. In the midst of it all I was organising all these meetings and discussing stuff and it became increasingly apparent to me that the most important thing we had to do was forge close links with the Dick Knight consortium – work out exactly where they were going and see if we could possibly get to support them.

PAUL SAMRAH: It was the first chance for people to meet Dick Knight and the consortium, Martin Perry of McAlpine's, Bob Pinnock, and I think the setting was superb. It was at the Hove Town Hall, everyone had a seat and it was conducted really professionally, microphones, the full works, everyone up on stage, and I think the consortium gained an awful lot of credibility.

TONY FOSTER: It was the only glimmer of hope we had and you just have to remember back to the reception the consortium had that day. It was very well supported and we had to go with it. It was another milestone.

TIM CARDER: It was actually a BISA meeting and it was packed out. This was the first opportunity any of us had had to actually talk to the consortium, certainly in public. We didn't really know who they were so they introduced themselves and explained what they were about.

I'm sure everyone came out of that meeting fully behind what they envisaged for the club and it was in such a stark contrast to Archer and Bellotti. We knew then that we had to get the consortium in and Archer and Bellotti out. They emphasised that they wanted to keep us in the area which was something that Archer and Bellotti just never seemed to bother about. The consortium also made the commitment there that they would stay, even if the club was relegated to the Conference, which was quite reassuring.

There was also a move to boycott all remaining home games. There was no way that people would have stood for that, even if they voted for it that night I don't think it would have stood up. There were 400-500 people there that night and that still left 4,000 maybe who weren't there that night – it wouldn't have worked.

MARC TWIBILL: Dick Knight obviously wanted us to boycott all the games until the end of the season. Looking back, from the point of view of getting rid of Archer that would have been the most successful, but from the point of view of supporting the team it could have ultimately ended in relegation so it was very hard to know what to do.

PAUL SAMRAH: We were reassured that if the club did get relegated out of the league that Dick Knight would still stand by us, which gave us great heart.

We felt that we shouldn't put money into the coffers of the present board. We then decided what our tactics would be and a number of people had mentioned about a possible one-match boycott and the game chosen was the Mansfield Town home game at the beginning of November.

25. Reclaim the ground

BOYCOTT OF HOME GAME AGAINST MANSFIELD TOWN –
9 OCTOBER 1996

BILL SWALLOW: The Mansfield boycott – we score ten out of ten on that one because the reason we didn't want to go in was not because we didn't want to support the team but because we didn't want to give Bill Archer any money. We didn't give Bill Archer any money. Then we broke in. And we saw the game, well at least half of it. It was absolutely brilliant.

PAUL SAMRAH: With Atilla, I decided to write to the players and manager Jimmy Case and the coaching staff of the football club, so we drafted a statement and I delivered this to Stuart Storer during the week leading up to the game.

[Extracts from leaflet:] 'Our anger is directed solely at the board of directors, the architects of our club's decline. It is our united view that however well you perform on the pitch, the Albion has no future whilst Archer is in control. We the paying customers who love the club dearly will not stand idly by to see this destroyed. The desire to change is therefore irreversible. We call on your support; this is your livelihood and our club. We are in this together. Win the game on Saturday and help us bring about the change that is so desperately needed.'

We then blew this up and put it on coloured paper and I stamped it all round and outside the ground.

STUART ADAMS: We worked at the turnstiles on the North Stand and that was quite fascinating. We were shouting out to anyone who had a season ticket who wasn't going in to give them to us so that the people who were going to break the boycott, at least they weren't going to pay.

KEVIN SHERWOOD: Some were adamant that they were going to go in. If you gave them season tickets, they said, 'What's the catch?' They were so suspicious and that was weird, that was what I couldn't get to grips with. Some people are completely uninformed and that's not their fault if they don't buy the *Argus* and don't listen to the radio, you can't rely on the club.

Albion's Supporter Groups say
PLEASE BOYCOTT TODAY'S MATCH

How can staying away possibly help?
It will show the country we are as one in our desire to rid the club of Archer and Bellotti. It will also reduce the club's cash flow – and Archer would ultimately be forced to sell a company starved of cash.

Why today?
The national media are here at the Goldstone because of the lack of Premiership fixtures. The widespread coverage will further embarrass Archer the businessman.

But I want to support my team.
We all support the team. That's why we've written to all the players assuring them of the fans' backing. They know our dispute is with the board, not them.

Staying away is the last thing any of us want to do, but, sadly, it is now necessary for Albion fans to make the **ultimate gesture** of any football supporter.

Think about it: one afternoon's football against a lifetime's attendance. If we do not *all* help to get rid of Archer and Bellotti, this club *will* fold.

But that's just sheer ignorance and that's just, 'I'm not interested in what's going on, I just want to watch Brighton play.'

LIZ COSTA: It was successful in that it galvanised Supporters groups of all sorts. Nobody expected us in the Supporters Club to participate and I think we gained a lot of kudos from people who had mistrusted us.

NIGEL SUMMERS: I've spoken to a few people since who went in and tried to ask them why. I've not really got a sensible answer but, again, it's all friendly. I wasn't on the miners' strike or anything but I imagine it must have been something similar. It was all really good natured and when people were going in nobody was calling them scabs or anything derogatory.

JACKIE MOONEY: If you went in or stayed out you did it because you loved the Albion and because you wanted to do what you thought best.

TONY FOSTER: I stood outside with two Mansfield fans that weren't going into the ground. They'd driven all the way and seen what was happening, understood the situation and stood outside with us at the back of the North Stand protesting with all our banners. I kid you not, the guy had broken down into tears. He said, 'What's happened with your football club, I would feel like a traitor as a football fan to actually go into the ground.' He was more emotional than I was. Unbelievable.

TIM CARDER: There was a theory at the time that if we deprived the club of money it would reduce the club's cash flow and Archer would ultimately be forced to wind it up or sell it. But the one-off boycott game got a lot of publicity. I think there were 1,933 people actually admitted through the turnstiles.

STEWART WEIR: The official figure was 1,933 but that takes into account the Mansfield fans who'd paid, the season ticket-holders who didn't turn up, and people who'd paid up on the day. I did a rough head count and I don't reckon there were more than about 800 in on that game. It probably just proves the point of how the campaign had developed from what you might call a hard core of 100 in the North Stand to 98 per cent of regulars that were going in there.

TIM CARDER: There was lots going on outside. It was the first time the chap from the Lewes bonfire society brought his models of Archer along there to explode ceremonially. I didn't actually go in although I wanted to. I went round the East Terrace and I could have, but I just couldn't bring myself to do it – I had really mixed emotions that day.

JAN SWALLOW: I remember going round to behind the East Terrace to one of the big gates and there was a whole line of big blokes lying flat on their stomachs and you could see under the gate – you could get quite a good view. All of a sudden the gates opened and we all ran in – it was absolutely brilliant – you felt like part of an army or something, claiming your territory back. Really odd. It was really exciting.

NIGEL SUMMERS: We started wandering round the ground and ended up round the back of the East terrace and a few younger people started kicking doors just in frustration and somebody said 'Let's go in.'
About six of us got up on to the turnstile and on to the terrace and we

walked down on to the terrace and all the Mansfield fans started cheering. From the left come a load of stewards and from the right a load of policemen, so step by step we start walking backwards towards the turnstiles. Then the gates burst open and everyone else comes piling in and there's bloody hundreds of people. I don't know how the gate ever got opened. People say a steward opened it. I never saw that.

STEWART WEIR: I was outside and I did all my work during and probably 20 or 30 minutes into it, and I was absolutely starving so I went over to the shop. For some reason I was in the car, I can't remember why, and I heard on the radio something like, 'They're breaking in, they're breaking in – they're in on the East Terrace', and thought, 'Shit.' I double-parked the car on a double-yellow line or something outrageous, ran around to the East Stand and most of them had got in.

CHRIS JONES: We went to get there at half-time and there was a buzz going on, you knew that something significant had happened. As we got in, loads of them ran across the pitch just as the game had stopped and took over the directors box. The Mansfield fans came along clapping and I felt empowered, I felt really, really good after that.

STEWART WEIR: The half-time whistle went and Erskine from *Gull's Eye* ran on the centre circle, and then 100 went on. The stewards and the police are just standing there – they're not doing anything. A few of the Mansfield fans came on and they were shaking hands on the pitch, they chatted and hugged.

NIGEL SUMMERS: Not the first of, but the latest in the series of, the football-fan love-ins.

STUART ADAMS: A Mansfield fan came on and about ten seconds later I was on the pitch myself. It just seemed the right thing to do with the Mansfield fans, and then of course storming up in to the directors box and watching the match from there with my son. My son's been everywhere this season. It was like retaking the Goldstone.

JAN MERRITT: I was outside and I didn't actually go in – I wish I had, in retrospect – but again, although it was illegal, I couldn't say that I felt anything wrong with doing it because there was no violence involved. I just felt so angry towards Bellotti at the time and when they ran across the pitch over to where he was, I thought, 'Good', you know? I wish they'd lynched him.

I mean, I'm a terribly non-violent person but I was just so angry with what was going on.

JAN SWALLOW: At half-time we went over to the West Terrace – I think there was one message on the tannoy that said 'Go back to the East Terrace' and we were all saying 'no way' and I remember saying to Anna, 'The only way they can get me out of here is if they carry me out.' Which was amazing, I've never done anything like this before. I wouldn't break the law . . . but then, there's no way I would have walked out of that ground.

BILL SWALLOW: We went and stood behind Jimmy Case. I remember him looking round as he came out of the dugout and being totally astonished at the transformed atmosphere in that ground from half-time – and giving us a smile and a wink as we stood behind him. Great.

TIM BOHANNON: I wasn't at the vanguard of the storming but I thought the protest was so much more valid – and the players responded, especially Stuart Storer. The Mansfield supporters knew what was going on and they were wholeheartedly behind everybody.

ANNA SWALLOW: We'd gone across the pitch, we'd stormed him out of the directors box and we'd got a point across, which is brilliant. That was a superb game.

TONY FOSTER: A couple of friends were reminiscing about that recently, when they got into the exclusion zone of the West Terrace and a very large Mansfield supporter pulled about five of them up into the directors box and said, 'Up you come lads, into your directors box.' He was huge, about 22 stone.

NIGEL SUMMERS: I was standing on the seat in the front of the directors box and the Mansfield directors stood for the whole of the second half and watched because they couldn't see sitting down. When the fans got behind the team, the team responded. We were 1–0 down and playing crap, the fans came in and the whole atmosphere of the place went from morgue to party-time. We got a dodgy penalty and equalised. The crowd had won the point, that's what it felt like. The only person who didn't turn up for the rest of the second half was Bellotti.

CHRIS JONES: I thought that was a very symbolic moment, reclaiming something, boycotting the game and then getting in to watch it. It was only 45 minutes but it was excellent.

TIM CARDER: What was good in this campaign was that events that were arranged – marches and demonstrations and all sorts of things – did act as a sort of pressure valve and relieve the pressure a little bit.

BILL SWALLOW: The degree of imagination that came out of all these things was just tremendous. They were different all the time. I actually think there was possibly a slight lack of co-ordination. The trick was, how could you have co-ordinated it a bit better without taking away the spirit? As Attila said at the Town Hall that time, 'If you've got an idea, go and do it,' and that was great. Perhaps it was anarchic but that may be what made it even better.

PAUL SAMRAH: I felt triumphant, I felt we had made a point, that we were supporting the team. The team were 1–0 down and they came back and drew 1–1 and Bellotti never reappeared for the second half. It wasn't lawlessness, it wasn't reckless, it was supporters having their say, 'It's our club.'

Tremendous, absolutely tremendous.

NIGEL SUMMERS: The crowd had got the Goldstone back.

26. 'Rochdale fans were absolutely superb'

ROCHDALE AWAY – 29 OCTOBER 1996

SARAH WATTS: When we got to Rochdale, having gone via Crewe, we all wanted to go and stop off at the Focus DIY head office. Of course Archer got word of it and gave everyone the afternoon off! We took a petition the *Argus* had done – we had 6,500 people who told Archer politely where to go – and tried to deliver it.

KEVIN SHERWOOD: We'd taken the *Argus* petition up to Crewe and deposited it outside Bill Archer's Focus DIY place on that industrial estate just outside Crewe. We headed off to Rochdale and of course it transpired that Bellotti was present in the ground as he liked to be at that time. That set the mood for the crowd.

STEWART WEIR: At the beginning of the season it was a foregone conclusion that Bill Archer would not be at Brighton games. It was only in the latter part of the season that he started to make appearances at away games. But Bellotti would be there with his wife and he just endured a whole torrent of absolute abuse. I don't know what the home directors thought of it all but I've no doubt that they would probably rather he had not been there. The fans were incensed by the look of him, by even breathing the same air as them, so that all their attention was put on to him and to chanting 'Archer Out' and 'Build a Bonfire'.

KEVIN SHERWOOD: Another dismal game. That was a pretty poor one – I think we lost about 3–0. The Rochdale fans were really supportive throughout the game and there was a mini pitch invasion at one point from the Albion end, where a group of about two dozen-plus Brighton fans went and joined the Rochdale fans behind their goal which was just a show of solidarity.

LIZ COSTA: The Rochdale supporters, to their credit, were absolutely brilliant because they actually led the 'Build a Bonfire' song. At one point I know some of the more volatile of our supporters said, 'Invade the pitch'. All of a sudden from behind me there was a mad rush and they all went zooming off, over the wall and round and they were in the end on the Rochdale terracing. They were swapping shirts with the Rochdale fans.

PAUL CAMILLIN: Rochdale fans were absolutely superb. We were 3–0 down and that was another top away trip because of the total moral support we received. With 20 minutes to go, we all strolled up on to the pitch, only three of us made it into the home end, got a brilliant reception.

A load of them swallowed me up into the crowd and said, 'Take your Brighton shirt off, mate.' They were absolutely fucking brilliant and said, 'Join us outside, we'll have joint protest against your board.' We kept the coach in for two hours that night, and in the end the police had to get the dogs in to get rid of us.

TIM CARDER: Whereas a few years ago there would have been an almighty punch-up in that situation, they were all swapping shirts, it was a general love-in and we were all supporting each other.

When your club's going out of existence, then everyone realises that they love their own clubs as much as we love our club. Ask a Rochdale fan what it would be like if Rochdale suddenly disappeared and he will understand – he'll get the same feelings that we get.

STEWART WEIR: The team, no doubt, did suffer with the atmosphere that the travelling Brighton fans brought with them. But what were they to do? The priority was to get Archer and Bellotti out and probably to a lesser degree Stanley, but I think Archer and Bellotti were the absolute main focus and it was awful.

STUART STORER: All I remember is we'd just been absolutely killed, 3–0 on the park. All I wanted to do was get on that bus, get home and get in my bed. And we had to wait around for three hours after the match because the fans wanted to get hold of Mr Bellotti.

KEVIN SHERWOOD: After the game we met up with the Rochdale fans again and there was a players entrance behind one of the stands. We were just waiting for them to come out and we must have stayed there about 40 minutes watching the players get on the coach.

They were just waiting and waiting and all of a sudden there was this big rush of stewards and they bundled this character on to the coach – head under the jacket. It was a typical post-game event. The coach pulled out, carried on off to the motorway and they've got a flotilla of cars and mini-buses following it. Heads off to the motorway junction, hits the roundabout which is the turn off to the motorway and just keeps spinning round and round about. And everyone was thinking, 'What's going on here?'

STEWART WEIR: It was almost the scene from the *Pink Panther* where the coach was being followed by several minibuses and cars.

The coach went round this roundabout four or five times to shake them off, eventually went back to Rochdale and Bellotti was smuggled out.

PAUL CAMILLIN: There was a rumour that Bellotti had been smuggled on under a coat and put in the toilet, so when it drove off we followed it and when it went back we thought Jimmy Case was on it. Case came out but Bellotti still didn't come out.

KEVIN SHERWOOD: Police are there and stop us getting in to the carpark and then all the players unload. A few local lads, wandering out of the sponsorship lounge said, 'Your boy's in there absolutely shitting himself – Mr Bellotti.' It seems it transpired that it was Jimmy Case who was bundled on to the coach.

PAUL CAMILLIN: We got on to the motorway and followed this coach all the way back and we drove alongside it and pulled in front of it to check he was still on it, then we got to the top of the M23. By this time it was about three o'clock in the morning and it went off towards Croydon. So it must have done one stop up in Croydon. There was a rumour flying round that Bellotti had three police cars waiting at the Goldstone. If that was true, it shows the total paranoia around the place.

KEVIN SHERWOOD: I was like most people. I just snapped. I couldn't bear to watch it any more without doing something. I think once you're over that threshold, what your emotions lead you to do, it's bloody frightening because some of the things that we did on our travels, like demonstrate in far-flung places like Doncaster and Rochdale, and you think, 'This is 3.30 in the morning and I'm stuck at some services waiting for the team coach to turn up just so I can scream abuse.' If you have time to dwell on it: one, you think you're daft and just want to go home and two, it scares you what you could do if you actually got hold of the bloke.

27. 'The FA's done fuck all' (Brighton chant, 1996)

PETITION TO FORCE THE FA TO CHARGE THE DIRECTORS WITH 'BRINGING THE GAME INTO DISREPUTE' AND MARCH THROUGH LONDON TO THE FA – 30 NOVEMBER 1996

TIM CARDER: There's a chap called Edward Grayson who's recognised as one of the foremost experts on sport and the law in this country. He wrote to the *Telegraph* a couple of letters saying that there is precedent for the FA to strip the directors of their position and appoint administrators into the club, and he quoted some case concerning Arsenal back in the 1920s, I think it was. This was seized upon by Paul Hayward and it led to a meeting in January.

PAUL HAYWARD: He's a barrister and he wrote a book called *Sport and the Law*. He's the country's foremost expert in the way that sport and the law overlap and he's helped players prosecute other players when they've been assaulted on the pitch and that type of thing. So he contacted me to say that he felt that there were legal precedents for the FA to charge the board, with 'misconduct' and 'bringing the game into disrepute'. When I examined the Articles of Association of the FA it seemed obvious to me that there were grounds for doing that and that if they failed to do so the FA were in breach of their own constitution and could be forced to do so by a court of law.

117

PAUL SAMRAH: Edward Grayson said that there is a precedent for the FA to take action against the board of directors. With Paul Hayward's assistance, a further letter again was published by Edward Grayson on 23 December saying quite categorically that there is a precedent for action to be taken by the FA and that he could take legal action himself to force the FA to take action.

TIM CARDER: It was on the basis of this meeting that we decided that we had to have this legal action in the background if the talks broke down. We employed a solicitor who Mr Grayson recommended who wrote a letter to the Football Association outlining the basis of our case and we received a reply back which was basically a rejection of that case but I think it did worry the FA to some extent.

DAVID DAVIES (the FA's director of public affairs): It is entirely true that a barrister wrote in the *Daily Telegraph* the FA, on a precedent of Arsenal in 1928, could and should have done this, this and this. I have to tell you that there were five or six equally eminent barristers who said absolutely the opposite.

Regardless of who was right – I didn't find the legal profession rushing to support that guy – but it's a good line, and don't think it wasn't seriously considered. What was certain – if you charge anybody with disrepute and they fight it, as for sure they would have done, that wouldn't have solved the future ownership of the club.

PAUL HAYWARD: They could have charged Archer particularly with Rule 26(a)(x): 'misconduct or any matter which in the opinion of the Council, is considered to be improper behaviour or likely to bring the game into disrepute'.

Having done that they could have ejected him from the game as they've ejected many, many people from football over the decades. They could have disqualified him as a club director, in which case the club would have gone into the hands of receivers. This is Edward Grayson's interpretation: it would have gone into receivership, not gone out of business but would have been held by bankers basically, and a new board would have been found. Clearly we knew at that time that a consortium was ready to step in.

They didn't do that because I think there's a paranoia at the FA about legal cases and I think they felt that they would land themselves with a complex legal situation.

PAUL SAMRAH: It was a great media thing. I knew deep down it was going to cost a fortune, and also one fan was going to have to put their name to the writ and, if we lost the case, costs would be awarded against that individual, we couldn't hide behind a banner of Brighton Independent Supporters Association. Someone had to put their name there, we would have needed a fighting fund of £10,000 from the word go and we just didn't have the time to organise massive fundraising like that.

TIM CARDER: I think it did galvanise the FA and probably helped ensure that they put pressure on the mediators and all parties involved to come up with a result that would satisfy both the FA and more importantly of course the supporters. So that's as far as the legal action went, but it was there in the background and we would have used it had it become necessary. We postponed it because of the sensitivity of the mediation talks.

LONDON MARCH, AWAY AT FULHAM – 30 NOVEMBER 1996

PAUL WHELCH: Attila, in a classic throwaway line at the end of the Hove Town Hall meeting, had said that he wanted everybody who'd ever loved the club to go to the Fulham match! It set me thinking and it was an opportunity, coming back to my role in London to see what I could do to organise something in London that would have an impact in that sort of situation. I initially went to the police and just said we were interested in having a march, no particular location, just a march. I wrote to the department that administers Trafalgar Square about having a rally. I copied it to Andy Naylor from the *Argus* and Radio 5, two days later it's on the Ceefax that we're having a rally in Trafalgar Square! I thought, 'Well, that is fascinating!' We were a very powerful political story.

I had a series of meetings with the Central Area Headquarters or the police area that governs Whitehall and the whole of Westminster. Over a protracted period of discussions initially they tried to persuade me not to do it and thought it was a very bad idea, but I stuck at it, realising that they couldn't really say that because at the end of the day it's their responsibility to police it. So in the end we agreed that a suitable route would be from Grosvenor Terrace, just outside Victoria Station to Hyde Park, which would work. Of course the advantage of that was that it meant two things, one is that we could start at Victoria Station which had a sort of spiritual location for Brighton supporters, and secondly that we could go pretty close to the FA in terms of the location of the march. Which then led to the suggestion that what we really ought to do was to have a petition so that we could actually give the whole thing some degree of coverage. We spent a lot of time trying to get the wording of the petition right.

PAUL SAMRAH: We just wanted action and the purpose of our march to the FA on 30 November was to actually force the FA to do something. That's what the petition was for. We cleared the petition with lawyers, we got 5,700 signatures. We had about two home games and people took away petitions and took them to work.

'We the undersigned demand urgent action by the Football Association to resolve the mounting crisis at Brighton and Hove Albion Football Club. It is our view that the club is in danger of being seriously mismanaged and that its present board of directors may be unable to sustain League football in Sussex. We therefore demand that action is brought by the Council and Football Association, in particular against chairman Bill Archer, and chief executive and deputy chairman David Bellotti, that they should be charged with 'misconduct, likely to bring the game to disrepute' in accordance with rule 26 (x) of the Rules of the Football Association.'

We wanted to be identified, it wasn't something that we needed to hide behind and so we contacted the press and it snowballed.

JAN SWALLOW: I thought, 'I don't want to just walk on it – I'm going to make a banner.' So we tried to think of different wording and I had this idea and it took me a week every evening making it out of an old blue sheet. I did it all in pencil first and then filled it in just using paint, you know, fibre-tip pens. Anna said to me, 'Why don't you just put "Piss off Archer" – it would be quicker.'

ANNA SWALLOW: I would arrive home on a Friday night to find my mum and her sister practically walking and turning corners with her banner up and down the hall – you know, 'What is going on with my family? We've completely lost it.'

PAUL SAMRAH: Paul Whelch had liaised with the police, he contacted the FA and told them you've got to have someone there to greet us when we arrive there and, again, we were blessed with good weather. We marched from Grosvenor Gardens up Park Lane, it was absolutely bizarre. You were hoping that there would be a lot of media coverage for it but actually I didn't see a lot.

NIGEL SUMMERS: I went up on the train. There was quite a lot of Brighton supporters on the train, but when I came out of the station there weren't any and I didn't know how many to expect. When I got over to that little triangle where we assembled, I couldn't believe how many people there were.

JAN SWALLOW: We all got off at Victoria and there were hundreds of people there waiting to go on the march. It was wonderful. As we walked along, people, especially tourists in their coaches, were looking at us thinking, 'What on earth are they doing?'

STEWART WEIR: I didn't do a count but it certainly looked close on to 1,000. It was leaving from just up the road from Victoria and there was this mass of people shouting 'Archer out, Archer out', just another example of how the fans would get together and do their thing. Again it's the first time that a club or fans have ever marched through London – there were three clowns dressed as Archer, Bellotti and Stanley which were quite fun to watch. We ended up at Hyde Park and they counted up the signatures and then went round to Lancaster Gate and knocked on the door – out comes some official, thank you very much – that's that. It looked good but what point are petitions any more? Is anyone bothered?

PAUL CAMILLIN: We brought a part of London to a standstill – that was absolutely superb.

ANNA SWALLOW: It was weird holding up Hyde Park Corner with the Albion, it was just fantastic. It felt futile in a way. A lot of signatures, which was great, and obviously my mum's brilliant banner.

LIZ COSTA: Now this is something that has never happened before. Football supporters marching through London – not even a London club, we had no right to be there. The fact that we were playing against Fulham that day is quite immaterial. It just seems to me extraordinary that the FA at the time didn't even take this into consideration, that we were being listened to by people who mattered. At that rally there were people from QPR, there were people from Tottenham, there were all sorts of people who joined that rally which shows that football, to a degree, is a universal language, and the supporters started to care and they started to listen.

PAUL SAMRAH: It wouldn't have been the same if it had been Manchester United. You could have had the march with 200,000 people doing that in Hyde Park with all the media attention from all across the world, if you were Manchester United, but it wouldn't have been the same.

It was our local thing. We recognised most of the fans on that march, we didn't know all their names but we recognised them all.

NIGEL SUMMERS: Everyone was very aware at that time about the importance of the media but of course the problem with the media is that they flog something to death and then it doesn't matter what happens, unless it's outrageous, it's not going to get printed.

PAUL SAMRAH: We wanted the FA to take action against Archer and at the rally we issued the press statement.

'We vividly recall the FA took no public action in the lead up to the club's final home game last season against York City in April. The resultant scenes were shown around the world with good reason, therefore we generally fear for public safety and order if positive action is not seen to be forthcoming imminently. The demonstrations have hitherto been peaceful and law abiding but we cannot restrain individuals from taking the law into their own hands. If the FA are in any doubt about the strength of feeling on the Archer versus the Knight consortium issue they should order the club to ballot its supporters precisely in accordance with Bill Archer's own written promises in a letter that: 'my intention is for the supporters to decide. I am not going to attempt to push water uphill, that's why ultimately you and the Supporters Club members will decide'.

'The FA has an immediate duty to resolve the situation.'

If not the FA, then who?

28. 'Sack the board'

SUPPORTERS' ACTION

LEAFLETS

TIM CARDER: The Tory poster of Tony Blair was out at the time so it was quite a current theme. The Tory one said 'New Labour, New Danger' and ours was a picture of the Archer demon with demon eyes in his sunglasses and the label was 'New Owners, New Hope'. I remember this was handed out in September and it said, 'I'm a loyal supporter of the Albion and I want you to step aside – you're destroying our club – please go and go now.' About a thousand of these were done and they were all sent on Monday 23 September to Mr Archer's very nice farmhouse on the edge of Blackburn so on Tuesday 24 he should have had a nice postbag.

PAUL SAMRAH: Suddenly we started to get these newsletters being produced, produced by 'normal reasonable law-abiding people who have finally had enough'.

NEW OWNERS NEW HOPE

HELP RID THE CLUB OF THE ARCHER DEMON

Dear Mr Archer

I am a loyal supporter of Brighton & Hove Albion and I do not want you at my football club. You have publicly stated that you will step aside if anyone can meet four conditions concerning the future of the club and a new ground. Mr Dick Knight's consortium has met these conditions, which you yourself are patently unable to fulfil, so I am asking you keep to your word. Open the books immediately, take your £56.25, and leave now. I believe you are destroying the club and that there is no future for the Albion while you continue to be associated with it in any way.

For God's sake go and go NOW.

Yours sincerely

Name....... *TIM CARDER*

Address .... *113 SURRENDEN ROAD*

.... *BRIGHTON*

.... *BN1 6WB*

....

If you agree with the above sentiments, send this card by first-class post on Monday, 23rd September 1996.

Affix stamp here

Mr W. E. Archer
Chairman,
Brighton & Hove Albion
Vine House Farm
Whinney Lane
Mellor
BLACKBURN
Lancashire
BB2 7EH

2 POINTS BIG DEAL!

IT'S OUR CLUB AND WE MUST STAND UP FOR IT

TELL THEM TO GO! NOW

DO WE REALLY WANT TO SPEND OUR SATURDAY AFTERNOONS SHOPPING AND WISHING WE HAD DONE MORE!

Mr. Kelly & Co. have again given the green light for **ARCHER, STANLEY & BELLOTTI** to continue with their destruction of the **ALBION**. In deducting two points , they have said; "do what you like and we will punish the fans if they dare protest against it!. All the **FA** care about is the big boys. As far as they are concerned, we can take a run & jump. Well chaps, we've got news for you; we don't give a **** about the two points. If the fans had wanted to abandon the Lincoln game to show their anger, they would have done so. If you don't start to bring your full powers to bear against these **CRUDE ASSET STRIPPERS & VERY SOON**, the fans will have no alternative but to consider the forced abandonment of another match. This will undoubtably have the full support and understanding of fans throughout the country who know that, if **BRIGHTON & HOVE ALBION** are destroyed whilst the **FA** stands by doing nothing, they could be next. This is not fantasy football, it's **REALITY!**

ARCHER, STANLEY & BELLOTTI HAVE, THROUGH THEIR ACTIONS, BROUGHT THE GAME INTO DISREPUTE, DON'T CHARGE THE ALBION, CHARGE THEM. KICK THEM OUT <u>NOW</u>!

WE ARE ALBION, AND WILL NEVER GIVE UP!

Produced by: Normal reasonable law abiding citizens who have finally had enough
A COPY OF THIS HAS BEEN SENT TO MR. KELLY

JAN SWALLOW: Adrian Wells at Detail Print produced them and there were quite a number of us giving them out all round the ground. Apart from the leaflets we did posters, and the 'Save the Albion' car stickers, we were writing and faxing the FA all the time.

LETTERS

NIGEL SUMMERS: The protests I can do I can do best throughout that sort of media. I'm not big enough to go chest-to-chest or nose-to-nose to anybody so I do it that way. I just started writing to people and it's just gone on and on from there. I wrote to all the Sussex MPs, I went to the library and looked up everybody in the Houses of Parliament, Lords and Commons, who list sport first and football second as their special parliamentary interest. I wrote to Companies House, the police, Sussex County FA, the Football League and it just went on and on.

TONY HYLANDS: I was sitting here so pissed off with what was happening to the club and I thought, 'I've got to do something.' I wrote a letter, like a dossier to the FA and I mentioned why has the ground been sold with no concrete plans for a new ground, why have they changed the Articles? This is the three-line reply I got back:

---

2 October 1996

Dear Mr Hylands
Thank you for your letter dated 28 September in connection with the above. We are doing our best to preserve league football in the Brighton and Hove area but our powers sadly are not limitless.
yours sincerely

Graham Kelly

To me, that was a fudge. I'd sat down for hours writing a dossier and sent it to the FA for them to reply two lines to me, I felt insulted. I thought the FA must stand for fuck all and the FA has done fuck all. To this day I would lay £100 on at the bookies, I'll go to my grave believing that the FA got involved purely through pitch invasions. The fans got the FA involved, because the FA thought there was going to be so much trouble with Brighton.

BANNERS

NIGEL SUMMERS: Brighton Bridge Club. No one's ever told me it's illegal. Somebody put one up and it wasn't me, at Sayers Common, and I thought 'That's a good idea', so I had a bit of wood in the garage and I put one up, and then a few more. It was getting a joke so we went out and started doing them properly, buying the wood, buying the paint, going into full production.

There was never any bad language, we never hung them directly over the carriageway and we never put anything defamatory. We didn't spray paint on walls or cause anybody any trouble. They weren't going to fall down on the cars and we hadn't damaged anything. They were temporary mobile signs.

One went up, and then two and then three and then ten and then 15, and then one morning they'd all gone. But, not to be beaten, we got some more. And I reckon we've done about 125 by now but the messages are always humorous. We were thinking of bringing out an I-Spy book of Albion road signs at one stage. They must have a hit squad on permanent stand-by, I reckon, but we'll keep on doing it because nobody's told me it's illegal.

'BILL ARCHER, ENEMY OF SUSSEX.'
(Bridge banner 1996)

ATTILA THE STOCKBROKER: If you provide the raw material the media will buy it if it's good and interesting and a bit witty and off-beat — like that banner, we had the one side of the banner which said in effect 'get off your knees' sort of thing and I thought, 'Well I've got a 15-by-three banner here, we must do something with that,' so I painted it up and it was in seven national newspapers.

'1901–97 – THE GOLDSTONE R.I.P.
SOLD BY MONEYMEN FOR PROFIT AND GREED.
WE WILL NEVER FORGET.'
(Banner 1996)

FANZINES (Gull's Eye)
IAN HART: If this hadn't happened, I would still be going to watch football. I don't think that the Gull's Eye would be going. This was like a shot in the arm for Gull's Eye, it was our Holy Grail, wasn't it, it was our cause.

We had to fight and we had to keep people informed 'cause I don't think that anybody else was.

ATTILA THE STOCKBROKER: Pivotal. Absolutely pivotal. It gave us a common focus that was uncontrolled by the media. It's made everything possible, it's spread the word and it's got things through. Occasionally the Argus would be brilliant and occasionally they would be a complete waste of time. If we haven't been able to get stuff in the Argus, we always had the Gull's Eye to

advertise our meetings and make sure people knew what's going on. People read it – that's the point. I mean, I never got a copy of the one with my poem in for the last game. It's got real respect and it bloody well should have because it's really good.

IAN HART: People said 'you're a bit out of order printing all the directors' addresses in there' but it got rid of Ray Bloom, didn't it? I printed Ray Bloom's address and he had a succession of packages in the early morning – pizzas and visiting massage and a proposed demonstration round his house and he resigned, so direct action worked. And I'm sure the Archers didn't like having to be moved out by the police from their house on Christmas Day because there was a bogus story saying that there was going to be a demonstration at their house.

ATTILA THE STOCKBROKER: The thing about *Gull's Eye* was that we didn't have to beg for anything. I didn't have to phone up four times to get a mention of a meeting or some sort of activity that we were doing. We put it in and it was printed and that was it. I genuinely do not have praise enough for *Gull's Eye*. The reason that it is read so avidly is because it does genuinely reflect what people feel on the terraces and it is loved by the fans.

It is a genuine creation of popular culture. It's the sort of thing that should be regarded as popular art. It encourages ordinary people to write who wouldn't be writing otherwise. Some of it's really funny and witty – even with the occasional spelling mistakes and gratuitous sexism – it's a brilliant

127

fanzine. I wouldn't like them to be politically correct or for the spelling and punctuation to be 100 per cent – it wouldn't be *Gull's Eye*. It's what they do.

FANZINES *(On the Up/Seaside Saga)*

MARC TWIBILL: I had lots of propaganda sent to my house and any protest that I thought deserved support I always printed but at the end of the 1995 season I was sent Bellotti's telephone number, address and fax number. At the time, just after speaking to him, I didn't think he deserved that. I felt he was caught up in the affairs of the club but obviously the same thing was sent to the *Gull's Eye* and other Supporters organisations and it all got out in the end anyway. But I did give 100 per cent support to all the protests – especially the peaceful ones.

JACKIE MOONEY: I always say it's just a fans' magazine. I think it's best the more people you can get putting their views in, it's just a voice for fans to say whatever they want to say. It's interesting for other supporters to hear what other supporters have got to say about the team, the club, whatever's going on.

SUPPORTERS' GROUPS

TIM CARDER: There was a loose sort of collection of supporters groups but each one was sort of doing its own thing while talking to the other factions – BISA and the Supporters Club were the two main ones, perhaps, they were always talking to each other, saying, 'This is what we're going to do this weekend – can we rely on you?' and of course we'd support both sides basically.

CHRIS JONES: Without them I think the whole situation could have seriously got out of hand. I don't think the owners of the club recognised what a service the organisers were actually doing to maintain public order. They kept the pot on a boiling pan and without them I think there would have been serious injury to people.

(Brighton Independent Supporters Association)

ATTILA THE STOCKBROKER: The Independent Supporters Associations really came out with the fanzine movement. The one brought about the other, effectively, and people have done them in different ways. Brighton Independent Supporters Association effectively is an anarcho-syndicalist collective, it has no leaders, no formal structure, no committee. It's a catch-all term for all those of us who are determined to do something to save our football club and to fight for its welfare so that we can come together under the auspices of something which is not the official Supporters Club and which is seen to be distinct from the actual club itself.

'I'm not interested in what's going on, I just want to watch Brighton play.' But the boycott of the Mansfield game produces the lowest home gate since the war (© Stewart Weir)

'The only thing that was ever said by supporters that annoyed me was "Oh the FA's passed the buck to these mediators"': David Davies attends a BISA meeting in Brighton shortly before the result of the CEDR negotiations is announced. Attila The Stockbroker looks on (© Stewart Weir)

'The roar that went up when he left the stand was absolutely incredible – it was like winning the game': David Bellotti, followed by his wife, leaves the West Stand, home to Fulham. This photo was famously run in The Independent *the following Monday (© Adam Scott)*

'He was living on borrowed time': Jimmy Case tries to calm the fans after the 2–3 defeat at home to Darlington. He was sacked the following day (© Stewart Weir)

'It's just like watching Brazil!': supporters from all over the world come together for the historic Fans United Day, 8 February 1996 (© Stewart Weir)

Stuart Storer, scorer of the last-ever goal at the Goldstone (© Stewart Weir)

'Steve Gritt's going for it, he's letting rip, he's out there, he's done it, and at the back of him the Hereford fans are motionless.' Stewart Weir describes this photo as the final whistle blows at Hereford (© Stewart Weir)

'One of the most sublime moments of my life': Robbie Reinelt scores the goal that keeps the
Albion in the Football League, away at Hereford, 3 May 1997 (© Evening Argus)

'It's almost as if the seed of the Goldstone was scattered across Sussex': the
last-ever game at the Goldstone Ground, 27 April 1996 (© Stewart Weir)

The Goldstone Ground, June 1997 (© Evening Argus)

Dick Knight, 1997 – the future? (© Stewart Weir)

PAUL SAMRAH: BISA is an organisation that doesn't have any members. It's just a banner. It's a way of bringing everyone together under a banner, we don't have to have membership cards or subscriptions or anything, we are the Brighton fans.

ATTILA THE STOCKBROKER: The whole idea for me was and is and will always be that BISA exists to have public meetings and do things. The day that anybody gets me to sit on a committee meeting or have a meeting to discuss what's going to be discussed at a meeting or anything like that, then bollocks. BISA is there as a forum for public debate and action and that is its sole purpose. Once everything is sorted, we may try and turn it into a membership organisation to raise funds for the development scheme or some aspect of the Albion's future development – but we'll have to wait and see how people feel about that.

(Brighton and Hove Albion Supporters Club)
TONY FOSTER: The Supporters Club has always been seen as the official supporter organisation by the club, as opposed to the fanzines. I couldn't comment on the past, but there's been more of a coming together between the two groups, supporting each other. We still do things in different ways, but it's whatever works for them. In relationships that have been developed, with other principal supporters or representatives, we get on reasonably well.

LIZ COSTA: The Supporters Club catered for a group of people who would not have under normal circumstances considered that a trip to the Concorde of a Monday night [where BISA meetings were held] would have been part of their agenda. The BISA meetings were very much for the North Stand element.
   I think even now there's still a certain amount of suspicion as to what we're actually into. Because we were officially recognised by the club, they saw us as being in the club's pocket. We weren't, because part of our constitution is that we're not. But if there was going to be any contact with the club from the supporter groups outside, the only ones that the club, at the time – and this is historic – would have talked to us is.

TONY FOSTER: I think the situation was so serious that we actually got together on things. Our actions ended up being not too dissimilar, to be honest, as well. The Supporters Club was certainly thought to be the official Supporters Club recognised by the club, when for the last two or three years we didn't recognise the board of the club.
   We've been quite happy to hold demonstrations all over the place, Hove

seafront opposite the Lib Dem conference, outside Focus DIY stores. Bill Archer knows about that, he knows Supporters Club people have been outside his stores. Peaceful, though. Leaving the ground before the end of a game, boycotting a game, we've all been involved in that.

29. Do It Yourself

BOYCOTT FOCUS DIY CAMPAIGN

LIZ COSTA: It was felt that perhaps the only way to get rid of Archer was to hit him in his pocket. The boycotting of the Focus stores, which Archer and Stanley were the major shareholders of, was targeted. Fanzines all round the country were circulated with various pleas for help because by this time the supporters of Brighton were desperate and the more we got other clubs on our side, the bigger the case we had.

TONY FOSTER: We ended up trying to do a trail of as many of the Focus DIY stores as possible, with away games and the like. We actually had other clubs with us from the Southern Division National Federation of Football Supporters at a couple of them. At Canterbury we had Watford, Wycombe Wanderers, Dover, Gillingham and another couple of teams with us there, supporting us; there were about 20 of us outside. We started getting other teams involved through the supporters groups and the fanzines. You went to away games and bought their fanzines and there you had articles saying 'Support Brighton in their hour of need', which was great. It wasn't just the coverage on the TV, it was other things, supporters making contact with other clubs.

TIM PITT: I've got concerns over the Focus DIY thing. It is all very well boycotting a high-profile company which Archer is associated with, but if we were successful − and our measure of success would be the failure of Focus DIY − I think there's too much social cost in terms of jobs lost and people that were innocent to Brighton and Hove Albion. All they want is a job in a local DIY store. Most of them probably don't give a hoot about football. So it may get at Archer but it needs to be something that only affects Archer directly.

TO THE GOOD FOLK OF LITTLEHAMPTON
FOCUS DIY

Did you know that the managing director and major shareholder of Focus is Bill Archer? We wonder if you want to spend your money in a store owned by Mr Archer. Please consider the following:

FOCUS DIY

* Bill Archer is also chairman and majority owner of Brighton & Hove Albion FC , Sussex's club in crisis.

* He took control of the Albion for just £56.25 and has never invested a penny of his own money in it.

* Under Mr Archer the club has sold its ground without consultation or negotiating to rent it back. He plans to move the Albion to Kent and has no acceptable proposals to return. His only scheme involves a retail park on the Downs, a plan that has alienated both council and community.

* Bill Archer was born in Shropshire, lives in Lancashire, and works in Cheshire. He has no known connection with Sussex and has rarely attended matches.

* There is a local consortium prepared to invest money in the club, which has identified a site for a new ground that the council leadership would support.

* The consortium has met all the conditions laid down by Mr Archer for him to step aside, yet he continues to block a takeover which would enjoy overwhelming popular support.

* Mr Archer insists his scheme is best, but has rejected a peace plan involving a neutral arbitration panel.

You may not follow the game, but is it right for one man in Lancashire to destroy the dreams of thousands of Sussex football fans by endangering the life of the county's only League club?

We firmly believe that the club will survive only if Bill Archer goes. You can show him your feelings by buying your DIY products from these stores:

Do It All, New Rd (A259), Rustington   Halls, 68 The Street, Rustington
Ockendens, 50 High St, Littlehampton   Wick Hardware, 143 Wick St, Wick B&Q,
Shripney Rd (A29), Bognor (A284)

Issued by Law-Abiding Loyal Seagulls, determined to save their football club

TIM CARDER: I compiled a list of all the Focus stores and distributed that generally – lists of directors of Focus.

I went on a few of these picket lines outside Focus stores and they were sort of 50-50. People took leaflets, the occasional person turned away, people said, 'Couldn't care less' – whether they actually did anything to affect Archer, I rather doubt. I remember a particular occasion at Stoke, for instance – we went to Stoke Focus DIY, handed out leaflets there, got a lukewarm reception, some people were receptive and some people weren't,

131

but we combined that with a match, Stoke v Tranmere, handed out leaflets there and of course it was a completely different reaction. Everyone was fully supportive of what we were doing – they invited me in for drinks into the little social clubs there and gave me a pint to keep me going while we were handing out leaflets, gave us complimentary tickets, everyone supported us, everyone took the leaflets.

30. The Coldean One

SIMON VALDER – 20-YEAR-OLD BRIGHTON SUPPORTER WHO RECEIVED YOUTH CUSTODY FOR MAKING THREATENING PHONE CALLS TO DAVID BELLOTTI'S HOUSE

JAN MERRITT: I think he was apparently one of many. He wasn't the only person to be making calls to David Bellotti. His number, although it has been said it was ex-directory, in actual fact had become common knowledge. I think it had even been printed in *Gull's Eye* and also there's a publicly available list of Liberal Democrat councillors where his number was printed.

Apparently these calls had been going on since June of last year but it wasn't until October, which was when Simon made the calls, that they had actually decided to do anything about it. At that point Jo Bellotti apparently got a Dictaphone, put it next to the telephone and recorded what was being said. They had a digital phone that actually displayed the number of the person who was calling and because, I think, being drunk he hadn't bothered to dial 1471, the number came up so they then decided to take action against him.

DAVE SWAFFIELD: He was just venting his anger as much as a lot of us had wanted to vent our anger on the man. We've all dreamt it, we've all put the thought through our heads what we would do if we saw him.

JAN MERRITT: It's very sad that it was taken to court and got to where it was. But of all the people to be sent to prison it was just unbelievable that it had to be Simon because he's such a nice guy and his mother is a single parent. She's brought him up single-handed, she dotes on her son and he had a job, was looking after her financially because of her health problems.

It was absolutely horrific at the court when the sentence was pronounced – she screamed, and that must have been one of the worst moments I've ever experienced. We were just absolutely numb when we heard what had happened. Just unbelievable.

ATTILA THE STOCKBROKER: Someone said to me, 'You wouldn't be too pleased if someone phoned up and threatened your mother' and I said, 'Hang on a minute, my mother wouldn't do what Bellotti has done.' It was provocation. If someone walked up to you in the street and said, 'You're a wanker, I hate you,' you are more likely to hit them than if they walk past you and smile. I totally support Simon and the sentence he got was outrageous but the fact of the matter is that it has been Bellotti's and Archer's activities that have led to that.

JAN MERRITT: We all said that we felt that under the circumstances, although we realised that he needed to be punished for what he'd done, that a non-custodial sentence would be the most appropriate thing because he didn't have any criminal record and was a very good character.

PAUL CAMILLIN: You could say Simon was stupid but there was so many like that, he wasn't the only one who made those calls. Simon was just a scape-goat and it really pisses me off that Bellotti went through with it. I just hope he is satisfied with himself.

31. 'They are a discredited board who've brought the game into catastrophic disrepute'

(David Mellor after Bill Archer's non-appearance on Radio 5 Live's 606)

ATTILA THE STOCKBROKER: We set out to capture the public's imagination, to do something which would be media-friendly, entertaining as much as possible, humorous in the circumstances. My position was that we wanted to go against the stereotypes of the football fan. As a club we probably have less of that element than anyone else of our size, I thought if we are clever and witty and we get the stuff across well, then we're going to get a lot of media support and of course we did.

PAUL SAMRAH: The York City so-called riot was when it hit the general awareness, but before that there was tremendous ignorance of what was going on. Nobody realised the significance of what was happening.

TONY MILLARD: As an Albion fan I had every sympathy with the actions taken by the supporters because it certainly seemed as if they were being shafted by the owners of the club. I could understand the depth of feeling and I could appreciate the depth of feeling and had I still been a supporter on the terraces I would have been very annoyed and very upset.

ANNA SWALLOW: I was working at the *Face* magazine and I wrote an article in which I called Archer, Bellotti and Stanley 'Villain number one, number two, number three'. I called Graham Kelly 'a deadbeat' and he wrote to the *Face* saying, 'Unfortunately, Ms Swallow, it's not possible for this deadbeat to do any more for your club.' His signing off was something like 'I wish you luck, but I'm afraid I'm not too hopeful.'

The editor rung the FA and said, 'Right, can we print this letter?' The secretary rang back and said, 'No, he doesn't want you to print the letter, you can print it all except the last line.' So I rang back and said, 'No, if you can be negative to an Albion fan, let's show it.' At which point they said, 'Mr Kelly will talk to you now', and we had this ridiculous conversation. We spoke for about three-quarters of an hour and I only wish I'd had a tape recorder. He was saying, 'Clubs go bankrupt, you've got to realise it happens' and I was saying, 'Well, what are you going to do about it?' He was saying, 'What's it got to do with me? I can't do anything about it.'

I got off the phone and I was just so angry.

PAUL SAMRAH: Paul Hayward did a superb article on Thursday, 12 December, which drew on the 'Putting the Record Straight' paper that we helped put together and then the *Guardian* on Friday, 13 December: 'Fined two points by the FA, adrift at the bottom of the league, a club is facing up to bitter death.'

PAUL HAYWARD: The sense that this struggle was a collective struggle was simply more pronounced in the case of Brighton and Hove Albion and more dramatic because the descent was so spectacular from FA Cup final in '83 to near oblivion 15 years later. I have to say that it caught the attention of the national media partly because Brighton is a fairly trendy place and a fairly cosmopolitan place and there's a strong media presence in Brighton. It did have this sort of romantic, spivvish image and that was of course exemplified, as we all know, by Jimmy Melia's white shoes and Mike Bamber. It's kind of a cigar-smoking club, Brighton, and people are seduced by that.

Journalists from national papers started coming to the Goldstone and examined the evidence more than they had previously and that together with the efforts of the supporters pushed it into the public domain. It certainly forced it on to the desk of Graham Kelly and those at the Football Association who perhaps had hoped that Brighton would quietly suffocate.

PAUL SAMRAH: I went on *606* with David Mellor down in Southampton. It was meant to be me meeting Bill Archer and, what a surprise, Bill Archer didn't turn up. David Mellor let him have it and we had a lot of air time that evening on *606*, Mellor was superb.

The press had picked up on the walk-out, the press had picked up on the boycott, the press had picked up on the march to Archer's house. Suddenly it had clicked, we realised as to what the national press picks up on: something novel, something different and well organised. You've got to have people at the front prepared to put their names to things, to do something and carry it through, and we did, we had a whole team of people who were brilliant.

PAUL HAYWARD: The question that's been preoccupying all of us over the last year – what can we do to stop this, what can be done? The glory is that people came up with so many constructive answers to that question, the fans came up with so many brilliant tactical moves to try and save the club and achieved that in the end. I know I reached points of total despair with it, thinking they're going to win, they're going to wreck the club and they cannot be stopped, they are either too stubborn or too mendacious.

There was this rolling campaign that got better and better and more and more impressive. The media interest was so enormous that I can't think of a single newspaper that didn't carry a major piece on Brighton at some point.

32. 'Don't Vote Bellotti'

THE SEAGULL PARTY

TIM PITT: Charlton and the Valley Party were the inspiration behind it – the fact that they had actually brought football into politics rather than the other way around and that was the first time football supporters were given

Brighton Independent Supporters Association

PRESS RELEASE (BRIGHTON ARGUS – FAO Matthew James)
14 JANUARY 1997
EASTBOURNE PARK COUNTY ELECTORAL DIVISION

Following recent local press reports regarding the forthcoming contest for the Liberal Democrat candidacy of the Eastbourne Park Electoral Division of East Sussex County Council, BISA has formulated the following plan of action in the event that Cllr. David Frank Bellotti seeks re-selection. Needless to say, BISA's opposition to Cllr. Bellotti cannot be overstated.

* Lobbying of Eastbourne Park Liberal Democrats to ensure they oppose Cllr. Bellotti's re-selection.

* Lobbying of Liberal Democrat councillors and other Liberal Democrat members and supporters throughout Sussex to ensure their opposition to Cllr. Bellotti's re-selection is registered with Eastbourne Park's Liberal Democrats.

* Members of BISA will form a peaceful presence outside Hampden Park Hall, Brodick Road, Eastbourne on January 28, where Eastbourne Park Liberal Democrats will be voting for the declared candidates.

* **In the event that Cllr. Bellotti is selected, BISA will nominate a candidate to oppose him in the East Sussex County Council elections on 1 May 1997. BISA's candidate selection process is well advanced and publication of the Notice of Election on the 24 March is eagerly awaited. The name of the BISA candidate will be released well in advance of noon on 4 April – the closing date for nominations.**

Press statement ends.

some kind of credit as having an influence in the way that the local authority was run. It was early May 1996.

We were initially going to launch ourselves as the Albion Party then. Really as a lobby group.

I then happened to see an item that said Bellotti was up for reselection at Eastbourne Park which is where he was the county councillor. I went to a BISA meeting soon after this article appeared with a draft press release saying that we would be looking to put up a candidate against Bellotti if he was reselected at Eastbourne Park, and launched it as the Albion Party with that press statement.

I got letters from BISA, from Roy Chuter, the official Supporters Club from Sarah Watts, Tony Hylands, John Campbell and the National Federation of Football Supporters wrote one, all urging Lib Dems down in Eastbourne Park not to select David Bellotti.

Then I had a phone call to say that Bellotti had gone absolutely ape shit on the Saturday, which is when these letters started arriving on the doormats of all the Lib Dems down there.

We all turned up at the selection meeting down at Eastbourne Park and we pretty much knew how it was going to turn out, but I did actually hear how the voting went and it was sizeable against Bellotti, significantly.

CHRIS JONES: He lost to a woman who looked like everyone's favourite granny, she was five feet tall.

KEVIN SHERWOOD: He pushed the suicide button on his political career. We went along to the by-election and that old girl was more or less on her last legs.

TIM PITT: So the great chant was 'There's Only One Olive Woodall'! She came out; she was absolutely marvellous; she loved every minute of it. I hope it conveyed a positive impression of football supporters to her as well.

We then heard the news that Pevensey didn't have a Lib Dem candidate and Bellotti was seeking the Pevensey candidacy. But they had to go with him simply because he was the only one.

On 5 March 1997 the *Argus* reported that the fans would stand a candidate against Bellotti and the next day the letters threatening litigation were received from Bellotti via the club's solicitors, Eversheds. Deliberate tactics or just coincidental timing?

Sarah Watts received a letter and I had it faxed through to me which was on a Wednesday or Thursday. I spoke to Roy Chuter, who had got one as well, and Tony Hylands.

Solicitors

10 Newhall Street	Telephone	0121 233 2001
Birmingham	International	+44 121 233 2001
B3 3LX	Facsimile	0121 236 1583
	DX	13004 Birmingham

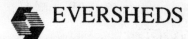 **EVERSHEDS**

FAO Roy Chuter

GET YOUR WRITS OUT FOR THE LADS

Some of you will never have been threatened with a
libel suit before. I'm privileged to have received such
a threat from solicitors acting for the esteemed Mr D.
Bellotti, so I thought I'd print it here to show what
happens...

Date   <u>26 February 1997</u>

Your Reference

Our Reference   **L TAE 162 Cs**
                BIRLIT/41684/1

Dear Sir

MR DAVID BELLOTTI

We have been consulted by our client, Mr David Bellotti, in connection with allegations
made you which were published in an undated letter addressed to East Bourne Park Liberal
Democrat, a copy of this letter is enclosed herewith.

The allegations attributed to you in that letter are grossly defamatory of our client. The
following defamatory meanings are conveyed:-

1. That since joining Brighton & Hove Albion Football Club ("the Club") our client
   does not striven to serve the Club's best interest but has allowed the Club to
   substantiate large financial losses; and

2. That our client has treated the fans with the disdain and has resorted to banning law-
   abiding and peaceful people from the ground for criticising him; and

3. That accordingly our client have lost all credibility and is unfit to run the Club.

Your allegations are utterly without foundation and thoroughly malicious. Firstly, as you
well know there is not a shred of evidence to support your claim. Our client has dedicated
himself to serving the Club and endeavouring to ensure it's survival and will continue to do
so. Secondly, as you well know our client, and more particularly the shareholders of the
Club rescued the Club from the brink of insolvency some years ago and the Club is
currently in a strong financial position. Thirdly, our client has not banned any law-abiding
or peaceful person from the football grounds. As you well know any individuals banned
from the Club have been clearly in breach of the ground regulations.

The wide publication of your false allegations throughout the local region will have caused
untold damage to our client's reputation. It has also caused him considerable upset and
distress.

BISA Brighton Independent Supporters' Association
4 March 1997
BIRLIT/41684/1
Page 2

In the circumstances, the purpose of this letter is to invite you immediately to agree to apologise and to withdraw your allegations in a Statement in Open Court in terms to be agreed, with a view to mitigating the damage you have inflicted. Our client also requires you to undertake not to repeat the same or any similar allegation about him, to make a satisfactory proposal for the payment of a sum in damages to him, by way of compensation for the degree of libels you have published, and to pay his costs incurred in this matter on an indemnity basis.

As a prompt apology and retraction of the allegation are of paramount importance to our client, your response to this will influence the level of compensation will accept to resolve the matter.

We wait to hear from you by return.

Yours faithfully

Eversheds

Eversheds

...Quaking in my boots, I was. So I sent it back to them, with the mistakes ringed, and this covering letter. I'm told that Eversheds in Birmingham have been doing legal work for the Albion. Isn't it a relief to know that the club's affairs have been in the hands of people who take such care over their work? Still, at least I understand now why Bellotti didn't take legal advice before he appealed against the two deducted points...

Dear Sirs,

I fear that someone must have broken into your premises and stolen a quantity of your headed notepaper.

Fortunately, the letter sent to me (copy enclosed) contains so many basic grammatical errors that I wasn't fooled. It is so sloppily written that it is reminiscent of one of Mr Bellotti's press releases. I'm sure it is reasonable to expect higher standards of literacy from a respected firm of solicitors - no such firm would allow such illiterate drivel to leave its offices.

I therefore send it to you in the hope that it will help you to identify the thief.

There is a faint possibility, I suppose, that it did originate in your office - in which case the corrections I have provided, free of charge, will give the writer a valuable lesson in the English language.

No reply so far!

Yours faithfully

Roy Chuter

Roy Chuter, B.A.Hons (First Class), English & Linguistics, University of Manchester.

9

SARAH WATTS: I just didn't know what to think and so I sat on my little stool by the phone, phoned Liz Costa and said, 'Liz, Bellotti's going to sue me.' That night we had the pub quiz and by then it was no problem, the Supporters Club were going to get the solicitors to look at it, so I knew that I wasn't on my own, everyone was fully behind it. I think we had a committee meeting that Saturday and everyone just sat there and agreed that my original letter was written on behalf of the Supporters Club as it clearly stated. We haven't heard from him since.

TONY HYLANDS: My immediate feeling was one of shock and horror, so I was on the phone to Liz Costa, Paul Samrah, Tim Pitt, various other people getting guidance and advice. Tony Foster calmed me down and said, 'We're all in this together and you're speaking on behalf of everybody else, we'll fight it, bring it over today.' So I took it over and handed it over to the Supporters Club and they're dealing with it *en bloc*.

TIM PITT: Roy Chuter just took it as a joke and put it in *Gull's Eye*. That was absolutely brilliant, the way he just tore into it.

TIM PITT: We then had a meeting down at Eastbourne and were saying, 'Shall we go with our candidate, shall we not?' I had made contact by that stage with the Conservative candidate. He came along to that meeting and in the end kind of talked the meeting round to believing that if we were to go with an anti-Bellotti candidate we could actually be counter-productive.

We found it was extremely difficult to run an anti campaign, the gist of it being that if you do so, you could actually be deemed to be supportive of the other party. As we believed it was going to be a two-horse race, if we were saying 'Don't vote Bellotti', it could've been perceived to be 'Don't vote Bellotti – vote Conservative', although that was never the line, it would just have been the way some people chose to interpret it.

Then at the final hour for nominations, three weeks or so before the election, a Labour guy comes on the scene and does exactly what we would have liked, put a Labour Party candidate up.

John Campbell was so keen to get shot of Bellotti that he was the major source of the funds that we had. This was the same John Campbell who sued the *Gull's Eye*. It just demonstrates how people have put their differences to one side and fought the common enemy and John has been absolutely marvellous. I was working with him and drafting out the full-page ad for the *Sussex Express* which is like local radio in that part of the world, big letters 'Don't vote Bellotti' – and again I found that we were probably running contrary to the law on the expenses side because we were paying for an ad that could push the other parties' expenses over their limits.

"A WAKE IN THE PARK"

For supporters, 1996 - 1997 has been the worst ever season in the 96 year history of Brighton & Hove Albion Football Club.

During the season, David Frank Bellotti held the position of Deputy Chairman and Chief Executive of the football club - employed on a salary of £40,000 p.a. by the owners William Ernest Archer and Gregory Alexander Stanley.

At a quarter to five on 26th April 1997, the Albion will have played their last Football League match at the Goldstone Ground.

To commemorate this end of an era The Seagulls' Party have organised a football match!

GOODBYE GOLDSTONE XI
(Supporters of BHAFC and invited guests)

V

PEVENSEY & WESTHAM XI

on THURSDAY 1st MAY 1997 at Pevensey Recreation Ground - Kick Off 6.30 pm
Match sponsored by John Campbell

The politically independent voice of Brighton & Hove Albion supporters.

Then Tony Hylands had this idea of a football match with Pevensey. I didn't really sort of think too much of it but then the penny dropped and I thought of course we can advertise the football match and still put the message across, so we had a half-page ad advertising this football match.

On the day of the election we got a few people down from about eleven o'clock onwards just to really drive around the streets of Pevensey. We had two megaphones on, on loan to us, just blasting out the message 'Don't vote Bellotti.'

John Campbell and I were out in the car for about an hour driving round and John was doing the megaphone absolutely brilliantly. 'To the good people of Pevensey, do not vote for David Bellotti, this man will ruin your lovely village like he has ruined our football club', echoing around the high street. We did this for about an hour and then went back and watched the football match in the evening and some guys went up to the polling station.

So I said to John, 'Do you fancy giving it one last sort of drive round and go up past the polling station?' There was Bellotti with Jo Bellotti shaking the hands of the voters and of course we drove past, John was giving it all the 'Don't vote for Bellotti'. We were like a couple of kids, absolutely in hysterics because Bellotti was standing there ashen-faced at this bloody message that was being delivered.

Having approached the polling station this copper stepped out in the road, stopped us and confiscated the megaphone. He said, 'Disturbance of the peace through using the megaphone, you need permission beforehand before you can do that.' We were in breach with the Electoral Representation of the Peoples Act.

Then on the Saturday morning after the election, John had a phone call from Eastbourne police to say that the megaphone was ready for collection. 'No charges, nothing further will happen and thanks very much for your efforts.'

Result
R. Thomas (Con) – 3,538
D. Bellotti (Lib Dem) – 1,961
D. Coughlan (Lab) – 1,111

NORMAN RAE (would-be Seagull Party candidate and life-long Albion fan): I am glad to be selected to assist in snuffing out the last burning embers of the blazing political career of David Bellotti.

33. 'Merry Christmas, Mr Samrah'

PAUL SAMRAH'S BAN FROM THE GROUND

PAUL SAMRAH: Christmas Eve 1996, I got in about nine o'clock having locked up and finished at work, opened up all the post and a few Christmas cards and then the final envelope, I'll never forget, was a letter from David Bellotti.

Dear Mr Samrah,
At recent games you have been seen to leave your seat to lead protests and threats to the directors box whilst matches have been in progress. In view of your behaviour inside the ground the club has decided to ban you from the ground until the end of next season. If you apply to the secretary a pro rata refund of your season ticket will be given.
Yours sincerely,
David Bellotti

I was just numb, I just felt sick because he had done it at a time when he knew I couldn't make contact with him or make any sort of representation. Christmas Eve, nine o'clock, what the hell do you do when you've got that sort of letter? I knew I hadn't done anything wrong, but I just felt that I'd been victimised. They had picked on me because maybe I was stirring things up with all the work that was going on.

JAN MERRITT: I know he writes for *Gull's Eye* and he's said things that Mr Bellotti perhaps wouldn't like but to ban somebody like that, I just find it completely beyond comprehension. Paul Samrah's never done anything illegal to my knowledge, he's just sat in the West Stand.

PAUL SAMRAH: So after the Christmas break and I'd taken stock I then dropped a line to Des Lynam, David Mellor, Bill Marsh at CEDR and Graham Kelly. Bill Marsh was most concerned because of the two fans that had been invited to see, represent and support us at mediation talks, one of them was banned and they didn't think that was very constructive. Graham Kelly was very concerned and he wrote me a nice letter back.

> Dear Mr Samrah,
> I am very grateful for your support for the mediation process and I very much share your hope that this succeeds and just defuses the risks which are currently causing so much disquiet. Your contribution is very much appreciated. Clearly one of the objectives of the mediation process is to attempt to heal the very poor relationship between the great number of supporters including yourself and the management of the club. In this regard I note that you have copied the letter to Bill Marsh who I am sure will take this up with the club. I am not able to intervene directly in matters such as this between a club and a season ticket holder, however I sincerely hope this matter can be resolved quickly. I am copying this letter to Bill Marsh with this in mind.
> Yours sincerely
> Graham Kelly

Which was very good of him. I must admit I thought that was rather nice and I didn't feel so isolated at that point.

JAN MERRITT: How dare somebody do such a thing? I can't believe the way he's treated them and banned people for no apparent reason.

34. 'Case Out!'

BELLOTTI BEING CHASED OUT. HOME TO DARLINGTON,
3 NOVEMBER 1996

TONY FOSTER: Mr Bellotti hadn't had time to warm his bottom on his seat and he had to leave. Quite unbelievable. He got a reception from everybody that was sort of still left – the season ticket holders in the West Stand, and he'd got a few comments from a couple of elderly gentlemen just to the side of him in the directors box, and then, all of a sudden, out from the North Stand popped about fifty or sixty people, into the exclusion zone – and he was away.

DAVE SWAFFIELD: As soon as he walks out in that box, everyone's just running and taking over that bit he's just closed and off he scuttled off again. That's the last we saw of the git at the ground. Again another great moment, a big, big cheer. The football was irrelevant, it was getting rid of him and seeing him run like the frightened little rabbit that he is.

BILL SWALLOW: That was absolutely brilliant. They talk about the youth of today but those lads who ran across, they were marching in quickstep – it was superb. It was so efficient and clinical and that was the end of David Bellotti being allowed in what ostensibly was his own football ground. Quite extraordinary.

SARAH WATTS: I have to agree with our ex-captain Steve Foster that one of the best moments of last season was the Darlington game when he walked into the box three minutes into the game and the fans ran across the pitch from the North Stand. He legged it and was never seen again.

TONY FOSTER: There were people there who weren't able to stand where they had been standing 40–50 years and they were wanting to stand there. But it was just for one purpose, for one person that he changed those ways of people because he had the power to do so. He totally flaunted his position.

STEWART WEIR: If a man can turn up at something and potentially cause a riot, which is what he has a habit of doing, then what are the rules? He should have stayed away and the proof of it was that the stewards voted, and I think it was after the Darlington game, the stewards said that if Bellotti turned up they would walk out.

JAN SWALLOW: I couldn't have sat there through a whole match with all that abuse coming at me. It's strange – he must be a very strange person, I think. At the same time I was quite worried about what would happen to him if they got him. I've never seen him move so fast, which was very funny.

PAUL SAMRAH: We were entering the Christmas period, we were adrift by about 11 points and Darlington was a game that really was a six-pointer for us because we could have brought them back into near the bottom place and we threw it away. I think we took the lead 2–1 and we then conceded a goal in the last minute to lose 3–2 and the atmosphere afterwards was just bordering on the revolutionary.

PAUL CAMILLIN: That was the most volatile crowd I have seen. I mean, people mention York, Carlisle and Lincoln but after the Darlington game everyone went a bit mental.

STEWART WEIR: The fans lost it, there was a hard core of about 50 that were going to rip Bellotti's head off. No doubt about it – doors were kicked in, windows were smashed. They lost their cool and they were going for it.

They were trying to break their way through the West Stand and I think with one charge they probably could have got in there. There were loads of coppers running across the pitch, the doors were being kicked and you could hear them creaking. They didn't get in and there was a lot of shouting and abuse being thrown and stuff like that but that then died down.

PAUL SAMRAH: It was just pure frustration that there was no one taking any notice of what on earth was going on. The club was just plummeting and we didn't know whether we should support the team during the game or chant against the board. It really was the pits. I think that was probably the lowest but it was almost unreal, you didn't believe it was happening and it turned out to be Jimmy Case's last game in charge.

DAVE SWAFFIELD: Sometimes the protests seemed really futile, you went round the back of the West Stand, did your chants and nothing seemed to be happening. Everything was on a downward spiral and you couldn't stop it, everything was going too quick. You'd think, what else can we do now? We've had the protests, we've had the FA involved; they didn't seem to be interested. The team were playing worse than ever, despair, total despair.

145

STEWART WEIR: Afterwards it was the strangest of all sights – this was 11 o'clock at night – Jimmy Case came out and actually talked to the fans for about 45 minutes and he was just trying to calm them down but they were just livid. They were really flying at him and before that time he couldn't really do a lot wrong, The focus of attention is not in the predicament of what's happening on the pitch, it's what's happening off the pitch. He was basically answering questions and people were saying, 'What's going on?' He was living on borrowed time.

JIMMY CASE SACKED, 4 DECEMBER 1996:

ATTILA THE STOCKBROKER: I always say I remember Jimmy for his great goals in the 1980s and for his brilliant team performances even up to about three years ago. I just want to ignore and forget about what happened for the early part of this season. I think he was in a situation he really could not cope with, I really do. I don't blame the guy, I think he was just in an impossible situation.

LIZ COSTA: He hadn't had managerial experience. He felt that at the time he accepted the job, he wasn't accepting the job from Bellotti, he was accepting the job for us, the supporters, and to keep the team together as continuity. It was the night before a Cup match and Liam had decided effectively that he had had enough of being shafted by the board. Jimmy was not financially in a position to turn round and tell him to stuff it and he felt that the team needed continuity at least for a while.

TONY FOSTER: A lot of people were relieved. I felt sorry in some respects for the guy. It wasn't working, though – I'm sure he'd admit it himself – it just wasn't working. And again, time for a change in that respect before it was too late. The fans had lost it and now with the chants of 'board out' we had 'Case out'. We were playing so badly on the pitch that people were sort of screaming at anything.

DAVE SWAFFIELD: He overstayed his welcome, he should have gone a long time ago because I think two more weeks and we'd've been in the Vauxhall Conference by now.

TIM CARDER: He'd stayed more or less neutral, but obviously Archer and Bellotti were his employers so he had to be pretty careful about what he said. He didn't win himself any friends, let's put it that way. I'd rather remember him as the bloke who scored the goals on the way to the Cup final rather than as a pressured manager, really.

PAUL HAYWARD: The period from the start of the season through to December when Jimmy Case was sacked, those four months were the darkest, most kind of intense and insufferable four months probably in any club's history. It was dark and cold and there was a horrible sort of hateful atmosphere on the terraces. It was like walking into an arms dump every time you walked in there. It was always going to go off at any moment. It wasn't enjoyable but every wet Wednesday or Tuesday evening you felt you had to be there, partly because of the sheer horror of what was unfolding in front of you. I felt the team at that point had downed tools, really, and whether it was because Jimmy Case was failing to motivate them or they were just completely dispirited by what was going on around them I don't know, but I don't think the players were performing particularly professionally at that time, and ex-players have said as much as well – Steve Foster and Gary Stevens and people like that have recognised the lack of effort, the lack of confidence in the players at that time.

I think the results of the second half of the season show that those players weren't as bad as they appeared in the first half when they were just in complete free-fall.

The game became almost an irrelevance. Everybody's eyes in the North would turn not straight ahead at the pitch but right towards the directors box. 'Oh Christ they've scored again, we're 2–0 down but forget about that, is Bellotti going to turn up?' It was an incredible state of affairs.

STEVE GRITT APPOINTED – WHISTLE PROTEST, 14 DECEMBER 1996

PAUL SAMRAH: On Tuesday, 10 December, in that week we had word that the FA were going to strip the Albion of two points for the Lincoln pitch invasion. That was Tuesday 10th, Wednesday 11th Gritt arrived and was appointed manager so that was a busy week in December.

We had a meeting on Monday, 2 December, a group of us who were just wondering about where we go from here. At that point we still hadn't heard the outcome of the Lincoln game penalty but we suspected that we were going to have a points deduction. We wanted everyone nationally to know that there were real problems at the Goldstone and we thought that really we've got to stop the game if that was possible, legally, without any of us getting arrested. Someone hit upon the idea of whistles and it was then agreed that for the game on 14 December just about two weeks later, we would have the whistle protest.

NIGEL SUMMERS: On the day he was appointed I thought I'd stop at the Goldstone and see what's happening. I pulled up outside there and I'm all dressed up, business suit, and there's all the Radio 5 and Sky and BBC South.

So I got my work folder out and folded it back-to-front so they couldn't see our company logo on the work folder and bluffed my way into the press conference and they asked me at the door for my press card. I just told them I was from a news agency and I was in.

I was sitting in the boardroom opposite Bellotti and everybody else. I thought that he hadn't figured out that I wasn't a journo. He looked very, very pleased with himself and said – it was the only time I've ever spoken to him – 'Oh, so you had no idea either?' and I said, 'No, we had no idea,' because when Steve Gritt walked in I must admit I didn't know who he was. I didn't recognise him. Then I asked Steve Gritt a couple of questions and when they showed it on the TV that night there I was and everyone was going, 'What the hell were you doing in there?' I'd just blagged my way in. I think that Bellotti did tumble me but it would have been a PR nightmare if he'd thrown me out. But when I look back on it, I'm sure he did know.

I said, 'Why do you want this job?' and he said, 'I've been out of football for a long time, I want a job.' And he didn't want the Brighton job, he wanted a job. When you or I go for a job, or anybody goes for a job, you do a bit of groundwork, you see where the land lies, you see where the company's going to, you see what their aims and objectives are, and you satisfy yourself that that's the job to go to. I think that he needed a job and I don't think he cared what job it was.

LIZ COSTA: Gritt, when he arrived, could not believe that things were as bad as everybody painted them. He couldn't understand why he was being pilloried himself because, in any other club, you get a new manager and he's usually applauded roundly by everybody – but of course he wasn't.

DAVE SWAFFIELD: I felt good because I knew he had a good record at Charlton, I knew he'd done well with Curbishley at Charlton and I was really surprised when he got booed, bit disappointed with the crowd. I remember seeing the graffiti and that was really embarrassing, all the spelling mistakes, that was just pathetic. The protests have all been quite intelligent and that was a real let-down.

'GRIT BELIEVES BELLOTTI BULSHIT' [sic]
(Graffiti on the West Stand wall)

STEWART WEIR: He came out to boos and hisses and stuff and there were a few claps but that wasn't aimed at him. I think that was a message to the board, a message to Archer saying that no manager should take this position because if you don't take the job as manager at Brighton, you'll be proving a point to Archer.

NIGEL SUMMERS: I was booing. I was right by the tunnel, or as near as you can get to the tunnel these days, and I was one of those booing.

PAUL SAMRAH: I was against him taking the job, I was against anyone taking the job. Even if Alex Ferguson came into the Goldstone as manager we wouldn't have greeted him with anything less then derision and boos and whistles and that was always going to be the way. The very fact that we did do that got us publicity and highlighted the fact that there was something seriously wrong at the club.

TONY FOSTER: Whoever the board would have picked would have had a rough ride. There were other people who'd made a connection between when Steve Gritt was the co-manager at Charlton, Greg Stanley's brother was the chairman at Charlton, and people thought, 'Oh, he's a Stanley man', and there's others who just wanted to give him a chance so it was a hellish mixed reception for him – in hindsight so unfair. I didn't take part in any of the personal abuse.

TIM CARDER: There were people who came out and said they wouldn't support anyone appointed by Archer and Bellotti and I thought that was absolutely ludicrous. We had to have a manager, we were adrift at the bottom of the League and we had to get behind the team and try and do whatever we could to get them up the table. Steve Gritt was appointed and I'd heard of him, he used to be joint manager at Charlton with Alan Curbishley. I remember the crescendo of whistling and booing that I could hear in Hove Park and found out later that that was the greeting for Gritt. I walked round to the back of the West Stand and there was 'Gritt is shit' and 'Grit believes Bellotti bulshit' and I just thought, 'This is absolutely stupid, let's give the bloke a chance.'

STEWART WEIR: We had the whistle protest and I spoke to one of the players a few days later and he said that it was fantastic. He said that the atmosphere was so good from the whistles, and of course the referee's whistle is a higher pitch from these whistles that were given out and with everyone blowing the whistle it was like one single tone. So the objective of disrupting or abandoning the game because of mass whistles didn't work, and it leant itself to creating a really intimidating atmosphere to the Hull players and of course they lost 3–0.

PAUL SAMRAH: I got 144 boxes of 12 whistles from an East End place in Bow which happened to be extraordinarily cheap and they were damn good whistles.

149

That morning we were going round with carrier bags with whistles distributing them at various pubs because we wanted it to be kept secret. We didn't know whether or not we'd get arrested by the police so we were sort of putting them in our shoes because I just didn't know whether or not we could land in trouble.

As it turned out we understand that the referee had been warned about this and he told the players that they could just watch his hand signals. It was like being in an Italian football stadium, the noise was just deafening. We walked into the West Stand and it was a barrage of whistles and the whistles kept going throughout the whole game.

TIM PITT: I was against the whistles initially because I thought it is not fair on the players. You have got all this commotion going on. As it was, I thought it was a brilliant atmosphere.

STUART STORER: Steve came, took over, he had his ideas, obviously his ideas worked for us, Jimmy's ideas didn't work for us. Maybe at another club they might've worked. Obviously when a new manager comes in everybody wants to do well. Really he just kept it going from when he took over. The crowds were getting bigger and bigger, 12 points behind at Christmas, everyone wrote us off and as we were crawling back, the crowds started coming back. Thinking back to the last five or six matches, the atmosphere at the Goldstone was unbelievable.

To be quite honest I didn't know what to expect when Stevie came. I didn't really know him, I'd never really heard of him. I knew he was assistant manager of Charlton with Alan Curbishley, but I was probably of the same impression as the fans, Steve's there just to do a job for the board. Steve being the man he is, he's very single-minded, knows what he wants, turned out to be the right man for the job.

35. 'In the Net'

ATTILA THE STOCKBROKER: I'm a complete technophobe and I'm hoping that I will discover it for my 40th birthday but the Internet was superb. That was one of the most creative things about the whole campaign for getting stuff together.

JAN MERRITT: I initially got involved in it because of my son, who is very much into computers, and one day he showed me that there was a Seagull Server. I mean, I'd never even used a computer before but he started printing out messages for me and I got very interested and I finally managed to get him to show me how to work it, and once I'd worked out how to use it and put messages on it myself, there's been no stopping me.

TIM CARDER: We decided to get in touch with those clubs that had Archer's Focus DIY stores near them and to elicit support from those clubs. So basically we were all allocated areas of the country to try and sound out via the Internet and to get support and contacts. My area was Lancashire so I traced web sites for Manchester City, Oldham, Rochdale, Preston, Burnley, Blackburn – I didn't bother with Man United because I thought they weren't going to be too interested. I sent a message to all these sites saying, 'We're desperate, we need help, there's a Focus DIY store near you. Can we ask for support?'

I went to these clubs and said, 'Would you be willing to put a link in from your web site to our web site so that your supporters can see this, jump to our web site and see how they can help to save Brighton and Hove Albion?' All the responses I got back were very positive and saying, 'Yes, what's it all about?'

WARREN CHRISMAS (journalist for *Escape* magazine): It's pretty amazing. There are people all around the world on the Seagull Server – people in Canada and South Africa, America, Malaysia are knowing exactly down to the last minute detail what is going on at the Albion.

I went to as many football web sites that I could find and built up a huge long list of the web page maintainers and just e-mailed them just to point their attention to our pages.

Several other web page maintainers of other clubs put a link from their site to Brighton so that people could easily skip across the Internet effortlessly to read about what was going on.

The Internet gave Brighton fans the chance to put across the true message that newspapers, at the end of the day, can't afford to waste pages explaining every last detail, and it attracted fans that really cared.

We had over 1,000 messages in the end and there was literally no more than about ten that were remotely malicious or bad.

TIM CARDER: This was the catalyst for the Fans United day. I don't know how many messages there were on there. Quite a few Palace fans wrote in saying, 'We hate you on the pitch but we don't want to see you go under – we want to play you again because we love the derbies.'

Every night I used to open it up and print off three or four more pages-worth and they were coming in from all over the world, all clubs basically, Palace fans, Portsmouth fans – all our traditional rivals – Millwall, the number of people who were saying, 'We can see things like this happening at our club', or 'We've been through this sort of thing, although it was never quite as bad as what you've been through but we appreciate the situation you're in and we fully support you.'

WARREN CHRISMAS: What pleases me more than anything is the fact that when Steve Gritt came in in December he really turned around the team and what we managed to do on the Internet was turn around the crowd.

TIM CARDER: In December a chap called Richard Vaughan put a message on, he was 15, we didn't know anything about him. All we knew was that he was a Plymouth fan and he put up a message saying, 'I think it would be a good idea if everyone who supports you turns up at the Goldstone ground in their own club shirts just to show you that we're all behind you.' This was where Warren Chrismas came in. He seized upon this message and this is where Fans United started. A date was selected when the England game was due so there were no Premiership games so we could get a lot of support from Premiership clubs, perhaps, and that's when it started to take off. We brought it to the Supporters Club's attention and BISA's attention and everyone thought, 'Yeah, excellent idea' because we knew how much universal support there was for us and we were pretty sure that we could attract a lot of support on the day. There was no reason to suspect that there would be any violence or anything like that.

JAN MERRITT: Richard Vaughan's suggestion was it would be nice for fans of all different clubs to get together to make a stand about the bad ownership in football and about the Brighton situation in particular.

It's wonderful to see messages from fans from not only in this country but all over the world, absolutely incredible, giving messages for support and saying that they would come down for Fans United – and just reading it, I know I thought that if all these people who say they're going to come do, then it's going to be one hell of a day.

The Brighton and Hove Albion Campaign Guestbook

Thank you for visiting the Brighton and Hove Albion Campaign pages. Please leave your messages of support in this guestbook we are keeping!

We sympathise with the Seagulls supporters in their struggle to survive!! So we (three Feyenoord Rotterdam supporters) try to be there on 8 Feb. to show our support. Archer BEWARE; Football belongs to us, SUPPORTERS!!
Erik, fred, willem
Holland – Friday, 17 January 1997 at 23:32:00 (GMT)

You stand up for the ordinary football supporters in this country who are fed up of directors who take over clubs for personal gain, not because they have any love for the club. As a Bristol City fan, we also experienced a very unpopular board who due to fan pressure were forced to resign. I hope you have the same success.
Robert Cowler <po0u6031@liv.ac.uk>
UK – Tuesday, 14 January 1997 at 15:25:14 (GMT)

It's great to see so many clubs represented here. This just goes to show football is bigger than one person or one club. Brighton and Hove Albion F.C. is an asset to the area in the same way a school or hospital is. These things should not be thrown away. From a Plymouth Argyle supporter in London. Keep up the fight.
Paul Luxton <p.luxton@ic.ac.uk>
London – Wednesday, January 08, 1997 at 16:47:11 (GMT)

All the best from a devoted WATFORD fan but I'll forego the away game at Brentford and be there for the good of English football everywhere. The people who do this thing to our national game need to be STOPPED. Why hasn't the FA come in on this? They're quick enough to fine players for misconduct. See you there.
michael rudd <michael_rudd@nt.com>
England – Monday, January 06, 1997 at 15:44:20 (GMT)

My son asked me a few weeks ago about what is happening at Brighton, now he looks out for your score on TV and listens for it at half-time/full-time at Vicarage Road – a 10-year old child cheering a club he didn't know a thing about until this sorry debacle. Long may the Seagulls fly, don't let those greedy b****s clip your wings. See you all on the 8th.**
Z
UK – Friday, January 03, 1997 at 16:18:51 (GMT)

One of my worst football memories is of watching Palace get stuffed at Brighton on Boxing Day 1979. But that's immaterial if one man is allowed to kill off a football team. Keep up the pressure. Don't let Archer get away with this.
Jeremy Nash <nashij@logica.com>
England – Tuesday, December 24, 1996 at 10:18:31 (GMT)

As an Arsenal fan I have been known to moan about our board from time to time but compared to the crap that Brighton are being put through our complaints are basically about nothing. I'm sure that 99% of all TRUE football fans are on your side. All the best, don't give up the fight and you will win in the end.
Justin Clarke <justin.clarke@dial.pipex.com>
England – Monday, December 23, 1996 at 14:35:35 (GMT)

Good luck with the campaign and keep up the good work. All true football fans realise that what is happening to you could so easily happen to any club. As a supporter of Pompey it is important that the south coast keeps the few teams that we have. 'Play up Pompey' and may the chant of 'Seagulls, Seagulls' be heard again at Fratton Park in the top divisions. There is now a link on the Pompeyweb courtesy of Pompeyphil.
Gary <gg@ee.port.ac.uk>
England – Friday, December 20, 1996 at 10:27:44 (GMT)

Although a Palace supporter, this is one occasion where I shall be giving total support to Brighton. For the sake not only of Brighton and Hove Albion F.C., but of football clubs and their supporters everywhere, football MUST win over the selfish interests of the few. Good luck Seagulls!
Graham Hart:
England – Thursday, December 19, 1996 at 17:12:58 (GMT)

I am an Aston Villa fan and I feel strongly about what is happening at Brighton. A football club is an institution, however big. Whether a club is the size of Villa or Moor Green, it should not be allowed to be closed down. A football club should be treated like a listed building, it should have government protection so that people like Mr Archer cannot do what they please with it. Also, a football club is more the fans, than the players, and directors, so they should be the ones who decide what happens with the club.
Joe Hewat <hewat@charis.co.uk>
England – Thursday, December 19, 1996 at 16:13:38 (GMT)

As a Palace fan, I'm not supposed to do this, but KEEP THE FIGHT GOING. You have the support of all DECENT Palace fans everywhere.

Neil Burling <neilburling<mis@dillons.eunet.co.uk>
England – Tuesday, December 17, 1996 at 11:15:02 (GMT)

Even as a supporter of the other team in deep relegation trouble, Hereford, I wish you all the best and hope you survive and I look forward to a happy day at Edgar Street at the end of the season.
Richard Webb <gripped@crux.u-net.com>
England – Sunday, December 15, 1996 at 22:32:52 (GMT)

Keep going. Football and its supporters must win. It's our game, not some businessman's toy. Football is all about the fans; without us there are no profits or glory. From an exiled Spurs fan.
Simon Read <siread@vossnet.co.uk>
UK – Sunday, December 15, 1996 at 18:44:24 (GMT)

I see the scum FA have now taken 2 points – who do they think they are? They wouldn't do this to Man United. It makes me sick what is happening to your club and it's an insult to your fans. I'm a Plymouth fan and I think that one week when we're away I'm going to come up and support your protest. I think it would be a good idea if LOADS of fans from different clubs turned up at Brighton (with their shirts on) and joined in. It would show that we're all behind you 100%. PS I'd love to hear from some Brighton fans. Mail me!!!
Richard Vaughan <r.vaughan@btinternet.com>
England – Wednesday, December 11, 1996 at 23:31:32 (GMT)

I think it would be a tragedy if Brighton were allowed to wither and die. As a Brentford supporter I know the struggles of being a lower league supporter. My message to the Brighton fans is this: keep carrying the fight on. You have the support of every decent football fan in the country. Good Luck. ARCHER OUT!
Paul <fitzsimo_e60@s.tvu.ac.uk>
UK – Wednesday, December 11, 1996 at 10:38:28 (GMT)

My mother was an au-pair in Brighton some 35 years ago, and I was so lucky to meet the people she lived with. They were Brighton fans and I fell in love with the club and specially Steve Foster's hairband, even got his autograph when he played for England B against Iceland about 10 years ago. I know the old man, Mr Dudley, is turning in his grave, so keep the fight up, both for the living and the dead. Ta ta.
Andri Sveinsson <andri@fjarvangur.is>
Iceland – Wednesday, December 11, 1996 at 09:30:08 (GMT)

Here's another message of support from a Sunderland fan. I have watched Brighton home and away this year and I have really fallen for your club. It

would be a footballing travesty of the first order if Brighton were allowed to die as it would set a precedent of other maniac chairmen to emulate. Football lovers everywhere should unite to stop this happening. Sack the board.
Pete Hindmarch <hindmarch@bris.ac.uk>
UK – Monday, December 09, 1996 at 16:03:20 (GMT)

Good luck from another Wycombe fan, hope you get rid of these people as soon as possible. Greedy jokers like these shouldn't be allowed to do this to your club or any other. I also think the FA could do more to protect clubs, and they should get their priorities right – if a player gets banned for 10 months for kicking ONE fan, what do you do with people who have kicked every single fan the club has?
Stuart Harvey <oscar@mail.bogo.co.uk>
UK – Sunday, December 08, 1996 at 13:09:03 (GMT)

As a Charlton fan, I totally sympathise with your plight. We found ourselves with no one to help us apart from a few genuine footy fans. I truly hope that you get your club sorted and whatever you do, don't give up! We've proved that you can turn it around. Why not form a political party? Charlton did it and got more support than you could imagine. Good luck to you.
Jeff Prior <sutlej@dircon.co.uk >
Britain – Saturday, December 07, 1996 at 00:47:47 (GMT)

I'm a Palace season ticket holder and you can guess that I'm not too upset to see Brighton losing games. However, the rivalry between our clubs does not extend to us wanting to see either going out of business and you have my full support in your fight against the money grabbers.
Bob Sinclair <100634.444@compuserve.com>
UK – Friday, December 06, 1996 at 12:17:17 (GMT)

---

36. 'Football! United! Will never be defeated!'

FANS UNITED, 8 FEBRUARY 1997

TIM CARDER: You have to remember that the Internet is not available to the vast majority of people, but people on it will talk to people who aren't on it and spread the word that way.

Fans United really started taking off after the New Year. There was a meeting of the supporters groups with Bill Archer and he was absolutely horrified with our idea for Fans United. He just thought it was going to be a mass punch-up, which shows how little he understands about the situation. It was totally unprecedented. Okay, you get England internationals where people go along in club shirts and they unite behind the England team but this had never ever happened before with one football club.

The day was really pretty misty to start with and I wondered if Archer had some sort of pact with Satan that he would actually get the game called off through fog.

I printed off 50 messages on card – messages that had come on to the Internet Campaign Guestbook and I stuck those up on the railings in Hove Park that led up to the clubhouse and they proved quite an attraction.

The first message I put up was a Crystal Palace message because I thought there will be Palace fans here and I wanted to show Albion fans that not all Palace fans are the scum they perhaps think they are and there are some behind us in our fight.

HELEN CHAMBERLAIN: I heard about it through Danny Baker's radio show. I checked the fixtures list and Torquay were at home that day and I just don't miss Torquay, but there was something that made me think this is just too big. But it took a hell of a lot to sacrifice a Torquay United home game!

You got this buzz as you were driving through the town where there was just shirts all over the place, everybody was in their colours and you kind of got that funny, prickly, you know, 'My God, this is really something so bloody huge.'

We got to outside the ground and walked around and what brought it home to me was the guy that I was with had a Sheffield Wednesday shirt on and walking towards him was a guy with a Sheffield United shirt on and they were eyeing each other up right until they walked past each other and they just nodded at each other and went 'Hello.' An Owl and a Blade who acknowledged each other's presence for the sake of football! And then we bundled into the ground and the same thing, grown men would come up to you with tears in their eyes, grabbing my hand going 'God, thanks for coming!', which made me feel so humble, like, 'I'm just a Torquay fan who has come along today.'

Where I stood I had a Sheffield Wednesday fan next to me, a Watford fan next to him then a Charlton fan, then there was a Blackburn Rovers fan the other side and there was a Wimbledon fan in front, even a non-league fan too.

I think what must have been in every fan's mind was, 'Jesus, if this can happen to Brighton it can happen to my club too.'

All the posters were saying football belongs to us, it belongs to the fans, you know, it doesn't belong to you two blokes who decide 'Oh yes, we are going to do this, we are going to do that', that is why I think a lot of fans were there because they knew it could happen to anybody.

It could happen to any club and there is nothing better than the force of people to change things.

TIM CARDER: I put Fans United day up there along with promotion days – it was just really moving.

In the North Stand we could see the Chelsea bloke standing up in the North Stand and he was leading all the songs – I don't know whether he was primed or not or had all these songs ready or not but he did a wonderful job, that bloke. I don't know if anyone ever found out who he was.

There were people from Germany and Holland and a lot of exiled Albion supporters came back for the day and I'm sure they thought it was really worthwhile. Of course we won the game 5–0 and Craig Maskell at the end ran up to the North End, kissed his hat-trick ball and threw it into the crowd and that just summed up a wonderful day for me. Here we were asking for our football back and Craig Maskell threw the ball into the crowd and made sure we got one.

I don't think it affected the stance of Archer or the FA or anyone in particular like that but it certainly renewed the enthusiasm amongst Brighton fans for the cause. Prior to that, crowds were hovering around the 3,000 to 4,000 mark. After that Saturday matches were eight, nine, 10,000 and I'm sure the presence of such big and such vocal crowds did have a major effect on the team and actually got us out of the fix we were in – you know, willing the ball in and willing the ball out of our goal. In the end we stayed up by virtue of having scored three more goals than Hereford.

The only disappointment really was that it didn't get the press coverage it deserved. Some of the broadsheets did good articles on the Sunday and the

Monday but by and large it was just ignored and the reason was that there was no riot.

A couple of Hereford fans were interviewed and asked, 'Why are you supporting Brighton today? Because Hereford could be in trouble and if Brighton go under it would help you.' And the reply was, 'It wouldn't help anyone if Brighton went under.' And I do feel sorry for him and all the other fans but life on the football pitch – winning and losing – is what the game's all about, or what it should be.

ATTILA THE STOCKBROKER: I had 15 Germans sleeping on my floor. They really supported us and we've had articles in about 20 German fanzines. The Germans were fantastic because they really are organised and they won their campaigns. For instance, the ban against all-seater stadiums – they won it. They said, 'We don't want to sit down to football,' and they won it. The Germans as a nation are very organised, it's a national characteristic so even the anarchists are organised.

Everybody from all over the country came and answered the rallying call and they were all supporting us and it was wonderful, just brilliant. It was a really moving day – great solidarity, people working together – fantastic, I can't over-emphasise how wonderful it was.

TIM BOHANNON: People came because they recognised that it wasn't just the club that needed help, it was the fans and the fans had been forgotten in the last few years.

Fans United was symptomatic of a different age – fans have seen what's happening to Brighton and Hove Albion and think they will continue and be as vociferous – and they'll need to be as rebellious.

I wasn't going to come down for the Fans United game because I really could not afford it but I went down and there were thousands of bloody people there and the official crowd was eight and a half. I think there was more than eight and a half, and I said to these people, 'Why are you down here?' and they said, 'Because we're football fans, first and foremost, we love football.' And you could see how the players responded, played Hartlepool off the park. That was the afternoon the chant 'Brazil! It's just like watching Brazil!' came into being. It may be ironic but it was the most wonderful term of endearment. People had come from Scotland, Newcastle, Kuala Lumpur, the States, Real Madrid, Frankfurt, they were there to show their solidarity in the most wonderful, wonderful way – it was enough to bring a lump to your throat.

I think Archer and Bellotti possibly thought they had a fight on their hands after that game.

PAUL CAMILLIN: I have never seen anything like it and probably never likely to see anything like it again.

A lot of it had to do with the fact that we were such a big club – only in 1983 we went to the Cup final. Brighton were a massive club, the biggest on the south coast, I would say.

IVOR CAPLIN: I was in my car on that day driving back from a conference and on Radio 5 they had one of their leading reporters at Brighton versus Hartlepool! That just shouldn't have happened!

LIZ COSTA: I know at one point I actually did break down in tears. I got on to the main road just before we went in to the ground and we were surrounded by Wimbledon fans with all their banners and two groups of Charlton fans and they were just so magnificent in their support and I thought, 'This is better than all our wildest dreams.' It was one of these things that was sort of spawned from an innocent idea – we really didn't know what it was going to be like, you couldn't possibly dream. I felt sorry for the Hartlepool players in a way because they really didn't stand a bloody chance. I think even Hartlepool supporters in the end thought, 'What the hell, we're joining in history here.' Although they were being stuffed out of sight they've not held it against us.

You look at the Sunday papers the following day – the tabloids didn't even mention it! There was no riot and they wanted trouble – they wanted all these thousands of fans from Palace and Portsmouth and everybody coming here and having a punch-up. Well, that wasn't what it was for.

Charlton sent seven coaches down to Fans United! There were loads of Charlton fans. And we had a banner up at Charlton the following weekend to say 'Brighton fans say thank you to Charlton'.

Anyway, with Fans United I think we made a lot of friends.

JACKIE MOONEY: I was there from early on and it was unbelievable, the amount of people, the amount of different clubs and the good feelings. Before the game I had not really given a thought to the actual game of football and I was astounded at how the players played so much better with the crowd behind them.

I'd taken a lot of phone calls from people from all over the place who either wanted to know what was going on: was it really all right if they wore their own club's colours, was I absolutely sure that they'd be all right and that they wouldn't get hurt or anything, and even if they couldn't come they wanted to send their best wishes to wish us well and to say what a good idea it was.

NIGEL SUMMERS: We went out the night before Fans United because we couldn't put the signs up any earlier than that because the Council would have taken them down. There were directional signposts to the ground for the fans from the other clubs. We heard the other fans being interviewed on the TV and the radio and they were saying, 'It's great, we come to Brighton and there are all these signs – we found the ground more easily than we ever did before.' It kept the media interested and it was in the *Argus* a few times. There was the 'Welcome to Brighton except Bill Archer' sign and there was the mileage signposted – Gillingham and Archer's house.

I went down to the ground about ten o'clock in the morning because we put the big six-boarder sign up outside the ground which was a message for Bill Archer 'From Ordinary Football Fans' with the accent on the capital letters!

When was the last time we scored five goals? No one can really remember and, yes, it was the difference between staying up and not. I mean, there are lots of reasons you can give for why we stayed up but that was just a perfect day. Bit foggy – my only criticism.

From then on the crowds got bigger every single game, one by one by one. I think it was officially 8,500 at the Hartlepool game and the next home game was something like 6,500, then it was 6,800, 6,900, 7,000 and it just went up and up for the rest of the season and that was really important.

BILL SWALLOW: The away supporters were brilliant all season – I remember the Mansfield supporters during the boycott match – they were particularly good. I remember the Barnet supporters chanting for Bill Archer to get out.

Fans United was extraordinary and it went beyond the narrow parochialism of ritual chanting for your own football club. You really felt we had something bigger at that match.

I think the Fans United day gave the Goldstone back to the supporters and back to the team. It became ours again – and didn't it show? We don't know, as supporters, whether we helped this team survive in the League but all the evidence suggests that we did because when we were there *en masse* we won. And when we weren't, we didn't and the coincidental evidence is there. And Fans United started that. Brilliant.

JAN SWALLOW: The crowds started building up from that day. I think a lot of people – in fact I know a lot of people who hadn't been coming because of what was going on – that was their form of protest. They came to that day and they kept coming and I expect they were telling a lot of their friends, 'Come on, you've got to come back.'

MARC TWIBILL: One of the best moments of my life as a football supporter. I met loads and loads of fans from other clubs. You had all the fans coming and buying the fanzine and they were all sort of chatting and saying their own points of view. I just felt it was completely friendly. I was worried that there may be trouble – you had Crystal Palace supporters there but people were just leaving them completely alone and it was friendly. I don't think I'll ever see anything else like that again and I tried to portray that on our front cover of our edition and we had a Seagull with his arm round an Eagle and the Gunners and Spurs together and I think that sort of summed up the atmosphere of the day. That's exactly what it was like – the fans putting aside their differences for the good of football for one day.

It's important that you do support the bottom teams and it's good to see that supporters from the top teams – the Premiership clubs such as Manchester United and Newcastle, Aston Villa – showed that they hadn't forgotten the roots of the game and came down to support our cause and I think that was a very positive step for English football as a whole.

It was a terrific day. Everything went well and I just felt there was such a carnival atmosphere outside the ground and I think that was the most enjoyable game since Liam Brady first took over at the club. I just felt there was such a positive atmosphere there and all the fans were behind the team.

SARAH WATTS: It was such a positive thing for football. I can still see myself in the North Stand and the Chelsea fan leading the singing and people jumping up and down around the ground saying, 'We hate Archer', it was a great day for football.

There were Wimbledon fans down in front, there was the Chelsea fans leading the singing, Newcastle fans, and it was just, 'Where are all these people coming from?' It was incredible.

STEWART WEIR: Fans United was probably the most outstanding day of this season. On the morning, I turned up early – I was there at about 9.30 to 10 o'clock and it was foggy, it really was cloudy and not nice and there was no one there. There were a few hot dog stands but it could have been any other day. I met Richard Vaughan and did a few snaps of him and we talked, and then I met some fans down from Rochdale, and they'd brought a fan from Poland who was a student and she was dressed in her colours. People started to arrive in dribs and drabs – a minibus-load from Southampton and a whole crowd from Norwich and an Aston Villa shirt walking down the road. It was so unusual to see all these different shirts and these different people and these different accents.

I was walking around and coming over the bridge there was this . . . just noise . . . that's what it was . . . it was just like mass noise. And there was this guy standing there, he was a German, Eintracht Frankfurt, with his flag and it was massive and an Arsenal fan talking to a Tottenham fan and there was a whole coachload that had just arrived from Sheffield and it dawned on me that 'This is fantastic – why are these people here?' Every one of those clubs had played at the ground but, 'Why are they here – what is their point?' And the point that they were trying to make is that football is for the fans.

The day was just outrageous. It was surreal. Official attendance was just under 9,000 but it seemed to me as if there were a lot more there and everybody had their own shirts and scarves and banners and stuff. There were a few banners from Germany and I saw someone carrying a banner with Real Madrid on it – I don't know whether they were from Real Madrid but it looked good. And of course Hartlepool had no chance – it was a 5–0 win.

I think the result of that day was that it made these fans from other parts of the country, from clubs that are in the Premiership and haven't got a problem, or don't appear to have a problem, it made them realise that Brighton is not a small club by any means and it could actually happen to anyone. Unless fans make a point of realising that this can happen to anyone, then their club could also be doomed.

TONY HYLANDS: Yeah, Fans United was a unique day. It was unbelievable to walk down the road with a Hereford fan one side of you and a Tottenham fan the other side and perhaps a Palace fan.

It's not my instinct to bottle them or beat them up because it's not in the context. We were all that day working for one common aim. To let the money men and the FA know that it belongs to people like us. We work our bollocks off for 40 hours a week earning money to pay them high prices to watch football, don't we? At the end of the day a lot of people can't understand football culture, it's in your blood.

For Fans United I produced 500 stickers. Did them at work, printed them in my lunch break, two hours' printing, two lunch breaks printed all blue and white and then the night before Fans United I sat from ten at night till four in the morning with a scalpel and a straight edge cutting them into single stickers and then got up in the morning and trained over to Fans United totally knackered. But at least by the Supporters Club getting stickers – I can't remember how much it cost them but they could sell at 50p or a £1 each – it made money for the fund.

CHRIS JONES: For me it was one of the most significant days and that has nothing to do with football, that was about community, an extension of community.

It was nothing like an England game. I used to go to Wembley in the '70s and early '80s and you saw horrible people there. I think it has probably changed now – then they were motivated by nationalism and also from a very kind of aggressive club point of view that they were there to represent their club. That day was totally different. I was standing next to three fans from Leeds, Ian Baird scored the goal and they all took their shirts off (it was quite a cool day) and they started waving their Leeds shirts in the air. I saw more Wimbledon fans than I have ever seen before and Charlton – both of those clubs know what it is like not to have their own ground so that was very inspiring.

One of my clients came down from Sheffield, he is a Sheffield United fan, a man with a good job and everything and he had been involved in the campaign against their former chairman and he came down and he said it was the best day he has had at football.

One of the insights into that game was that it was the first time since I have been watching Brighton that an Albion game has been well marketed.

TONY FOSTER: It was great Bournemouth fans joined us, that was brilliant. I spoke to a lady in the week leading up to it and she said, 'Can I bring my collection tin along?' – it was good she was there.

I was one of the organisers of the day. We hired the rugby club in Hove Park, tee-shirts, stickers, badges, things like that and we helped with the press, myself, Liz, Tim Carder did information packs for the press, and those were distributed out to all the newspapers and the like.

We invited members from the supporters clubs, Affiliated National Federation of Football Supporters. We had a southern meeting beforehand and we got quite a few people that way. I think that was probably the best football day they've ever had – and their team wasn't even involved, you know – it's amazing. Obviously the fanzines invited people as well and there were other events going on – the clubs had invited people and the clubs became meeting places. We were in the rugby club from about nine in the morning and people were coming in as early as that. You know, people were filtering in and you'd be thinking, 'Christ, what kit's that?' And sort of 'Flipping heck – welcome Wycombe!' There was a Glasgow Rangers fan and a Celtic fan – I mean, where else would you see that?

Bellotti and Archer. They didn't comprehend it, they just thought it was going to be a massive punch-up.

STUART STORER: Unbelievable! Warming up in front of the West Stand there was such an atmosphere, carnival atmosphere, it was like another 20 per cent on your gate.

PAUL SAMRAH: It was a totally unique day. We were on a roll, we felt that the home games were going our way, we became invincible, impregnable at the Goldstone ground, it was back to those promotion days where we were scoring goals and the football was very attractive, they were using the wings and crossing the ball in and it was exciting.

Archer and Bellotti said, 'Please issue a statement asking for calm and for there to be no trouble, we would really like you to do that.' And we said, 'Well, of course we'll do it, it's not a problem.' They were really worried that we wouldn't do it. It was a kind of real negotiating tool. It sort of elevated us to people with real power.

WARREN CHRISMAS: One Wednesday afternoon before Fans United I thought, 'Hell, Danny Baker is only down the road at Broadcasting House, literally two minutes from where I work, why don't I go and print out the Guestbook and take it down to him?' Ultimately all I was looking for from him was just a recognition of what was going on at the Albion and he, in fairness, had said quite a few things about Brighton in the preceding weeks.

So I sent this letter to Danny Baker, literally just a paragraph on the end saying that any fans that want to come down, come down on this day, come together and, as I say, the main part of the package was the Guestbook.

He came on the radio at ten o'clock and within 15 seconds of coming on air he said, 'I've just received this amazing package' and I'd literally only delivered it like half an hour before the show and he came back to it a couple of times during the show and was really enthusiastic about it and that was how it was born out of that. A lot of Brighton supporters have been listening to Baker and so it went ballistic from there.

The moment that it actually hit us was when we came out of the Hove Park Tavern, it must have been about two o'clock and we just looked down the road just outside the North Stand and there was the biggest fucking queue and I hadn't seen a queue like that in a long, long time at the Goldstone.

I've got a video tape of the game. I didn't notice it at the time but the reaction on the players' faces when they come out at the beginning of the game is just amazing because they are looking around and after playing in front of 3,000 or 4,000 for so many weeks and listening to all these 'Archer Out' chants and suddenly there was maybe 10,000 or 11,000 in there of fans who were really getting behind the team!

It started off as a demonstration and ended up in a celebration of the fact that Brighton were there and we love football and that we wanted to do something about it and it was pretty special.

I still believe to this day there was probably fans of every single English League club there even if they weren't wearing the shirts, there were so many other fans there, that there would have been.

DAVE SWAFFIELD: What a brilliant day that was, another highlight of this dismal two years. You felt you're not alone here and it was a protest against what was going on in football. Went to the pub beforehand, got there quite early and you walked in it was like multi-coloured football shirts – Southampton, Portsmouth, Newcastle, Sunderland, Preston North End, people who'd come down especially for this, you couldn't thank these people enough. 'Thanks for coming, thanks for coming.'

37. Goodbye Goldstone

MERIDIAN TV PROGRAMME, SUNDAY, 9 FEBRUARY 1997

WARREN CHRISMAS: We'd all had such a great time at Fans United and everyone was still buzzing on the coach going over to Meridian to record the programme. We weren't made to feel very welcome and it was a bad programme. It was bad PR for Albion supporters, it just didn't go right. At the beginning of the programme Geoff Clarke says there will be plenty of opportunity for Albion's fans to ask questions, and there never was and before we knew it, it was over and it wasn't until it was over that everybody started to get really angry.

PAUL SAMRAH: Fans United on the Saturday was a brilliant day – the Sunday, the 'Goodbye Goldstone' debate on Meridian TV, was a disaster. We went in there rather naïvely thinking that all the facts surrounding the furore about the club will be explained in a balanced view and it wasn't. Dick Knight was not going to attend because Bill Archer wouldn't attend. Well, to our surprise Bill Archer was there, David Bellotti had the cheek to turn up and also arrived with his wife which was even more galling because in our negotiations with Bellotti he'd asked us to refrain from any verbal or other attacks on his wife and we naturally assumed that, really, she would take a back seat.

Regrettably things got out of hand and we didn't get our case across in a professional way and it ended up being a shouting match and I was glad the programme ended when it did because I think we could have done our cause an awful lot of harm.

Bellotti is brilliant in front of the cameras, he's a superb guy in an interview – he can answer a subsidiary question and miss the main question. Archer came across as a nice guy sitting in a studio in Liverpool.

As soon as I came out of the debate I rang Dick Knight and said, 'Did you know that Archer was appearing?' and he told CEDR because it was a CEDR agreement that they wouldn't go. Driving back the 60 miles from Southampton we felt cheated, we felt hijacked and the most annoying thing was that we knew it was down to us. It wasn't anybody else really that had let us down, it was ourselves that let ourselves down.

LIZ COSTA: The 'Goodbye Goldstone' programme was a total triumph for Archer and Bellotti. And this having taken place a week after Bellotti had said to us, 'Please leave my wife alone', he brought her into that studio. She had nothing whatsoever to do with that programme – she had no input, was not expected to have any input.

Archer was there with a patch over his eye, we were told, because he had corneal problems. The neutrals, the people who didn't really know what was going on or had chosen not to take any notice, must have thought, 'What the hell are the supporters on about? Archer and Bellotti are so totally feasible.' Well, that's how they bloody wriggled their way in in the first place, by being feasible.

TONY FOSTER: To some extent we were stitched up on that – as far as I'm concerned so was Dick Knight and the consortium. Things were edited, we had to re-do quite a bit and at the end of the programme re-record certain bits that probably didn't come across on the programme.

PAUL SAMRAH: I am afraid it was the low point of our campaign.

38. 'We are staying up, I said we are staying up'

TIM CARDER: After Fans United, people started realising – you know, we'd won 5–0 and we had closed to within three points by then – people started seeing that perhaps there was a possibility of getting out of this situation. It did really hit home that people had to get behind the team rather than just protesting about Archer and Bellotti, which is what it had been for the first four months of the season, and the support was absolutely fantastic after that – there was a chance and we took it.

DAVE SWAFFIELD: Not that we didn't ever support the team, but the direction of our cheering was towards the team now. It was just like going back in years again, the nervousness, I hadn't felt that for years, scoring early on and then having to suffer 40 minutes of total barrage by the opposition team, the biting of the nails. Things were starting to happen off the pitch, not as fast as everyone would like, but the main thing was we were watching the team again and playing quite well, scoring goals and beating the top teams which is how it should be.

People could see the end of the Archer/Bellotti era, because I know a lot of people didn't want to go because of those two. That's not the right attitude in my opinion, you should be there to fight the bastards and shout them down as much as you can. The drifters could see a bit of light at the end of the tunnel and it dragged them back.

NIGEL SUMMERS: I think the fans can take credit for lifting the fortunes of the team after Christmas. Do the fans then take the blame for not getting behind the team before Christmas? I don't think you can have one without the other.

PAUL SAMRAH: We felt that we'd done our bit in getting the Football Association to do something, getting the CEDR talks underway, they seemed to be going down the right line, it seemed to be hopeful, it seemed to be optimistic. We thought, 'Right, we've done our bans, we've done our boycotts, we've done our marches, we've done everything else, let's get behind the team', and the team were responding, so it did seem to be working in our favour.

DAVE SWAFFIELD: One of the amazing things was having to leave the pub early. Before it'd been leave the pub at quarter to three and just walk straight in the ground, whereas now you'd leave at quarter past two so there's no queues. As you walked down to the ground you'd think, 'Bloody hell, there's queues at the North Stand, something's gone wrong, they've shut some gates or something.' It was back to football again, and supporting the team.

BRIGHTON v LEYTON ORIENT, 8 MARCH 1997

PAUL SAMRAH: So we're waiting for an agreement to be reached at CEDR which still hasn't come, people are getting a little bit tense. We went into the Orient game on 8 March and after going in 2–0 up at half-time who could have forseen the events that followed?

STUART STORER: As I remember we came out absolutely on fire, we scored two goals in ten minutes. I think we scored straight from the kick-off, we were so fired up for the match. We went in 2–0 up, everything was happy, the fans were singing and chanting, came out second half, after seven minutes we were 3–2 down! I don't think I touched the ball second half. We battled our socks off to get back in the match, Ian Baird made it three-all and everyone was so happy and relieved that we got the equaliser. Straight from their kick-off they scored right away.

DAVE SWAFFIELD: I made a terrible decision from moving on my place in the North Stand for some reason, I don't know why now. We went 2–0 up really early and then they pulled two back. At that point I went, 'This isn't right, I'm going back to my normal place, the reason this is happening is because I'm standing where I am, not where I should be.'

STUART STORER: All I can remember is the Orient lad who scored, Carl Griffiths I think it was, giving it the old gun salute to the Brighton fans. I think a couple of them took exception to it, ran on and tried to have a go. I didn't really see much of it, but I just saw one of the fans had Butch Wilkins' leg. The fans were brilliant then, you'd expect a lot more fans to run on, but they all booed them when they got arrested, especially with another possible points deduction, which would have been absolutely vital again. But to be fair to the majority of the crowd they just got them off the pitch, got on with the match and luckily we were given a very dubious penalty and McDonald slotted it home. That match had everything – goals, sendings-off, last-minute penalties, crowd trouble. It must've been a hell of a game to watch.

PAUL SAMRAH: I think we all felt ashamed to be Brighton fans, all our hard work was in danger of going completely down the pan.

A few fans went on the pitch, punches were aimed, Wilkins was attacked, the referee was attacked. It just left us all numb and fortunately we came back and drew 4–4 but the football was irrelevant. It was totally sickening, we had behaved ourselves so well throughout everything, and we came out thinking after what the FA did after the Lincoln game when it was a peaceful walk-on, walk-off demonstration with no police involved, here we had seen the sight of police chasing fans on a football pitch, the players getting involved in a mass brawl with supporters and the guys being booed off and we felt they couldn't fail to take action.

JAN SWALLOW: You can protest in so many different ways peacefully, and we'd done that, we'd done it in a dignified way. This was totally undignified and, you know, one of them could have hurt Ray Wilkins. There's no way that you direct your anger at players or the referee. I know that some of the players were gesticulating at us in the North Stand and I suppose these were just full of emotion, hot-headed young blokes who couldn't help themselves.

DAVE SWAFFIELD: That's the big difference: before it was like applause, 'do your protest, come off.' And now, as soon as these people ran on the pitch, it was like, 'Get the fuck off, what are you doing, you idiots'.

That showed the total change to where it had been before, the negative side that had now changed on to the footballing side, things had changed off the pitch, now we had got to make the team stay in the League.

One of the fans was thrown back by the police into the North West Terrace and the fans started beating him up.

PAUL SAMRAH: The press comment afterwards was 'football thugs', 'Brighton thugs', 'hooligans', 'kick them out the League'. You had Orient's chairman, Barry Hearn, and their manager making comments which were probably hyped up. Nevertheless the only other time we had seen national TV coverage was the York City abandonment and it was a stark reminder that to the average person who doesn't know anything about football, Brighton fans were thugs. Totally wrong, but that was the way that it came across.

PAUL HAYWARD: I remember arguing with a colleague of mine about the Orient incident. He was saying, 'Well, that's it, Brighton have got to lose more points for that, they just surrendered all the sympathy they'd built up over the preceding months.' And while I thought that was an act of complete stupidity, I've got a problem with punishing 8,500 peaceful people for the actions of three or four idiots. I think it would have been unjust.

28.3.97 – the FA announces that no action will be taken against Brighton for the Orient game.

170

JANUARY 1997 – MAY 1997

39. 'Dick Knight in – Dickhead out'

PAUL SAMRAH: Paul Whelch liaised with Mike Appleby from the FA and organised a private meeting at the Mill Hotel in Sudbury on the 16th November. We said basically that there was a tide of lawlessness prevailing at the ground, that we were concerned that someone was going to get hurt. And that the FA had got to do something because we couldn't account for people who wanted to take the law into their own hands. He went along to the game at Sudbury and heard the chanting and it came home to him, I think.

We then had a meeting on Wednesday 20th November in Eastbourne with the A21 Club and Ivor Caplin also came along and I outlined there that Paul Whelch and myself had a meeting with the FA the following day to hand over a dossier on the case for bringing the charge of 'bringing the game into disrepute' against the directors. So on Thursday 21 November at 12.30 p.m. we turned up at Lancaster Gate and met Mike Appleby and the FA's solicitor and handed over the dossier. We stressed in no uncertain terms that lawlessness was just a game away.

DAVID DAVIES: I was deeply concerned about the state of the negotiations, and I was also aware of the level of concern of people whose opinions I value had about the extent of the breakdown in relationships in the club, and the Archer/Knight thing. There seemed to be no common ground whatsoever.

The position was so unusual that, at least on behalf of the supporters, we had a responsibility to do everything we could to try to find a solution. This is potentially a very big club, what was it doing at the bottom of the Third Division? The fact that the ownership had developed in the way it had, that the club had declined in the way that it had, that the breakdown in morale was cataclysmic. And my motive was to say if the worst were to happen I want to be clear that those of us here have done everything we conceivably could have done to avert that and to give this club a long-term future. That means if you are looking to sort out a long-term future, there are certain things you don't do, if the legal advice is such, that might give a good feel to those who hate one side or another – for example, charging people with bringing the game into disrepute and all that. That, in terms of giving a long-term future to that club, might have the absolutely opposite effect.

MARC TWIBILL: I think people felt that the FA didn't really care about a small Third Division club. 'The Premiership seems to be the be-all and end-all' is how we felt. They didn't really seem to be taking any strong action. I think the fans had a right to be very angry and I don't think without our continued pressure the FA ever would have taken any action.

TIM CARDER: I think that one of the problems was that although they could charge Archer and Bellotti with bringing the game into disrepute – I'm sure that could be proven, I think the circumstances of the York City game would probably have been enough although I'm no expert – but what do they do? They punish them, they throw them out of football, but that doesn't actually change the ownership of the club. They can prevent Archer and Bellotti and whoever being directors of the football club – there's nothing the FA can do to change the ownership of the club.

PAUL SAMRAH: It is difficult for the FA because they can't control private limited companies. Their powers were severely limited. They also knew that they would face, with Archer, an enormous legal backlash and these things would drag on. They probably thought that charging the board with bringing the game into disrepute would not change the ownership problem and we recognised that deep down.

PAUL HAYWARD: The Football Association now is preoccupied by what they would think of as bigger things like World Cup bids, the Premier League, pay-per-view and Sky TV deals and all the rest of it, they are wrestling with an almighty multi-million-pound industry. Faced with the demise of Brighton, I think initially they chose to quietly ignore it. Again it was the fans and the attention that it received in the media that forced the FA to become involved in December when they set up the mediation process.

ATTILA THE STOCKBROKER: We put sufficient pressure on the FA and we made them ashamed. There was shame in the voice of Kelly and Steve Double and we made them ashamed of their lack of power.

DAVID DAVIES: I was trying to find an innovative solution to their problems. I talked to all sorts of people that I know and one of these organisations that was mentioned to me was CEDR, the Centre for Dispute Resolution – 'short sharp shock' mediation was what it was. I got on to them and then there was the problem of paying for it, because you don't employ these people for sixpence. Of course that opens up the issue of 'if we pay for it, do we pay for every club', our old-friend precedent? I know people can turn around and say, 'Oh it's chicken-feed relative to whatever the television deal is' and all the rest of it. It isn't chicken-feed. And we went into it having no idea how long the mediation might last, but it shouldn't last too long because it's 'short sharp shock' mediation.

PAUL SAMRAH: We had a breakthrough two days before our march in London. Following our meeting we had with the FA, they knew about the petition that was going to come their way, they were aware of the lawlessness and they issued their statement which said they'd called in CEDR (that was the 28 November). That was something positive. Archer, the Friday before the Fulham game, welcomed the offer of arbitration and warned the supporters against 'pressing the self-destruct button'.

ATTILA THE STOCKBROKER: Acting on the basis that there was nothing they could do about it, they then went to the CBI and this was where the CEDR came in. They didn't realise this but this was the ultimate accolade for Archer – to be called into the CBI – it was like, 'I'm really important, I am, the CBI are taking an interest in me.' He loved that, I could tell. He loved the sparring and the being so important, and they were all saying, 'He's very successful, you have to respect him, he's very successful.' And I said, 'Well, you probably don't want to hear this from me, but he's probably successful because for the last 18 years people like him have been encouraged. In my kind of society he wouldn't be successful – far from it.'

PAUL HAYWARD: I think the mediation process was well-intentioned but the fact is that it took months and months and an awful lot of money to achieve what the FA should have achieved by enforcing their own rule book and getting to grips with Archer and the rest of them directly. I've heard it said that they spent upwards of £50,000 on that mediation process and when it was set up they promised a 'short, sharp mediation' (as they described it). But that turned in to a sort of marathon process in which, because the parties concerned were forced to sign confidentiality agreements, nothing really emerged and so again supporters were groping in the dark, the club was ticking towards the possible end of Brighton and Hove Albion and nobody knew what was going on. We were assured again and again that it was all in hand and that things were being sorted out but I think we were entitled to ask questions of the FA and the mediation process and that right was denied to us. I regret that and I think it was wrong.

DAVID DAVIES: The only thing that was ever said by supporters that ever annoyed me was, 'Oh, the FA's passed the buck to these mediators.' Not only had we not passed the buck, we had brought in professional people who deal with this sort of problem and paid them.

Open letter from the Football Association to Bill Archer, 28 November 1996:

Dear Mr Archer,

As you know, a number of representatives of the FA have been involved for some time now in seeking to resolve the position of Brighton and Hove Albion Football Club following the sale of the Goldstone Ground.

As has been made clear on every occasion we have had any contact, the overriding purpose of the Football Association's involvement has been to ensure the future, in both the short and long term, of a professional football club in the Brighton and Hove area.

Brighton and Hove Albion FC has been for a considerable period a full member club of the Football Association and a member of the Football League. It is of course fully acknowledged that Brighton and Hove Albion FC is a company and, as such, its directors must be allowed to make business decisions in the way that it feels are appropriate in the best interests of its shareholders. Many people, however, care deeply about the club and its future, including the Football Association.

The history of the club over recent years is well known; there is no need to go over again the sale of the Goldstone Ground and the reasons for that decision. What is a matter of great debate is where the club is to play after this season ends. This is the same position we were in last year. It seems that, for whatever reason, little has changed.

I have of course seen the recent letter from the Football League to club secretaries in relation to the issue of ground-sharing. The Football Association fully supports the stance set out in that letter.

I have personally been involved throughout the Football Association's efforts to mediate between the various interested parties, including the club, the Councils, potential purchasers and the supporters. Previous attempts to broker a way forward have failed.

However, the Football Association is available still at any time to give whatever assistance it can in achieving this goal. At our meeting towards the end of September, a proposal was made that a separate independent mediator might be brought in. We believe this to be the best way forward and are now willing to retain, at our cost, the service of the CBI to achieve this. I would urge you to take up this offer.

As a separate but extremely important issue, I have to say that it is difficult for anyone involved in the game to ignore the unrest amongst the paying supporters of the club, and the apparent ill-feeling amongst the Brighton and Hove community as a whole. This seems to centre on the rift that has arisen between the directors and shareholders on the one hand, and the supporters of the club and Councils on the other.

It is a paramount concern of the Football Association that the safety and security of all who attend matches is a priority. I am personally very concerned as to the possibility of continued crowd disturbances leading to someone being seriously injured.

I would appeal to the club, its directors and shareholders, to have as their paramount concern the needs of the community in which the club holds an important position.

I will be making the contents of this letter public. I look forward to hearing from you as soon as possible.

R.H.G. Kelly

Chief Executive, the Football Association

PAUL SAMRAH: Paul Whelch and myself were invited to CEDR for a first just sort of getting-to-know-each-other session as representatives of supporters at CEDR's offices, Friday, 13 December, 8.30 at St Katherine's Dock in London. Just ourselves, nobody else to meet the two mediators David Richbell and Marsh. So we turned up on that Friday armed again with the pack that we'd given the FA, including the 'Putting the Record Straight' dossier.

Bill Archer's public statements from 'Putting the Record Straight'
Document by Paul Samrah and Dick Knight:

BBC South Today, 4 October 1996

I haven't been convinced by the consortium that they have the funds to build a new stadium.

BBC Radio 5 Live, 5 October 1996

I've had two meetings with Dick Knight's consortium and they had an opportunity at the first meeting (22 August) to demonstrate that they have the funds to take the club forward. They were given a second opportunity (FA meeting, 30 September) to demonstrate they had the funds to take it forward. They didn't do so.

BBC Radio 5 Live, 10 October 1996

Mr Knight says that he has the funds to develop a new stadium. He had the opportunity in front of the FA when Mr Kelly and the rest of the FA people were there – he then couldn't demonstrate that he had the funds.

Answer: the consortium provided documentary evidence at the FA meeting and earlier to Archer and the Brighton Argus, that they fully met all the pre-conditions under which he publicly promised to step aside.

Daily Telegraph 14 October 1996

Various consortia have attempted to take over the club but none have shown where they would build a stadium. A letter from Cllr Caplin states a site has been found and that the council have agreed to support an application 'as a matter of urgent priority.' It would save a lot of time, money and distress if it is offered to the club's board to consider. Maybe supporters should now be asking councillors for a few answers.

Answer: at a meeting on 22 August, Archer introduced a further condition – if the consortium could prove evidence that it had identified a site and the site would be supported by the local authority in planning terms, then he would be prepared to negotiate the transfer of the club to the consortium. The consortium supplied Archer with the information – Caplin's letter was part of the evidence. It was also presented to the FA. Archer was seeking to obtain information about the proposed stadium development.

BBC South Today, 4 October 1996

If anyone can demonstrate that they can build a stadium better than me, and they have more funds to build a new stadium better than me, then I will genuinely step aside.

Answer: the consortium has.

BBC Radio 5 Live, 10 October 1996

We have the funds to build a new stadium.

Daily Telegraph, 14 October 1996

We have the funding in place to build a new stadium.

Answer: Archer has produced no public evidence of his funding resources.

BBC South Today, 4 October 1996

I knew that it would be me and Stanley, who would have to put the money in, put our assets in. We actually put the security up for saving the club in 1993.

BBC Radio 5 Live, 5 October 1996

I took a decision with Greg Stanley in 1993 that we would take this club forward. We would actually invest in the club. What really saved the Albion in 1993 was hard cash – two million quid's worth of hard cash.

BBC Radio 5 Live, 10 October 1996

Myself and Greg Stanley took the decision that we would bail the club out.

We had to inject another £2 million to keep the club afloat. I reluctantly took the decision in 1993 with Greg Stanley to actually put funds into the club.

Answer: the only hard cash invested was an £880,000 bank loan, secured on the Goldstone. At this time Archer gained control of the club for a personal investment of £56.25 by promising the then shareholders repayment of their personal loans in 1996.

The Stanley Trust loan has been in place since 1992 secured on the Goldstone and is attracting interest and a penalty. The terms of the loan will result in the Trust taking an estimated £400,000 from the club in addition to the sum loaned.

BBC South Today, 4 October 1996

The books are an absolute irrelevance, we are shortly to produce the statutory accounts anyway.

BBC Radio 5 Live, 5 October 1996

Now this irrelevance about the accounts. There's no skeleton in the cupboard.

Answer: despite repeated promises to give the consortium access to the club's books – the last at the meeting of 22 August once the stadium evidence condition had been met – to date Archer has failed to do so.

The books are very relevant to gain a full picture. And given that the accounts when published will only show up to 31 May 1996, management accounts from then are needed to show a clear picture of the club's current financial status.

BBC South Today

I have been watching Brighton and Hove Albion for the last eight years. I would go to every match.

BBC Radio 5 Live, 5 October 1996

I only don't go to the games because I'm not permitted to.

Answer: Archer joined the Albion board in 1990. He rarely attended matches – home or away – even prior to 1995, the start of the current troubles.

PAUL SAMRAH: I remember Paul Whelch saying to Bill Marsh just as we were leaving, 'If you think you can solve this problem that we've got at the club you are probably better off going out to Bosnia, that's probably an easier job' and he was probably not far wrong.

We were then invited along on 31 January for a talk with the board, to meet Bill Archer and have discussions about the club mediated by CEDR.

We were a bit sceptical because we thought, 'Why should we be involved in these discussions? All we want is for the Knight consortium to take over the club.'

LIZ COSTA: I had got a phone call at work from Bill Marsh, from the mediators, and he said he wanted representation from the supporters, 'Who should be invited and how do you perceive what we should be doing?' I thought, 'This is unheard of, they're actually asking our advice.'

We were ultimately all invited to attend and that was myself, Tony Foster, Paul Samrah, Paul Whelch, Attila, and Norman Rae from the A21 club.

We were invited to this meeting on the Friday and it was a bit upbeat when we got there. We were there for half past nine and at quarter to ten Archer and Bellotti arrived, I refused to be in the same room as them. And they said, 'Oh no, they're not going to be involved in our discussions. We will have our discussion and if we think there is a point where their input would be helpful, then they will be called in.' So our meeting went on until near enough lunchtime before Archer was called in and he was given quite a rough time.

Originally we were told that we had to sign this confidentiality agreement which Attila refused to sign. At the time, we weren't really sure so we all signed it but in fact there was nothing discussed on the day at any point that was not anything that we could come back and say, 'This was what happened.' But there was always the chance that something could have been let slip that could have jeopardised the continuation of the talks. I, personally, wasn't prepared to jeopardise that. The future was almost in our hands, if you like.

PAUL SAMRAH: Attila said that if there was anything that was going to be discussed that was confidential he would leave the room, he didn't want to be party to any kind of confidentiality and I admire him for that – it was excellent. We continued and in actual fact throughout the whole day there wasn't anything discussed that was confidential and Attila remained in on all the meetings. He didn't want to shake his hand. I remember he said, 'When he comes in I'm not going to shake his hand', I said, 'Well, when he comes in I'll start the chant "Stand up if you hate Archer!", all stand up.' Archer, when he came in, actually walked round the back of our desk to shake hands with each of us individually, so not to shake hands would have been blatantly rude. In fact Attila did shake his hand and we sort of winked at each other.

179

ATTILA THE STOCKBROKER: I genuinely get the feeling that Bill Archer enjoys being a hate figure. He loves confrontation and I do think genuinely that he makes concessions when you lay off him rather than when you really have a go at him.

At this meeting, I've got to hand it to the guy, there were six of us there, livid, and I was really laying in to him and he was giving it back. Some of the others were rather intimidated by him and yet if I made a specific point where I wasn't attacking him he would go, 'Yes . . . well, you know . . .' and he kept trying to get round us, especially me. He would come up and say, 'I want to work with you, not against you.' And he was genuinely trying to get us on his side.

PAUL SAMRAH: We had been warned by Bill Marsh that if you push Bill Archer into a corner he will get very angry, and the best way is to stand back and he will be remarkably tolerant and approachable. We adopted that approach initially, and then we slightly fell into the trap of then going in to push him back into a corner with a barrage of, 'You haven't done this, you've lied on this.' We physically felt we'd put Archer in a corner, he was in front of six of us – of course Archer then came out absolutely fighting. He completely lost it, 'You can't tell me what to fucking do. You haven't put any money in that club, you haven't come up with money to buy the club, all you ever do is bloody demonstrate and argue, can't you just bloody well accept that we've sold the ground, all this business, there's no capital gains, you're talking crap'. By this time it was about 1.30 p.m. and rather sensibly Bill Marsh and David Richbell said, 'We should have a lunch break, let's cool off.' So Bill Archer left the room and went upstairs to have lunch. We had about four or five hours of talks, it really was extraordinary, here we were representing the supporters of Brighton and Hove Albion Football Club, it was quite a major thing.

LIZ COSTA: We knew we were getting nowhere – it was just like butting your head against a brick wall with him.

PAUL SAMRAH: So, having had a 45-minute break, Archer came in again and that was probably the best meeting we've had, about an hour and a half. He'd calmed down and we'd realised that you can't put him into a corner, we respected that and kept our distance. We had a very frank exchange of views, perfectly calm, made it clear what we expected to happen and why we expected things to happen and we backed our arguments up.

ATTILA THE STOCKBROKER: I said to him, 'Tell me, why are you doing this? What are you getting out of this? Do you like being hated?' And he said, 'Well, my family think I'm mad too. My wife says "Why the bloody hell don't you jack it in and leave them to it?" But she knows that if I start something I'm going to finish it, and I'm the ogre who gave away the family silver.' All this crap.

PAUL SAMRAH: All of us made some very valid points and all of us were very focused on the point. Bill Archer, at the end of it, said, 'Look, you've got to see David Bellotti, he's been here all day, you've got to see him, notwithstanding the Paul Samrah banning thing, he's a broken man, he's just lost the seat, he's been deselected.'

So he came down about 4.30 p.m. – he'd been waiting all that time upstairs, he looked under pressure and we just grilled him. Liz Costa just went for it and Archer was saying, 'Go on, answer the question', treating him with utmost contempt but the upshot of it was we got an agreement. We said it was unsafe for the board to attend games and we'd agreed with Archer that the board were not going to attend any game, home or away.

I went off with Bellotti into a private room and we discussed with Bill Marsh my ban being lifted. Bellotti said to me, 'I want the ban lifted as well' and I thought, 'Well that's quite interesting given it was you who instituted it.' 'Oh well, it's not quite as simple as that,' he said, 'I will lift the ban and give you the seat back as long as you do not lead demonstrations inside the ground.' I said, 'I don't lead demonstrations, I take part. Anyway you're not going to be there, David, so that won't be a problem because that's been agreed.' He said, 'Well then, you can sign something to that effect to say that you won't be leading demonstrations inside the ground and we'll give you your seat back, that's fine, no problem.'

I thought, 'Fair enough, I'll accept that', so he turned to Bill Marsh and said, 'We've got an agreement, we'll give you a seat in the South Stand.' I said, 'Sorry David, what do you mean a seat in the South Stand? I'm a West Stand seat ticket-holder.' 'Oh, I don't think that I can give a West Stand seat back, because that's where all the organisers are and I don't want you with them.' So I just said, 'Well fine, you haven't got an agreement, I'll just walk out. Does Bill Archer know that you're giving me a precondition?' As soon as I mentioned Bill Archer, he completely back-tracked and said, 'Oh well I'm sure that we can give you your West Stand seat back.'

So I agreed to liaise with my solicitors and Bellotti agreed to liaise with the club's solicitors and they then issued a press release:

> It was agreed that the banning of Paul Samrah from the club grounds will be lifted, the progressive opening of the East Side of the ground will commence which was agreed and whilst accepting that directors have responsibilities on match days there will be no overt presence in the stand that may cause adverse reaction.

Basically saying that the board will not attend games, which was a break-through, really.

NIGEL SUMMERS: They talked about bringing in CEDR in November and they appointed them in December with an idea of having a solution by the end of the year. How many times have you heard the expression, 'An announcement is planned shortly.' I'm just sick of the sound of it and when people are reading this book in ten years' time, I wouldn't be surprised if 'An announcement is expected shortly'.

DAVID DAVIES: On a Wednesday evening, 12 March, I got off the train at Birmingham International and walked across the carpark and my mobile phone went and I got a call from CEDR saying we'd reached a provisional agreement. And I am quite happy to say it was one of the best moments of last season – probably the best moment of last season for me. So many people within football had said, 'No chance!' Significant numbers of people had said this is the ultimate intractable problem.

TIM CARDER: Obviously one or other side or both sides had shifted position and I rather think it was the consortium who had shifted position to allow Archer to remain in on the deal. Up to that time they had probably insisted that it must be a complete takeover or nothing and Archer had insisted that he wouldn't be giving the club away despite what he'd said previously in the summer. I think probably the consortium allowed him in on the deal and that was what clinched it. I remember hearing on the radio that Greg Stanley had come out of the meeting and everything was on and the deal was apparently signed there and then. But we knew nothing. We just knew that a deal had been struck and we went into limbo. With the Doncaster game coming up, the last one ever at the Goldstone, this was the same sort of situation as with the York City game – we didn't know where we would be playing or who was going to own the club, so something had to be done. Eventually they called a press conference in that week leading up to the Doncaster game.

DAVID DAVIES: There's no secret that my relationship with Dick Knight is very good, as it is with all the people in the consortium. But I understand full well that the supporters don't want platitudes, they want a solution to the long-term future of the club. Which is precisely what we've invested time, effort and money in. There's absolutely no question that, for some of us, the hours that have gone in to finding a solution to this problem is nobody's business.

PAUL SAMRAH: The final game at the Goldstone was coming and still we didn't have an announcement, still we didn't know that the agreement had finally been concluded.

In actual fact we understand that on Thursday, 17 April, Dick Knight and Bill Archer went out for dinner because on Friday, 18 April they were summoned to the FA to be told, 'You'd better deliver on an agreement before you have the final game at the Goldstone', less than eight days away. They were being told to get their act together and fortunately they did. Friday 18 there was a press statement to say there would be a press conference on Tuesday 22 when details of the deal would be announced at the Metropole Hotel off Edgware Road in London.

DAVID DAVIES: When on 22 April we got everybody to sign the memorandum of agreement, it was a red-letter day in its own way. Yes, I was quite pleased with myself. But our role had been played, at that point. And there is an agreement in principle, as of 22 April. Nobody in the FA has signed the document. We were the brokers, hopefully the honest brokers, of an agreement.

PAUL HAYWARD: Right to the wire it was a chaotic procedure. We were all sitting there in the foyer wondering what the hell was going to happen and suddenly this cab pulled up and Archer got out. You could see everybody, even journalists who weren't particularly involved in the Brighton story, stiffen and the whole foyer of the hotel seemed to tense up as soon as he walked through the door. And I remember looking at him very straight on and trying to make eye contact but he avoided eye contact with all of us.

In everything I've ever written about Brighton, when I've tried to call Archer to get his response on things, he's seldom returned my calls. The same with Bellotti, neither of them have ever been available for interview, as the phrase goes. It was supposed to start at 1 o'clock but it started actually at 1.20 p.m., and we sat there with our notebooks and tape recorders wondering what the hell was going on, and there was a feeling even then that Archer might still be being obstructive or that the final details hadn't actually been sorted out. They finally came out at about 1.25 p.m. and everyone had their say. Dick Knight was brilliant, actually – he was incredibly warm and human and talked about his dad and how much it meant to him. And I asked Bill Archer whether, in view of what had happened during his time at the club, whether it would have been more honourable for him to resign and allow the consortium to take full control – and what he did was extraordinary – he apologised, or on the face of it apologised, for 'all the pain he had caused over the last two years.' Which I thought was an amazingly hypocritical response.

STEWART WEIR: Archer referred to the club as 'Brighton and Hove DIY', which is a wonderful Freudian slip.

PAUL HAYWARD: When Bill Archer had had his say, which was a sort of stream of consciousness, most of which was unfollowable as some of his public pronouncements are, I noticed the body language of everyone on that panel. There was the policeman, John Smith, ex-deputy commissioner, who's going to be on the board, there was David Davies in the middle, there was Dick Knight and other members of the consortium — everyone started shifting uncomfortably in their seats when Archer started talking, even the journalists did as well.

It was almost physically painful having to sit through Bill Archer taking credit for and joining in with the salvation of the club, when he had share some of the responsibility. I remember thinking 'I can't wait to get out of here — there's something not right about this'. It was wonderful to see Dick Knight taking that great stake and having all his hard work come to fruition and, again, he was very impressive.

But the rest of it, or Archer's involvement, I found hard to take, and really I felt sorry for Dick Knight still having to deal with the guy. He tried so hard to get complete control of the club and there he was still stuck with Bill Archer.

CEDR press release 22 April 1997

Following several days of mediation over the past 20 weeks we are pleased to give details of the settlement agreed by the present owners (Bill Archer and Greg Stanley) with the consortium led by Dick Knight. The main points of the settlement are as follows:

Restructuring of the football club

The new shareholding is agreed as follows: consortium 49.5 per cent, present owners 49.5 per cent, Martin Perry (McAlpine's) 1 per cent.

This means that the present owners have given up overall control but retain a significant interest in the club. In addition, following a suggestion from the Football Association, two new independent non-executive directors are to be appointed. These independent directors are Sir John Smith (former deputy commissioner of Metropolitan Police) and Richard Faulkner (vice-chairman of the Football Trust).

The new board is unanimous in the view that these independent directors will bring invaluable experience to the running of the club. Under the new arrangement Dick Knight will become chairman of Brighton and Hove Albion FC.

Future club management

The final membership of the board of management has yet to be agreed but will include a representative of the supporters. All current directors' roles will be reviewed by the new board.

Temporary playing facilities

All parties agree that playing locally next season is a priority. There has been publicity about temporary facilities at the Corals track and negotiations will continue on the solution. However this is not the only possibility being pursued. It is recognised whatever arrangement is made it will require Football League approval. Such approval has not yet been given to ground-sharing with Gillingham.

Permanent stadium

A planning application will be made for a permanent stadium and commercial development in the Brighton and Hove area within the next three months. The scheme will include a 15,000 seat capacity initially with plans to extend up to a 25,000 seat capacity in the future.

Conclusion

This has been a long and difficult mediation and has involved significant movement on all sides. It should be recorded that the official purpose of the mediation laid down by the Football Association was that professional football should continue to be played in Brighton and Hove and that the future of this historic club should be assured. We believe that aim has been achieved.

The parties have confirmed that this settlement is firm and will not be affected if Brighton are relegated.

There are many people to thank in achieving this, not least the supporters for their patience and trust that all would be well in the end. Also the media. Mediation is a confidential process and so there has been little or no information to be given out. It has been frustrating for us and undoubtedly frustrating for you but most of the time it has been respected and worked well.

Finally thanks to the FA who, after calling CEDR to mediate the dispute, have held their nerve and given us time and space to help the parties find a solution.

PAUL SAMRAH: I accepted the deal. Archer was no longer the majority shareholder, which was the bottom line, and that was the best that we could hope for. It was clear that Archer was not going to walk away from the development of the new ground and we have to accept that.

ATTILA THE STOCKBROKER: Knight and Perry went in there 100 per cent-or-nothing and ended up with 50.5 per cent between them. As long as it is what it says it is, it is a huge victory because 50.5 per cent is overall control.

I would still say that I don't think Archer has made any money out of this because the people that we trust who investigate these things see no evidence that he has actually taken money for his own personal use. It's an ego and control thing plus obviously the opportunity of making a lot of money in the future out of the new development. But the ego and control thing is the most important and so to get overall control away from Archer is a major victory with the proviso, of course, that the McAlpine element is not ever going to side with Archer. I can't possibly see that Perry is going to side with Archer against Knight. I mean, quite apart from anything else, if he did there would be hell to pay for McAlpine's. So to get that 50.5 per cent is a major victory and it's a victory by the supporters and a result of a season of total pressure and campaigning at all levels plus the media support that we've had, plus the eventual involvement of the FA, who did do something.

TONY HYLANDS: I still feel the big press announcement two weeks before the end of the season was a publicity thing. It was a PR exercise to stop any rioting, to make us believe that it was all sorted.

BILL SWALLOW: I think there were six words that really stuck in my gullet about that deal and that was 'forty-nine and a half per cent'. As long as Bill Archer is running the football club or is, in some way involved on the board of the football club, then there's a cuckoo in the nest.

TIM CARDER: I won't forgive him. I hate and loathe him as much as anyone else but I can live with the fact that he's there as long as the Albion have a future. While he was in sole charge I saw little future and that's what we had to bring about. We had to bring about a change in the ownership somehow, that Archer would no longer be in sole charge and we could actually look forward to having a proper future.

MARC TWIBILL: There were lots of questions raised about Knight and it was very easy for emotions to run high again and for people to become unsettled. It did go slowly but at the end of the day perhaps we've got a compromise. We're halfway there and I think now we've just got to give it time to sort of work itself out. Dick Knight was never going to be able to come in, wave the magic wand and everything was going to be okay again. There's been much damage done at the club and it's going to take a long time to repair it.

BILL SWALLOW: What must happen is that Bill Archer, must be removed from the football club board as quickly as possible. If he sits there at the back taking a rake-off from the football club development, so be it, that's how life is, but I don't want him to have any right to sit in the directors box at Brighton and Hove Albion. And until that's done, the deal won't be completed.

TIM CARDER: I certainly think the FA, now they've been through this, should take some note of what they've learnt from it and act upon it. But it's such a high financial world that football clubs move in these days, how much power does the FA have over clubs? If they're going to be taken to court every time they try and invoke some regulation and it's found to be against some European trade law or whatever, then they're going to be pretty much toothless tigers and almost anything could happen to any football club.

ATTILA THE STOCKBROKER: I don't want Archer to have any further involvement in Brighton and Hove Albion Football Club. Now, if some people turn round and say, 'We don't like Archer but we've now got the board we wanted and things are moving forward', and they want to stop the campaign against Archer or put it on the back-burner, then those of us who don't agree will argue our case. I can't believe that the majority of the fans would ever say that, I don't think any of them will ever accept Archer. I'm a very forgiving person but I would never forgive Archer for what he's done. I mean, we're quite prepared to ignore him, the day he withdraws all interest and involvement in Brighton and Hove Albion Football Club I will forget all about Archer. I've no intention of carrying on a campaign forever but as long as he is involved in the club, he will get it.

> Dick Knight, the chairman-elect, issues a statement to fans through the *Argus* – 23 April 1997:
>
> When Liam Brady asked me a year ago to become involved in the problems at the Albion I did so because I wanted to help the club I love, the team that I've followed all my life as a fan. How could I have ever dreamt 50 years ago, when my father first took me as a small boy to the Goldstone, that I would find myself in the position I'm in today?
> I step into the role of Albion club chairman with some humility, knowing how much the club means to thousands of fans like me. I want to thank all Albion fans for their resilience, patience and, above all, marvellous support for the club in its hour of need.
> Given all the circumstances, I'm satisfied with the outcome. My co-directors, the FA and CEDR are satisfied and I hope the supporters will be satisfied too. For the good of the club the time for turmoil and confrontation must now be over. We must all now get on with rebuilding the Albion.

> The new board will work together to achieve the following key
> objectives:
> - An injection of finance into the club, initially in the order of £2 million;
> - Rigorously pursue all our options to ensure Albion will be playing its
>   home matches locally next season;
> - Finalising our plans for the permanent stadium.
>
> Another important objective of the new board is to have a regular dialogue
> with Supporters representatives.
>
> The club's immediate future is in its own hands. Nothing less than six points
> will do, because, realistically, I don't believe we can get the two
> deducted points back. On Saturday, the last ever game at the Goldstone,
> I'm sure the team will rise to the occasion. There won't be a dry eye in
> the place, whatever the result. But I pledge that this board will bring
> brighter days back to the Albion.

40. 'Going down Old Shoreham Road – to see the Brighton aces!'

JAN SWALLOW: We got there very early and we wanted to be there as long as we could be. Normally we get to games just before three o'clock but we got there about two, I think, and there was a brass band playing. That got me going because I hadn't seen a brass band playing down there since I was at school and I didn't know they were going to do that. I thought I'd prepared myself but that took me by surprise.

STEWART WEIR: Doncaster was a huge game. It was a game of lasts. When you think about it – it's the last time the hot dog stand's going to be there, it's the last time the players will go in, it's the last time the press will walk in, it's the last time the turnstiles will be used, it's the last time the players will come out for a warm-up, the last time Fred Oliver walks around selling his *Argus*.

TONY HYLANDS: For me personally it was just a very weird day. I couldn't believe that I was walking down Hove Park for the last time, I couldn't believe I was going through the North Stand entrance for the last time, I couldn't believe I was watching the game for the last time and I couldn't believe that I was never ever going back there again. It was weird.

PAUL HAYWARD: Brighton are quite honoured by this in the sense that a lot of clubs were vacating their grounds at the end of the season but none of them attracted the same kind of attention that Brighton did. There was really an influx, of not just regular football writers, but sports feature writers who were interested in this phenomenon of Brighton finally leaving the place where they've been for 93 years, and by then the deal had been done so the temperature was slightly lower than it would have been. I remember being crammed into the press box with people I wouldn't normally see at Brighton and them looking to write evocative pieces about Brighton being ejected.

There was this sense of the whole town flooding towards the Goldstone Ground, a kind of precious lost feeling, and the last time that we were ever going to get it.

MARC TWIBILL: I'd spoken to a few people who were in the know and they told me that they'd heard that we would be staying at the Goldstone for another year as long as we stayed up. It was only going down to the Goldstone last week and seeing the pitch and the stands already being knocked down that it was able to sink in with me.

TIM CARDER: As well as it being the emotional occasion of the last game we were also absolutely desperate for those three points. That was the more important thing at the time than saying goodbye to the Goldstone.

STEWART WEIR: The Doncaster game was the crescendo, the peak was going to be that last game at Hereford. But for the time being everyone was focused on Doncaster and what the ground meant to them. You could see it in everyone's faces before the game started, you know they were looking around and they were probably looking around at where they first stood or where they were standing for their best game – because everyone's got their best moment or their best game or their best memory.

There was nothing less than a win required because had we lost or drawn and Hereford had won at Orient . . . Everyone was on about this conspiracy of Hereford at Orient – are Orient going to do us any favours because of what happened a few weeks previous?

PAUL SAMRAH: This was the game of course that Dick Knight had taken his seat in the directors box. We'd had the Last Post at the start of the game at the ground, there was a wreath on top of the dugout and it was the last time we'd hear 'Good old Sussex by the Sea' coming out of the tannoy. It was a very emotional day but we were immune to the emotion from the kick-off. We were just concerned for getting those three points.

We just could not believe that Orient would beat Hereford and the game kicked off second half and the chant '1–0 to the Orient' started to go round the ground.

DAVE SWAFFIELD: I still had in my mind that it wasn't going to go, the ground would still be there, it wouldn't be destroyed. When they played the Last Post, I was blubbing my eyes out.

TONY MILLARD: I was doing joint commentary with Jim Proudfoot and he handed to me for the last eight minutes because I had been reporting on the Albion for so many years. I have to say that, whilst delighted with the result, I finished up in tears because I knew it was the last commentary I would be doing at the Goldstone in a press box in which I had sat for many years.

PAUL SAMRAH: We'd had our Ian Baird sent off so we were down to ten men as we entered the second half, then there was a substitution, McDonald came off and Reinelt went on and Stuart Storer scored a magnificent goal.

It's quite fitting that the last goal ever scored at the Goldstone should be scored by the PFA representative and player that had really performed outstandingly well since Gritt had taken over.

STUART STORER: We knew if we lost, that was it, we were out of the League. Scoring the goal against Doncaster, it was just like someone had taken a piano off my back, the pressure was just so enormous. They came for the draw I think and there wasn't many chances created in the match and luckily that one just fell nicely to me, like, and I just banged it in.

Unbelievable feeling, especially when the final whistle went. To know that we had three points in the bag, Hereford had lost and we had to go and get a draw, that was such a big lift for us. Although we still had that whole week to go before Hereford, we were on such a high, I just couldn't see us losing. I've got a load of pictures of the goal, a big collage and looking in the background and seeing all the faces, there's such delight, it made me proud that I could cheer up so many people. At the time I was more worried about the three points.

STEWART WEIR: Sitting behind the south goal, it was just like everything happening in slow motion, really, you know, the ball came over, it rolled, it hit the post, it went out and Stuart Storer crashed it in – and the whole ground went crazy. End of story, end of game.

STUART STORER: Going around Brighton in the next couple of weeks, realising it was the last goal at the Goldstone was an even bigger thrill for me. At the time I didn't realise what I had done, all I'd done is scored and got the three points.

TIM CARDER: When Hereford's result at Orient came across – they'd lost – we knew that it would only take a draw the following week to stay up so really it was absolutely rejoicing at the end rather than any malevolence. It was sorrow at saying goodbye to a dear friend, the Goldstone Ground, but also rejoicing at the fact that we now had a very good chance of staying in the League. So along with thousands of others, I went on the pitch and took my little bit of turf. It was a bit sad to leave with the sound of seats being smashed in the background but it didn't upset me in any way because I would rather the fans took the ground than the bulldozers. I've got my little bit of turf in the garden and hopefully it's growing new shoots and regenerating and all these other symbolic little things that will reflect in the club.

I remember seeing people coming out with the toilet seats. It was bizarre seeing what people were carrying away. I remember seeing these two blokes walking down Newtown Road with these huge advertising hoardings. Quite how they were going to get them home or what they were going to do with them, the mind boggles.

NIGEL SUMMERS: I wasn't as upset at leaving the Goldstone in the Doncaster game as I was in the York game, which doesn't make sense at all. It was exactly the same scenario but I think maybe the fact that we won and everybody was on the pitch like we'd avoided relegation was a bit scary because we obviously hadn't at that stage.

PAUL SAMRAH: People took away all sorts of things, the clocks, the seats, the turf, a St John's Ambulance woman was cutting up the goal netting.

JAN MERRITT: I must admit I was rather disappointed with the last match at Goldstone against Doncaster. Having experienced Fans United perhaps I expected that there was going to be an atmosphere like that, I know it's different but it didn't quite match up to that.

PAUL HAYWARD: The dismantling of the ground at the end, the *News of the World* decided that this was a riot of hooligan behaviour, and Jeff Sweet of the *News of the World*'s first question to Stuart Storer when he came into the press conference was: 'What do you think of the dickheads out there?'

Storer said, 'Listen, you've got to understand that these people have been through a lot. It's their ground, it's got a lot of memories for them and good luck to them.' Jeff Sweet's question wasn't a question, it was a statement — he had presupposed that the people were as he described them, 'dickheads', and he showed a complete lack of understanding of what the whole thing was about.

I remember standing in the press conference listening to Steve Gritt and all we could hear was this sort of metallic twangs and bangs and bumps with people ripping up bits of the seats. But there was a sense, both among the police and most of the journalists and certainly amongst the players and staff of the club, that this was an entirely appropriate way for people to take what they wanted from the ground.

I didn't regret the passing of the Goldstone that day. I felt sad because a lot of memories had been buried, but I felt that the club was shedding a dead skin.

SARAH WATTS: When I finally walked out of the ground I cried. I knew in myself that I was never going to walk out of it again and that really hurt.

NIGEL SUMMERS: I've never been back to the Goldstone since then and I won't either — I can't bring myself even to drive down the Old Shoreham Road. I can't do it.

PAUL SAMRAH: I was one of the last to leave at the back of the North Stand at about 5.50 p.m. I walked away and I've vowed never to go past again. That's it, this chapter is closed.

PAUL HAYWARD: It's entirely understandable that people should want to take their own personal memories of the Goldstone and it's almost as if the seed of the Goldstone was scattered across Sussex. You could almost hear the rumbles of the bulldozers that day and every time you drove past it subsequently you wondered whether it was still going to be there or if there was going to be a load of guys in hard hats and cranes smashing it to bits. So the idea that all those seeds have been scattered in the wind across Sussex and have landed in homes and front rooms and gardens is quite appealing.

STUART STORER: The passion here is amazing. I walked off against Doncaster, the last game at the Goldstone, I was virtually in tears, the passion, the place being ripped apart, you just get so involved with it, it's crazy and I've only been here two years.

TONY HYLANDS: Didn't want a bit of the net, didn't want a cross bar, didn't want a seat, didn't want anything, didn't want to be reminded of it, horrible.

Didn't shed a tear or anything then, just walking about in a numbed disbelief that that was then the end of it. The end of an era, 30 years of my life I was going there, come to an end.

From *Gull's Eye* issue 100
GOLDSTONE GHOSTS

As bulldozers close in upon our old, beloved home
and those who stand to profit rub their hands
So we gather here together in sad, angry disbelief
and for one last time, our voices full the stands
This is no happy parting, but a battle-scarred farewell
though victory hopes are mingled with the tears
and I, like you, will stand here as the final whistle blows
with memories which echo down the years . . .

*   *   *

The Chelsea fans threw pennies. Old ones. Sharpened. I was eight.
A target in the South Stand with my dad
and he got rather battered as he held me close and tight
and confirmed my view that Chelsea fans were mad!
And there, on those old wooden seats, I learned to love the game
The sights and sounds exploded in my head
My dad was proud to have a son with football in his blood -
but two short years later, he was dead.

Eleven. North West, on my own. (My friends liked chess and stuff.)
'Now don't go in the North Stand!' said my mum.
But soon I did. Kit Napier's comes curled into the net.
Oh god. The Bournemouth Boot Boys! Better run . . .
Then Villa in the big crunch game. A thirty thousand crowd.
Bald Lochhead scored, but we still won the day.
Then up, and straight back down again. Brian Powney, brave and squat.
T.Rex, D.M.'s and scarf on wrist, OK?

And then the world was wonderful. Punk rock and Peter Ward!
(And not forgetting Spider, tall and lean)
The legendary Walsall game. Promotion. Riding high.
Southampton – Spurs: that stitch-up was obscene.
The final glorious victory. The pinnacle at last.
The Arsenal game, midst fevered expectation.

Those Highbury gods tore us to shreds: we learned the lesson well.
Steve Foster was our soul and inspiration!

Man City came, and Gerry Ryan waltzed through them to score
And mighty Man United bit the dust
Notts Forest, and that Williams screamer nearly broke the net.
The Norwich quarter final – win or bust!
And, after Gordon, Liverpool were toppled one last time.
The final curtain on those happy days.
And then the years of gradual, inexorable decline -
Sadly, for some, the parting of the ways.
But we stayed true, as glory days turned into donkey's years.
Young, Trusson, Tiltman, Farrington. Ee-aw!
A Wilkins free-kick briefly brought us hope. 'Twas not to be.
The rot was deep, and spreading to the core.
We found our voice, and Barry went. Hooray! But worse to come.
Though just how awful we were yet to know.
Dissent turned to rebellion, and then to open war
As on the East the weeds began to grow.

The Goldstone sold behind our backs! Enraged, we rose as one
against a stony Northern businessman.
We drew a line, and said: ENOUGH! And as the nation watched
the final battle for our club began.
We fought him to a standstill. Fans United. All for one.
A nation's colours joined: a glorious eight.
And finally, the stubborn, stony Archer moved his ground
And made way for our own collective Knight.
The battle's only just begun, but we have won the war.
Our club, though torn asunder, will survive.
And I salute each one of you who stood up and said No!
And fought to keep the Albion alive.
And one day, when our new home's built, and we are storming back
A bunch of happy fans without a care
We'll look back on our darkest hour, and raise our glasses high
and say with satisfaction: WE WERE THERE.

But first, we've got to face today. The hardest day of all.
Don't worry if you can't hold back the tears!
We must look to the future, in dignity and peace
As well as mourn our home of ninety years.
For me, the Goldstone has an extra special memory

Of the football soulmate I so briefly had.
He, christened me John Charles, and taught me to love the game.
This one's for Bill. A poet. And my dad.

ATTILA THE STOCKBROKER
26 April 1997

for loyal Brighton fans, past, present and future
(Here's to the treble: Archer out, Tories out, Brighton staying up!)

41. 'A crap game at a run-down stadium, a five-hour drive away from home'

HEREFORD UNITED v BRIGHTON AND HOVE ALBION, 3 MAY 1997

TONY HYLANDS: The most important game in our history.

KEVIN SHERWOOD: Any victory Brighton ever has in the future, if they win the European Cup in ten years, it will never mean as much as that Hereford game.

IVOR CAPLIN: Staying in the Football League was absolutely crucial because it does generate money and it does generate other things in terms of any new developments, and staying in the Football League was crucial.

TONY HYLANDS: We met up at 6.30 a.m. on the Saturday morning and we left Eastbourne at 6.40 a.m. on a coach, 46 of us from the A21 Club. It was a very, very nervous trip up, until we got past Slough, everyone started to wake up. We weren't allowed in Hereford until 2 p.m. so we pulled into this lovely little pub by the side of the road. First coach to pull in, got tanked up, sitting outside in the beautiful sunshine, then another coach pulled in and then a minibus pulled in, and then some cars pulled in. In the end it was just Albion fans, the whole pub inside, outside, all the gardens, a mass sing-song, just to ease the tension.

STEWART WEIR: I was down at the training ground on the Thursday and I got

195

a call from Hereford to say that I couldn't have a press pass for the game. My knees went to jelly and my last two years of existence flashed before my eyes and I thought 'Shit'. I tried to explain to them what was happening and what I was doing and that even though I'd got no divine right to a press pass, I thought I'd faxed them early enough. Anyway I phoned round and begged and got on my knees whilst I was talking to them on the phone and they relented on that.

STUART STORER: We went up on the Friday morning. We stopped at Ross-on-Wye, nice hotel overlooking the river. We was up to about 10.30-11.00 a.m., everyone was just sat around. We were so relaxed it was quite frightening, but obviously we'd had so much pressure since Christmas, I think we'd got used to it.

ANNA SWALLOW: Me, my dad, my mum and Paul Samrah all driving up to the match and we got there at about 11.30 a.m.

Then Paul Samrah said, 'Of course you do know that we're going to be on *Football Focus*, you don't mind, do you?' and we were like, 'Oh my god, I'd better comb my hair.'

It was Paul first and then my dad, then my mum, then me and Harry Gration from the BBC was doing the day. He was saying, 'This is daddy Swallow, this is mummy Swallow and this is baby Swallow' then at the end 'And the most important supporters this afternoon for the Seagulls will come from the Swallows' and my dad was so proud.

The weird thing was we were standing on the pitch and Bellotti and his wife sort of crept up in the stand. That's when they were trying to throw him out. This was all going on whilst this interview was going on.

STEWART WEIR: Out of the blue he turns up. I didn't even see him get dropped off but I saw him walking towards me with Jo, his wife, and he's there. It was like, 'Shit, this is the most important game – ever – he's turning up and there's going to be a riot. If all of Brighton knows he's here and things are going bad, we're going to be in trouble here and it's going to be his fault.'

For some strange reason he sat down in the foyer, he didn't go to the executive bar or wherever people go, and then I find out that Hereford are not allowing him in. He's been told to stay in the entrance because they're not at all happy with him turning up. Paul Samrah and quite a few other fans are talking to anyone they can, Hereford stewards, the police and just saying, 'You cannot let this man in because there's going to be trouble.' So all these complaints go through and I'm sure it's impressed on them but it turns out that he is eventually allowed in.

PAUL SAMRAH: We did the interview with *Football Focus* and as we came out of the ground just by the offices I saw David Bellotti sitting with his wife, Jo. I was very polite and said, 'Hello, David, do you think it's wise that you are here today?' Perfectly calmly because there was no point in being angry about it. He turned round to me and said, as though he'd never met me before in my life, 'I don't enter into any discussions with anyone on match days'. I thoughtto myself, 'That sums up the bloke, the arrogance, the slick comment.' I was speechless, I just had to walk away, I mean what do you say to that?

TONY MILLARD: His appearance at Hereford was one of the most negative public relations exercises anybody in their right mind could have produced. Despite being asked by Herefordshire police, Hereford United Football Club, the Football League and the Football Association not to come, he still apparently considered himself to be bigger and more important than any of those.

LIAM BRADY: He revelled in it because it's his only claim to fame and he can't get it any other way.

PAUL HAYWARD: It really was a great road trip. I kept telling myself all the way there that whatever happened I had to write a piece that was balanced and wasn't pro-Brighton and that takes into account what Hereford have gone through. I think they would have given me permission to write a personal memoir, but I chose not to do that because I felt it would have been too indulgent and I did want to balance Brighton's salvation with Hereford's decline into the Vauxhall Conference.

The whole day was incredibly special – being part of this convoy, this pilgrimage, passing all these cars with Brighton fans and scarves and flags hanging out the back. There was a sense that we were all moving towards this climatic 90 minutes which was going to decide everything one way or another.

TIM BOHANNON: I'd prepared myself for Brighton to go down. There was a period of time when I was maybe 14 or 15 when if Brighton lost then it ruined my weekend, I was in a bad mood, horrible to everybody and over the years I got used to it, so if they fail, you don't experience the loss that you should do – like a defence mechanism. But it came to a stage after Steve Gritt had become manager, maybe mid-February, when I said to my girlfriend, 'I have to feel this, I have to feel everything because this is one of the most important things that has happened in my life.'

197

DAVE SWAFFIELD: One of the really important things over the last two years has been the people you go with. It's really important to have a group, I'm sure there's loads of these little cells all over Sussex where you've got a group of people who've come together just through watching and their love of the Albion and that's really helped at times. To be a lone supporter at these times would have been really difficult, you all feed off each other and that's been really important.

TIM BOHANNON: I was driving down from Manchester, meeting up with my friends who'd all come together over the last two years because of what had been happening, beyond and purely for the love of the Albion.

DAVE SWAFFIELD: I didn't feel too nervous beforehand, I started getting nervous when we got into the carpark and the police helicopter was flying overhead. One of the nice things was walking into the ground and there was one of our pals that had to come from somewhere else, and it was big hugs, really emotional thing football, it really is. So much depended on us getting this draw and not losing.

JAN SWALLOW: It was Paul Samrah, I think, said, 'it was like the feeling you get before going in to an exam', everybody was being quite quiet and slightly hysterical at the same time. Of course the first half was so dreadful.

TONY HYLANDS: Couldn't get a drink in Hereford 'cause all the pubs were shut, so walked down to Tesco's, bought some cans. Quite innocently drinking our tinnies and the whole security force of Tesco's came out which was a real good laugh 'cause we was just ripping the piss out of them. Then we walked from Tesco's back to the little Subbuteo stadium. As we walked past a pub on the way to the ground all you could hear was 'Fuck off, Brighton, fuck off, Brighton.' It was full of Cardiff City fans who'd come down, which wound us up. So my mate Chris, says, 'I'm staying here.' I said, 'Look, I want to see the game. I don't want to get done over, I don't want to get nicked, I want to go to the game.'

What a terrible end to put away supporters in, that end for the Brighton fans. Almost had a carpark in front of it, I thought it was disgraceful. They paid eight pounds to get in and then they couldn't see the game at all 'cause you're looking up. How can you look up to a football pitch? I walked in and straight away I thought, 'I want to see this game, there's a steel girder across there', so I climbed up the wall, got on this steel girder in the roof and I had a television view of the pitch. I had one arm round a girder and that's where I sat for the whole game.

TIM BOHANNON: The support was absolutely incredible. I particularly like the chant 'We are Brighton, super Brighton from the South' – and I can't concentrate on the game if I'm singing, which is awful. If we're 3–0 up then that's fine but . . . Once we kick off, that's it, my arms are folded or I'm biting my thumb nail and looking very serious and, quite honestly, the way we were playing against Hereford I haven't seen us play quite so badly for a long, long time. I didn't know it was an own goal until I got home and my girlfriend told me, I didn't know it was Kerry Mayo.

TIM CARDER: It was an absolutely awful game to sit through. I was up on my feet shouting and doing things that I never normally do at football matches, I was just so worked up. I remember going berserk at the referee at one point, which is something I rarely do, but he gave a free-kick when I thought he was going to give a drop-ball and I just went absolutely mental at him. I was just so wound up and worked up at the situation, I was wringing with sweat at the end and it was just absolutely awful. Everyone around was the same basically – I remember in the first half we never got a look in.

STEWART WEIR: That first half was probably the worst 45 minutes I've ever had. It was probably worse than the last minutes of the Doncaster game. There was no way that I thought we were going to win this game. Throughout that whole season we'd only had one away win up at Hartlepool and this was probably one of the worst first halves that I've ever seen. We're not going to make it – no way, we're going down to the Vauxhall Conference and I thought to myself, 'Shit, I've never been to Dover and Stalybridge Celtic and whoever else'. We've got no divine right to the Football League but it's an outrageous thought to think of a club this size playing in the Vauxhall Conference. It doesn't tally, it doesn't register. How the hell are they going to cope with a thousand to a couple of thousand fans visiting them? How are we going to cope? If we don't make it up in the first season then we are going to be doomed.

JAN MERRITT: The tension was absolutely indescribable. When that goal went in for Hereford I just thought, 'Well, this is it.' We hadn't looked like scoring. I just thought, 'I can't see us coming back from this' and I saw people pacing up and down, people crying, people with their heads in their hands, I had a lump in my throat. I thought that everything is completely wrecked now, we're down.

PAUL HAYWARD: In the press box we all looked at each other at half-time and said, 'Brighton are down, Brighton have gone', because the first half was so abject that there was no way they were going to score in the second half if they were going to perform like that.

I was just sitting there at half-time and working out how to compose myself and trying to prepare myself for it so that I knew how to deal with it at the end. It was an amazing feeling that – thinking that something bad is going to happen in 45 minutes and you'd better be ready for it. You're going to feel fairly appalling about it but you've also got to do a job. You've got to walk down on that pitch and speak to the Hereford chairman, the Hereford manager and the Hereford players and write about their great escape as well as Brighton's calamity and I was utterly convinced at that point that Brighton were going down.

PAUL SAMRAH: I thought to myself, 'If we can hold out till half-time at 1–0, we'll be all right.' At half-time Attila came up to me and I said, 'It's going to be OK, John, we're only 1–0 down, had we conceded that second goal . . . it'll be all right, have faith.' We did play appallingly in the first half and Hereford should have gone 2–0 up, but they didn't, they kept it 1–0, which was tremendous. I was really up for it, I think a few were despondent but a few recognised that this was it, the biggest 45 minutes in the football club's history.

STUART STORER: When it came to the crunch, I think bottle won it on the day. We was a bit more used to the pressure than I think Hereford were. First half, we were terrible, they were right up for it; I don't think we were ready for that. Our plan of action was to go out and hit them, early doors. They bombarded us, I think we got in their half twice first half. I remember walking out on the pitch for the second half and someone saying 'A lot of your fans are in tears', we'd been playing that badly. Luckily, second half we went out and played a bit better and at the end of the day we got the result, that's all that matters.

TONY HYLANDS: Half-time I stood there and looked up and said, 'God, I don't believe in you. You've given me shit over the last year, if Brighton go down I'll never ever go to church again and be a Christian.' The game kicks off second half, Brighton are a different team.

TIM CARDER: The second half they did look as if they'd been warned that, basically, they'd probably be unemployed if they lost that game, so they looked as if they were up for it. Storer had a storming second half although he didn't look fit. When he was running, he was really going in for tackles and trying his heart out.

McDonald wasn't having all that good a game and so Reinelt came on for him. Maskell volleyed it and it hit the far post with the goalkeeper diving and we were just up on our feet willing Robbie to get to there first, which he did and slotted it home. I just remember shouting 'Yes, yes, yes' for about a minute and hugging people next to me.

SARAH WATTS: He stuck it in and everyone was just leaping to their feet, I was sobbing and screaming.

TONY MILLARD: I was doing the commentary with Gerry Ryan alongside me both of whom, myself and Gerry, had strong Albion connections. It was a memorable occasion for many reasons. I certainly went over the top, I made Jollop and Pierce seem positively quiet when I screamed Brighton's equalising goal.

JAN SWALLOW: We were standing behind and to one side of the goal and we couldn't see very well because the steps weren't very steep, there was flat ground in front. I'm quite short but we'd obviously scored. It was unbelievable. I'd never felt anything like it. That must have been the most precious goal I've ever seen – or not seen.

DAVE SWAFFIELD: Absolutely amazing, everything going absolutely wild. Then of course we had what we'd been suffering for the last two months probably, getting the goal we wanted then having to survive it and we came under a lot of pressure.

JAN MERRITT: When we got that equalising goal that was absolutely brilliant, we've done it but we've still got time to go, what if Hereford score again? The tension then was even worse, waiting for the final whistle to go. I think the second half started late and I kept looking at my watch thinking, 'When's the whistle going to go?'

TONY HYLANDS: It was Maskell, wasn't it? He was on the edge of the box 20 yards out, it hit the post then I see Reinelt running in and I just jumped up in the air and nearly broke me neck 'cause I nearly fell 50 foot down. I managed to grab hold and I was just singing and dancing along with everybody else. It was such a tremendous feeling. It seemed to go on forever that second half, I didn't think it was ever going to finish.

STEWART WEIR: I was sat behind the goal and Robbie Reinelt comes through and whacks the ball in. And that's it – the whole world goes crazy – well, the stand behind me goes crazy. I looked at my watch, there were 20 minutes to go and I thought to myself at that point: 'I'm not even going to look at my watch, I'm just going to go into auto-drive and just not think about anything, I'm just going to occupy myself.' I remember looking at the fans and it was heads-in-hands time, it was looking at watches, it was whistling. The noise that was coming out of that end was outstanding.

TIM BOHANNON: It was the purest form of elation I have ever experienced for all of about five to ten seconds. I remember jumping up and celebrating the goal and taking the sharpest intake of breath I've ever had, shrinking right the way back to the back of the stand and thinking, 'Oh Fuck, we've got 30 minutes left – plus injury time – we've got to hang on.' Towards the end of the game I couldn't celebrate, my legs turned to jelly, it was like being punched on the chin, and I was standing next to Dave Swaffield. I couldn't understand how he could still be celebrating when everything was still at stake.

I was looking at my watch every two minutes saying, 'Go faster, for Christ's sake, go faster'! Maskell's one-on-one – if he ever reads this – he was slack, he had the keeper to beat and it was tame, he should have scored – then I would have been celebrating. Then five seconds later they were one-on-one less than ten yards away from Ormerod and he shot straight into his arms.

I remember we were right on the corner of the stand which banks on to Edgar Street and looking at people outside the ground obviously listening to what was going on and thinking, 'You have absolutely no idea what's going on, you're not experiencing this – my bloody team that I have supported for God knows how many years could go out of the Football League.' The injuries went on for eternity, every time someone went down I remember thinking, 'Another ten minutes bloody injury time – my heart can't stand it'.

TIM CARDER: It really was the most stomach-churning event that you could possibly imagine. We started off, we were in the League, and then we were out of the League for 40 minutes, then we were back in the League but at any moment another goal would have sent us out of the League. It was a real roller-coaster ride through 90 minutes of torture, really.

I remember Maskell breaking away and could have scored but didn't so we had to continue on this roller-coaster. But the main thing of course was a minute into injury time and the Hereford number nine got through and just had Ormerod to beat. The ball was travelling quite fast and he just sort of got a toe to it and he could only chip it in to Ormerod's arms and our hearts could go back from our mouths into our chests, basically. I was scared stiff at that point because I don't think we'd have come back from there. There was about three or four minutes of injury time after that – eventually that was it and we knew we'd done it.

STEWART WEIR: There were about ten minutes to go and I started to think, 'Let's get a shot of that moment – that whistle going.' So I went round and I saw the Hereford manager and he looked as if he was shitting himself. Brighton had turned the corner, they were starting to play well and the Hereford players had lost it. The Hereford fans were silent, they looked shocked. They'd had six days at the very bottom and we'd had something like 210 days and we were used to it. We know what it's like to prop up everyone else and that's probably what ultimately told – that they were staring at something that they hadn't really experienced for any length of time. I remember sitting literally a foot away from the feet of Steve Gritt, John Jackson and Jeff Wood and them shouting something like 'Come on, ref, how much more fucking time have we got?' The whole of that bench, and probably the whole stadium, were looking at the ref. Just before the whistle went it was as if the whole of the Brighton bench went quiet – not quiet, but they just stared at the ref – and then he went and blew and that was it. It goes without saying that the Brighton fans exploded, but the whole of that bench lifted three feet off the ground, everyone was yelling and I took this picture of Steve Gritt just as that moment happened. Looking at the picture now, Steve Gritt's going for it, he's letting rip, he's out there, he's done it, and at the back of him the Hereford fans are motionless. They're sat and there's one guy just standing there.

JAN MERRITT: I had this feeling of sorrow for Hereford because I knew how I'd been feeling thinking it was going to be us and, seeing how they were reacting, I felt very sad for them. I was just thankful that it wasn't us and at least next season, whatever happened, we've still preserved our League status.

ANNA SWALLOW: I've never been that happy in all of my life. I mean, I haven't been married and I haven't had a baby so I wouldn't know about that but I've never been that happy, I just burst into tears. Even a massive bloke next to me with a tattoo on his head burst into tears, it was brilliant. Then we just went bonkers and Dick Knight arrived and I went over the wall and kissed him. Apparently it got caught on Sky Television.

TONY FOSTER: People were hugging and kissing members of the same sex, for Christ's sake! There was a lot of emotion as a lot of it drained out of people and the pressure – it was a release, it was like the cork came off.

SARAH WATTS: Afterwards it was just brilliant. It is just intense emotion and colour, a lot of blue and white. I know that it was really tough on Hereford to go down the pan, because we knew what they were feeling like, we'd sat there for 40 minutes and experienced it, we were facing it ourselves but we survived and it was a real fairy tale.

DAVE SWAFFIELD: When the whistle went that was my absolute best Albion moment. It meant such a lot, after everything that had gone before, the last two years.

TONY HYLANDS: They blew the whistle and I just filled up and I thought, 'I'm going to bawl my eyes out, I can't hack this', and I'm a big macho hooligan and I am going to turn around, look to the back of the stand – and I saw all these skinheads just bawling their eyes out and I just burst. I just started crying my eyes out. I released two years' emotion, it just all came out. I don't apologise for that fact, that was such an emotional feeling – we had a future.

TIM BOHANNON: I had tears in my eyes and a lot of other people did. I don't know if it's wrong – with getting married, having children, sensible adult things that people go through and this is essentially a football match – but for six months we'd been at the bottom of the table, been the worst team in the whole of the Football League.

BILL SWALLOW: When the final whistle went, I have to say I couldn't believe it. I just wanted to sit down very quietly. I didn't really join in the cheers and shouts that much for two reasons: I couldn't believe it had happened, and I felt desperately sorry for the Hereford supporters. So we hung around after the game and I remember going up to Robbie Reinelt after the match and saying, 'I'd just like to thank you very much indeed for doing that', and he said, 'Well – it's my job, innit?' and that was what it was all about. It was a funny feeling when that match ended. I didn't leap up in the air, I just thought, 'Thank God for that'.

DAVE SWAFFIELD: I went down to find my son who was standing at the front. I've taken him to see the Albion since he was six, maybe, and he hasn't seen any success with the Albion – he's thirteen. He went to Wembley with the play-offs where we played absolute bollocks, all he's seen is struggle with this team, really. You always want your son to support the team you support, that's just a natural reaction, you want him to see success as I've seen success with the club and sometimes I've doubted his commitment – he's young, he's got other things he wants to do.

I went down to look for him and there he was, down the front, hugging his mate and they were both in tears and I thought, 'Yes, you're there, you're an Albion fan, you're going to be with this club forever now.' Seeing him in tears with relief was just absolutely amazing. That was just the best bit, that really was. As important as the Albion surviving, it was seeing that. I actually hugged him like I haven't hugged him since he was a baby, it was just incredible.

TIM CARDER: The riot police quickly came across the pitch. The Albion fans, by and large, stayed behind the barrier and the players threw their shirts into the crowd. Steve Gritt and Dick Knight and Ivor Caplin were there shaking hands and giving interviews. It was just fantastic and it was like winning a Championship because we'd been resigned to being in the Conference and we got out of it, so it was as if we'd won the Conference Championship perhaps – that was the sort of feeling. Utter, absolute relief but you couldn't help feeling sorry for those Hereford fans. They were distraught and it could so easily have been us and, as I said earlier, some of them did come down for Fans United and gave us support in our moment of need – so I would like to think they'll come straight back up.

PAUL HAYWARD: I was in the overspill of the press area and I was surrounded by Hereford fans who were very good-natured and obviously as committed as the Brighton fans behind the goal in their own way. When the final whistle blew, the women around me broke into hysterical sobbing and the men just bowed their heads. A classic men/women thing – the men did their best to show grief but they suppressed it as men do, but the women just dissolved into floods of tears and walked out very slowly. They really were like mourners at a funeral, they walked in that respectful, slow-funereal pace and down the steps and out forever and that was the last any of us would ever see of them probably. I remember some fans sitting on the terraces completely frozen – just completely still with the pain of it – and at the other end of course was the pandemonium and the joy and the pleasure that one gets from walking through prison gates or out of a hole in the ground after that long in captivity. No one on the planet I should think could begrudge Brighton supporters the happiness they felt in those moments. They worked for it, they never stopped fighting, they stuck with what seemed for a long, long time a hopelessly lost cause.

NIGEL SUMMERS: I didn't much enjoy watching us having sent the opposition down. I'd rather it was A N Other club somewhere else in the country watching them go down.

IVOR CAPLIN: I'd been asked by a number of press people which was worse – the tension of election night or the last 25 minutes at Hereford and I made it clear that the last 25 minutes at Hereford were far worse than election night. I've been going for 32 years, the last 25 minutes were very, very tense indeed at Hereford and a great feeling at the end of it all.

I didn't go on the pitch deliberately but it was the only way to the press box and I'd already agreed to do an interview with the BBC whatever the result. It was only as I was walking down to the press box that the supporters started shouting, so obviously I went over because I could see one or two people I knew in the crowd and I just went over to say hello and it turned into a lot more than that. But it gave me an opportunity and it gave Dick an opportunity to say thanks to the supporters, because the supporters have been firm in their views about keeping the club going and it did, both on and off the field.

DAVID DAVIES: When they stayed up it was fantastic. I was thrilled for all the individuals who'd put a lot of effort in.

STEWART WEIR: I had a quick chat with Steve Gritt and asked if there was any problem getting into the changing-room, and he said, 'Yeah, no problem.' On the way in there, just before the turning into the changing-room, is Bellotti. He leans over, puts his arms around Steve Gritt and says something like 'well done' and Steve Gritt — I didn't see the front of his face but what I saw from the back — just walked straight on. So I think it goes without saying that Steve Gritt is not the world's greatest fan of David Bellotti, judging by that moment.

So getting in to the changing-room it was cans open and 'Things Can Only Get Better' — the volume was up full blast but the speakers had actually blown some time ago. They were just absolutely overwhelmed. I don't think it had sunk in.

STUART STORER. I was in tears that day as well. Having been here two years at the club, it was just a relief to do something like that. Obviously, our jobs were on the line, kids to feed, careers to uphold. I always think of the worst scenario that can happen and I make sure that it don't. Obviously you think about it all week, but when you get on that pitch, I think it's like any other match — but the trouble was there was so much tension out there and there was so much on it that we couldn't afford to lose.

IAN HART: Steve Gritt has achieved the most an Albion manager has ever achieved. Because he came in and the crowd weren't interested in him, it was a lost cause and he turned it round. The man's a star and he's a top bloke with it as well.

SARAH WATTS: We finally got outside the ground and Attila came round and Tony Hylands and in the end we got a photograph of Tony Hylands, Roy

Chuter and me – the three that Bellotti was trying to sue.

It was just amazing and then this guy came up and said, 'Thanks for all you have done. I was one of those people who were saying "why don't we do something?" and I was letting other people do it, I wasn't prepared to do it myself and you were doing it.' It was more than one of us, I would say that there was about 50 hard core who were leading and coming up with the ideas and making things happen.

PAUL SAMRAH: I went on the pitch and did an interview for Southern Counties Radio, hugged Dick Knight on my way up and shook hands with Steve Gritt, which was brilliant. We all stayed behind and waited for the team to board their coach and we didn't leave Hereford till about 6.45 p.m.

We drove back and passed cars, pubs with Brighton fans, and then we came into Brighton and went to a club. It was like my student days, I ended up having a hamburger at 2.30 a.m.

TONY HYLANDS: We left Hereford and we found that same pub and it just filled up with all Brighton fans and that's where we stayed. We just sung the whole way home on the coach. We sung every song from 'Bohemian Rhapsody' through to all the Jam numbers, as well as all the football songs and if you can imagine 46 pissed-up blokes singing 'Bohemian Rhapsody', it was like *Wayne's World*, it was just a brilliant laugh. Of course it took me a week to come down. I couldn't come down at work, you're walking around going 'Brighton this' and 'Brighton that' and they don't understand what you're going on about. That stuff is important to me.

PAUL HAYWARD: It turned into a lovely evening. There was this nice soft sunshine and Hereford's full of these lovely kind of egg-box hills and it seemed to be lilting through this lovely landscape, passing pubs where a lot of Brighton fans had stopped at these pubs for a drink, horns were hooting and flags were waving and every time you hooted a horn everyone in that pub waved. There was this amazingly joyous exodus back to Brighton.

People talk about bursting with happiness and you knew that there was no celebration that would have been adequate, really – that would match the physical intensity and the pleasure that everybody felt that Brighton had finally escaped and things really did seem better. Maybe we were going to have a new ground, maybe next year there would be a brief ground-share, maybe next year we'd be pressing for promotion even, with a team that on the evidence of the second half of the season was probably going to perform fairly well next year with Steve Gritt in charge. Everything seemed right – and summer was coming and the Tories had gone.

207

ATTILA THE STOCKBROKER: We got to the end of the season and it was one of the best weeks of our lives — the announcement of the deal, followed by the victory at the Doncaster game, then the General Election result, and then Hereford. I was certain that we were going to do it at Hereford. It was illogical but I just thought, 'We're going to do it' and it was wonderful. It was just a brilliant, brilliant, brilliant experience — there's no other way of putting it, really.

KEVIN SHERWOOD: Let's face it, it was a draw — it feels like a 50–0 win but it was a draw, but you can never get any more pleasure than you did at that moment. It was a crap game but I've watched the video five or six times already and no matter what we ever do, nothing will ever sum up the emotion of that day. It summed up the end-point of two years.

DAVE SWAFFIELD: I've been to Wembley twice with the Albion, I've been to Newcastle and seen them promoted, I've never, ever felt as nervous as I did at that game.

PAUL SAMRAH: I was able to go into work and hold my head up high, being so proud to be a Brighton fan. It was just back to football and we stayed up. Forget the stadium, forget the new board, forget Bellotti, his name wasn't mentioned, it was irrelevant. It was about the players, it was about Steve Gritt and it was about Brighton and Hove Albion Football Club staying up and hoping that next season will be totally different.

TIM BOHANNON: I've never experienced emotion like that — apart from when I first fell in love. My eyes met this Irish girl across a crowded art gallery in Leningrad and that was it. Love at first sight, I've never experienced anything like that where your stomach is being torn out, your entrails are being torn out because you cannot be with this person — but the emotion of the last two years, culminating in that one final game was stronger than anything I've ever known before.

PAUL HAYWARD: For me, personally, the whole thing was instructive because I've got this very privileged position which allows me to move in the élite of football and sit at the Noucamp or the San Siro and watch the most technically accomplished footballers in the world play football in front of 70, 80, 115,000 people. It's easy to get drawn into that world and forget the basic nature of the allegiance to a football club which is unaffected by the quality of the football — it becomes irrelevant when you get the strength of devotion which was evident at the Goldstone Ground.

That was the absolutely universal theme in relation to football and its followers and it was incredibly uplifting to see it demonstrated so consistently and so nobly by Brighton supporters. I was just in awe of them, really, throughout the year. I probably never said that to any of them but I remember feeling consistently astonished by what they were prepared to do to try and save the club. Curious, being a journalist in that sort of situation because, even being a Brighton supporter, to some extent you are suspended above it or to the side of it. You're on the outside looking in. I had a very deep sense of watching other people behave in an amazingly admirable and tireless way. I'll never forget that.

There's a sense that whatever Brighton do from here on they are going to have to do something pretty spectacular for the fans to feel the same depth of emotion that they were able to feel this year. It was horrible and harrowing and exhausting in many ways but at the same time, because it enabled people to throw themselves into it and be so utterly committed to wanting to win, wanting to defeat this kind of ogre, I'm sure a lot of people felt strengthened by that and felt that their lives were changed by it. They felt that they had stood up for themselves and stood up for something they believed in – they felt massively empowered by it. And I'm sure that a good top-ten position in the second division or even the first division will make them feel good but they may never feel that same sense of empowerment and of having their voices heard. Because it was a triumph – in a crazy perverse way it was a triumph – Brighton finished 91st out of 92 League clubs but they could easily have had a civic reception and an open-top bus ride because Brighton were saved.

TIM BOHANNON: One of the most sublime moments of my life.

PAUL HAYWARD: In between the Doncaster and Hereford games I saw an England International and I saw Barcelona play Real Madrid at the Nou Camp, but neither of those games came anywhere close to the Brighton glory at Hereford – a crap game at a run-down stadium, a five-hour drive away from home.

LESSONS TO BE LEARNT

42. The Football Association

PAUL HAYWARD: The football authorities aren't really controlling what's happening at a lower level, you're getting these people who are coming into football who either have no feel for the traditional allegiances in communities like Brighton or they don't care for them.

TIM CARDER: The FA did let us down to start with. I don't think they had the will or the guts to stand up to Archer. I think he was riding roughshod over them and they should have taken action right at the start when the Articles of Association were found to have been changed against the rules of the FA, and certainly it took them three or four months to actually rectify that – and that, to my mind, was unacceptable.

BILL SWALLOW: What I do know is that the FA's public relations and public face generally were uninspiring, which is one of the things perhaps it has in common with much of football. No sense of communication with the fans. My dream is that the new consortium, who have not got off to a good start on that, will regard that as a priority. We felt again like abandoned Yugoslav refugees, like feudal serfs, like ignorant supporters. We were left out of it, and mother – who should be looking after us at Lancaster Gate – didn't seem to be interested.

CHRIS JONES: Whilst the Football Association ultimately half-delivered, it should have started a lot earlier. I think it is ludicrous that you have to seek planning permission to put a dormer window in your house, but you don't have to have any vetting to own a football club. If their rule book didn't allow them to do anything about the situation then the rule book needs to be rewritten.

JOHN CAMPBELL: The FA should vet people who get involved in football clubs. They have the power to do it. One of the things the FA could do is insist that the FA have a charge over the land with any football club at every level because you've got to trust the FA. It would have to be agreed to, the directors would have to have a financial interest, but the FA could turn round and say, 'Well, we own your ownership, we are the ones that give you the franchise to operate the football club'. If they'd had a charge over the

Goldstone it would have meant this couldn't have happened.

PAUL HAYWARD: I think in December 1996 the FA should have convened an inquiry and set out to remove Archer from the board. It doesn't matter that it was a private company and that Archer was merely the majority shareholder, the FA still had the power – it has draconian powers, really – to act.

There's lots of examples of things they could have charged them for – they could have investigated the York City riot to see whether they knew beforehand that they were going to sign the lease-back deal with Chartwell because if they'd announced that, clearly there wouldn't have been a riot.

NIGEL SUMMERS: The Football Association over many issues this year has said, 'It's not us, it's the Football League' and the Football League has said, 'It's not us, it's the Football Association'. Isn't it a complete nonsense that we've got two governing bodies? So, we need one governing body for football and we need to have laws or rules for being an associate.

PAUL BRACCHI: When people have power at clubs and pull the purse-strings, are intent on a course of action, it is very difficult for fans to stop that going ahead. I think the FA certainly came in too late in the day. I would say in some way they helped save the club by brokering the conciliation talks. I certainly think for a certain amount of time the FA should hold its head in shame for what they didn't do at Brighton. They say they didn't have powers, in the end they couldn't even bring themselves to publicly criticise Archer for actually changing the Articles of Association, they couldn't even publicly make a statement saying they were wrong to do it. They didn't do anything, so I think that they were culpable.

STEWART WEIR: Football is about money and it's about making money but the biggest aspect of football is that it is answerable to the fans and the community. And I think the buck ultimately stops with the FA. The FA have got to realise that they have a far greater responsibility than they would like to admit to the fans. This will happen again unless the FA change their rules and have greater powers of looking into a club's affairs. I think the loophole at the moment is that if a club is run as a company, the FA rules don't allow it to intervene or look into a club's affairs because it comes under company law.

43. The campaign

IVOR CAPLIN: I think the supporters of the Albion – and wider than that, Fans United – have really shown how supporters can take charge of the football club. I don't mean that with any disrespect to Dick Knight or Bob Pinnock, they are clearly going to be the board and they run the football club, but what I think the supporters have done is that when decisions are being made that are wholly wrong, as was happening in Brighton and Hove Albion, then the supporters can stand up, get united and actually say, 'This is wrong and we're going to tell you why' in a passionate but effective way. In other words, without the need for hooliganism. The legitimate demonstrations of Fans United, the walk-out, the letter- writing, the march around the town, the general publicity, the march in London, all of that was actually the supporters as one saying, 'We want this matter resolved.' I think in the end it's political with a small 'p', but I think the supporters were excellent. We've seen the very, very low points and now we have to go up.

MARC TWIBILL: I was against any violent protesting which I felt might have a negative effect on the club. I felt that peaceful protests were the way. There are ways of doing things which has often been proved through trades unions of making your point in getting what you want through peaceful means, and violent means at the end of the day can often do more harm than good.

SARAH WATTS: Suddenly we were having pieces written about us and we were being given half-pages in the *Guardian* and *The Times* – it was serious writing. It was OK to be a Brighton fan and you could admit it now! You could be proud to say that you were a fan of a small club. I think that's part of what our fight has been about – it is OK, and nothing to be ashamed of it.

PAUL SAMRAH: At the end of the day if you've got money, you can buy into a football club, if you haven't got money, you can't. The great thing of all of our campaign was that we managed to bring a consortium on to the scene. Liam Brady convinced them that there was the potential because of the fans' support and we wouldn't have been successful if we didn't have the consortium – we still needed someone with money to do something, take over and give us hope. All the marching – we could have marched to Timbuktu – if there was no consortium out there, no people who wanted to take over the shares, we wouldn't have achieved anything. We couldn't. Liam Brady deserves an awful lot of credit.

STEWART WEIR: I think that what happened with this club was that it bonded a lot of people together in a reasonably short period of time and in a lot of ways. What's happened here has actually made the fans realise what they could have lost and what they've got. The community has yet to realise it – they don't realise what they've got with a football club.

WARREN CHRISMAS: As a fan I didn't realise how much work some people have put into saving the club and not just in the last two years with all the financial trouble, five years ago, whatever. There's a few dozen people that work that hard and if you sit down and think about what would've happened if those people hadn't been around, you can almost certainly say the club probably would be dead by now. The Supporters Club and BISA were always at each other's throats but they've united for the common cause, they wanted to get rid of Archer and they wanted to save the club – but it will be interesting to see what happens in maybe three or four years' time when we have a new ground and everything is settled down.

TIM CARDER: In a funny sort of way I think some of us will miss what we've been doing over the last two years. We've been so busy organising things, handing out leaflets, demonstrations, you name it, we've done it. Some of us won't know what to do with our spare time in the future.

I think it's certainly united factions within the club and got people together who perhaps before would have shunned each other in the *Gull's Eye*/BISA side of things and the Supporters Club side of things. I think there's a lot of respect from both sides now for each other and it's built up a real fraternity within the support of the club. The active campaigners, I guess when you think about it, are a small minority of the support of the club, 50 or so people have been involved in organising things.

KEVIN SHERWOOD: I think now would be a fantastic time to form a new supporters club with representatives of each one. You've got a common aim. Don't let's say, 'Brilliant, we did a great job, we've got a stand, we've got a football club, let's look to the bright side of this' and all go back to what we did before. We ought to keep meeting up. That's the representation we want, that's the input you want going into a board in an ideal world. It would be a shame if it was all wasted now we've done so well to substantiate those links between supporters. Look at *Gull's Eye*/BISA and the Supporters Club, you'd never have got those round the table because they were seen as the sober, more conservative side of the club, but we covered everybody and that is a brilliant achievement.

TIM CARDER: Just as I think Archer and Bellotti were pig-headed and weren't going to give up the fight, we were the same, really. However bad the situation looked (we were going to go out of the League and going to be uprooted from Brighton and Hove and Archer and Bellotti were still going to be in charge at the end of the day), we never gave up and in that respect we were very similar to the dreaded pair.

ATTILA THE STOCKBROKER: Our greatest victory has been to show the world that football fans can be intelligent and witty and inventive, and run a campaign to save the thing they love and attract wide support from all different sections of the community and, of course, from the media.

The funny thing is that, for me, who has been involved for much of my life in left-wing political activity of one kind or another, football was one of the areas of my life which was a kind of oasis where I just went along to watch the game.

What was really good and the reason we got so much media coverage was that there were so many diverse people involved in the campaign. We haven't always seen eye-to-eye but over the last year and a half Liz Costa has done some really good stuff. When we were trying to get rid of Barry Lloyd, our ex-manager, she was very pro-Lloyd and it was like 'Don't have a go at the club' but when she realised what was going on she's been really good. It's been great from a media anti-stereotype point of view to have a woman, and an older woman, as one of the main spokespeople for the fans, she's got total respect and I salute her and Sarah Watts and all the others from the Supporters Club. And then you've got me, who's quite unorthodox in the way that I live and what I do, and that's been quite good copy for some people – writing poetry about football and justice rather than smashing up telephone boxes – you know, it's that anti-stereotype thing. Then you've got someone like Paul Samrah, who's your typical kind of middle-class City person. There's all these different people, and then the Internet people and the fanzines and then the more traditional-type supporters doing their own thing as well – people like Tony Hylands and Nigel Summers. We've all come together and learned from each other and, as I've said so many times, it's been brilliant for me just to have worked with and made friends with all these people from different walks of life, very different kind of social outlooks and backgrounds and aspirations. As much as possible it's been good fun as well as very important. I have never at any point thought, 'Fuck me, I wish I wasn't doing this.' Sometimes it involved an awful lot of work, and certainly it has involved a considerable amount of personal disruption over the past year, but it's never been a chore and I've always thought I was doing something worth while.

STUART ADAMS: Releasing a few balloons wasn't going to cut it, writing a few polite letters, no matter how well they meant, wasn't going to cut it – but it was the direct action that swung it for us and put us on the map and people took us seriously.

PAUL HAYWARD: I think supporters from everywhere around the country will look at the Brighton story as a model for future resistance movements. I think that will be the blueprint, really, for any set of supporters wanting to rescue their club.

44. Ownership

ATTILA THE STOCKBROKER: The football club, as far as I'm concerned, is owned by the fans. It is our club. Without people to watch it, it has no function.

IVOR CAPLIN: The mistake for me in what has happened is that you didn't have football people running the club. I think someone who's running the club day-to-day needs to be a supporter but they need to have the business ability to run the club as well. And I think that applies to the board as well, they've got to be supporters first, and if they're supporters first and have got strong local connections, as Dick Knight does have, then that is actually going to enhance the team.

JOHN CAMPBELL: I said when I came on the board 15 years ago, 'Football clubs don't belong to individuals, they belong to the community, we hold them in trust,' and unfortunately that view was not shared by these directors and so it is a business. I agree that it is a business but you should never lose sight of the fact of what the main business is. It's football and supplying entertainment to the public. I will never accept that public companies and football clubs are good bedfellows because you are trying to satisfy two masters, one is a shareholder and wants a dividend on his shareholding and the other is a supporter, the most important thing he wants is a winning team. He doesn't care if the shares aren't worth anything.

BILL SWALLOW: A football club is an intangible concept in a sense. It is almost impossible to say who owns it. It is rather like saying, 'Who owns Christianity?' And the answer is, 'No one does'. But nevertheless, it is the fans who are an essential component of what the club is. They are part of the club, if not its owners.

Clearly there must be far more community involvement through councils and so on. I wouldn't like Brighton to be turned into an anonymous plc.

IVOR CAPLIN: One thing I am quite firm about is that the local Council, local authorities, the community, should have a stake in the stadium, which means that someone can't do what Bill Archer and David Bellotti have done at the Goldstone Ground. Once you've got a local authority stake in there that will never change. Political control will not change that and therefore that community holds its own stake in that football club, in the ground, and I think that's a fundamental part of insuring the future of football, rugby union, whatever.

DAVE SWAFFIELD: Never trust chairmen, whoever they are. I think chairmen have got to come from the community and even better if they're a known fan of the club, it's a bonus and I think we're lucky that we've got one. Because they've been on the terraces they know what it's like so, I think we'll get a fairer deal from chairmen like that. When Dick Knight came in and when you learnt about his background and how long he'd been supporting the club, you felt that's the sort of people we want. You don't want the money men like Archer.

PAUL WHELCH: It's absolutely essential for football club owners to take the view that if the fans say, 'Sorry, we don't have any confidence in you and there is clearly an alternative option for the benefit of the club', that owners should sell up and go! I don't think people should regard football clubs as their personal property, if there is a viable alternative solution.

PAUL HAYWARD: The brightest lesson and one that I hope every football director and chairman learns is that you cannot destroy all the traditions of something which people love. You can't walk into a place and destroy it in the face of people who are sustained by that tradition and who are prepared to fight for it and who would say that they felt love for it – you cannot do that and get away with it.

PAUL SAMRAH: I think that all fans have got to study the club accounts; they have got to ask questions and not just accept answers at face value. I think you have to ask for evidence to support the answers that the board are giving you. We have to recognise that each football club is a private limited company and if you are not a shareholder you can't demand things to be done and expect them to be done – there are reasons why things aren't done the way we would hope them to be done.

CHRIS JONES: If I buy a pair of trainers and they are crap and they fall to bits, no matter how good the brand is, I will take them back to the shop and I will get my money back, and if I don't get my money back I will never buy them again. You can't do that in football and that allows people who control football to take liberties with the people who are their paying customers.

LIAM BRADY: It wouldn't happen at Arsenal. We had a very rocky start to last season, we had no manager, but we had good people at the club to make sure that the ship was steered in the right direction and results were obtained until Wenger came. The board knew what they were doing and they bit the bullet for the few months that they had to ride the storm. I have a lot of contact with the board now, in the position I'm in, and I really feel that the people who run Arsenal are custodians of the football club. If they make money while they're doing it, well, I think the fans are willing to accept that.

LIZ COSTA: A football club belongs to the fans. Without the fans, without the supporters – and I don't care how big the club gets – without the supporters there is no club. If you want it, fight for it. It's your club, you've earned it, you pay enough money in week-in, week-out supporting it, whether it be buying shirts, whether it be turning up at the turnstiles or even just buying one of the fundraising things which cost you 50p a week. It's your club – and you have a right to that club but if you want it, fight for it.

DAVE SWAFFIELD: The supporters own a football club. That's what I'd like to see, I'd like to see the supporters have shares in a club. It'd be good for the club and it'd attract people who perhaps aren't such avid supporters as some of us.

TIM CARDER: I personally think that the club should have its majority share-holding owned by a supporters trust. My idea would be to see a supporters trust with a controlling share interest in the club but it wouldn't be able to make decisions on the day-to-day running of the club like hiring and firing the manager, anything like that, it wouldn't receive dividends. The only thing it would do would be to safeguard the existence of the club and it would only be able to vote on matters such as where the club plays, what loans are taken out by the club – things that would be deemed to actually affect the very existence of the club. There are too many clubs that are becoming plcs and floating on the stock market and once that happens I think there's no chance of that really happening. But at the moment at the Albion we've got a private limited company with a limited number of shareholders and I would like to see 51 per cent of those shares in the hands of a supporters trust, under the conditions which I've outlined, which do not affect the day-to-day running. The idea of that is that potential investors in the club are not put off. Potential investors, if they're good investors, are there because they want to help the club and see their investment as helping the club rather than speculators who are just there to make money out of it.

ATTILA THE STOCKBROKER: In an ideal world, which we haven't got, I don't want any bloody consortiums or businessmen involved in football at all. It should belong to the fans, it should be our club. We should be able to finance it, we should have our own people in place. In Germany the stadiums are mostly owned by the Stadtrat, the local council, the Presidium is the equivalent of the board and it's voted for by the members of the club, who are the supporters. Anybody can stand for that and obviously you are elected to it because either you are a wealthy businessman with lots of money who says, 'I will put x amount of money into this club – I will do this, this, this and this', or in some cases because you are a very active, well-known, well-liked local supporter. Obviously, by the very nature of it, the majority of the people who are elected are the rich businessmen but they are elected by the supporters and they have to give a commitment of what they are going to do and they are not private limited companies, they can't actually then say, 'Right we are going to take this club over and destroy it.' Now obviously it isn't like that in this country. It is extremely undemocratic and it's a question of having the kind of capitalists you like rather than capitalists you don't like.

LIAM BRADY: I think directors of football clubs are custodians for the people who support that football club. And if they make a success of it then they are entitled to the perks; if they make it successful and they go to Wembley and they gain promotion then they are entitled to claim responsibility for that success. They are custodians.

TIM CARDER: Although I don't really envisage my plan of a supporters trust having the majority shareholding in the club, I certainly think a shareholding should be issued that ordinary supporters could come in on – like shares at £5 or something like that. Apart from raising money it would also spread the ownership, not in any major way, but it would allow supporters to feel they owned a part of the club. I can imagine thousands of homes across Sussex having a little certificate on their wall saying, 'One share in Brighton and Hove Albion Football Club Limited.'

45. Supporter representation

IVOR CAPLIN: I think what's absolutely essential is that the chairman and the managing director of the club meet on a regular basis with the supporters representatives. Those are open and transparent meetings and if there are problems they are talked about at that early stage so that never again does the club get into this very closed environment that it's been in, in the past two or three years. Whether you actually have one person sitting on the board as a non-executive director, I'm open to persuasion as to whether we could achieve that properly in the Brighton and Hove situation – but certainly regular meetings with the important people who are involved in the day-to-day running of the football club is vital.

SARAH WATTS: It doesn't matter who runs Brighton and Hove Albion now, the Supporters Club will never be extreme but they're not going to be yes-men anymore. We'll say it politely and we'll try and find ways of giving them an alternative if they don't agree with what we're doing – but we're not yes-men any more.

PAUL SAMRAH: I was always sceptical about getting fans on the board because I always used to think that the directors were fans! Probably so far as Brighton and Hove Albion are concerned that probably wasn't the case, or if it was then their PR machine was so dreadfully appalling and they didn't realise it. They should have had a fan on the board so that they could have been told that their PR was absolutely outrageous and dreadful and then maybe we wouldn't have been in this mess that we are in.

TIM CARDER: I certainly would like to see supporter representation on the board at Brighton and Hove Albion and every other club. Perhaps that's something that the FA could bring about.

PAUL CAMILLIN: I mean everyone goes on about supporter representation, but I don't think you need that. All you need are regular updates, a board that keeps you informed. They have got to have a look at how a supermarket would treat its customers, or a service industry. It is a service, football, a leisure service, entertainment as such. If you go to the cinema, you don't expect to be treated like you are at football and it is the same thing now.

LIAM BRADY: I don't like the idea of supporters representation because how open can you be? You've got to be discussing at boardroom level whether you should sell a player or whether you should buy a player, whether a player has been misbehaving badly and you've got to get him out of the club for that reason, and if you've got someone who's representing the supporters, who's expected to tell supporters what's going on at boardroom level – how would that work?

When you're dealing with people like Greg Stanley, Bill Archer and David Bellotti I don't think you would have changed much. You probably would have found a lot more about what was on their agenda – but I'm actually against it.

TIM BOHANNON: All these clubs that have become plcs, the shareholders are not the people who have bought the shares, the shareholders are the fans, the people who have been going for all their lives – they are the people who should own the club – I'm not talking about a great socialist/communist ideal because it wouldn't work, but they are the ones who should have a certain amount of say in what is going on.

46. The people's game

ATTILA THE STOCKBROKER: Just to watch a game of football is one of the simple pleasures of life, but it's also a hell of a lot more than that. It's also about culture, people coming together, a shared identity, a shared interest and, for me, who operates, it's fair to say, on the fringe of mainstream society as a poet/musician, it's one of the areas which I really treasure in that it brings me into regular contact with people from a completely different world, different social background, different aspirations.

A football club is, of course, far more than just the players or the pitch. It is the fans. I can't get away from my political beliefs here. I do believe that football is the people's game and that the fans are the people who should be taken as the number one concern, not some bloody Stock Exchange flotation. And I would like to see radical steps taken by this new government to do something about that.

SARAH WATTS: I was a Tory and I was conservative small 'c' as well. I wouldn't

221

think about voting Tory now. I'm far more socialist – my general outlook. Part of it is to do with all this.

ATTILA THE STOCKBROKER: It's like with the miners' strike and anything else. People learn through their struggle, they see what's happening, they get angry about it, they come together to do something about it and in many cases – not all, of course – it makes them draw conclusions about other things as well.

DAVE SWAFFIELD: It's caused misery at home when things have been bad and I can't talk to anyone, loads of people don't understand why. People don't understand football fans, only a football fan can understand a football fan.

PAUL SAMRAH: I wouldn't say I miss it, but I really got a buzz out of the togetherness. That's what was so good about it. People from all different walks of life, different areas of Sussex together on a Saturday afternoon and those friendships that I've made I hope will be with me for the rest of my days. I know they will because we will all be Brighton fans, we will. John Baine [Attila] and I have totally different political views but I tell you, you could never wish to meet a more dedicated bloke.

JAN SWALLOW: We have suffered, because it's never been off our minds since the ground was sold and since we had the first inkling that something was going on. It's built up more and more and more until – I know sometimes I've thought, 'All I've thought about today is the Albion'. You know, whatever I'm doing, it's in the back of my mind.

ANNA SWALLOW: I think you cannot take people's dreams away. If someone loves something you can't destroy it. If you try, and that someone is part of a collective mass, you can't do it. Brighton and Hove Albion still exists and all the better for it, I hope.

LIZ COSTA: I think we've all learned a lot about one another. Our own strengths and weaknesses have all come out and the thing that I've found, I mean over all these years, is that football is a huge family.

I've got a new grandson and I am desperate to make sure that there is a football club for me to take him to. He deserves and he has the right to be able to go to a football ground and support his local team. As far as I'm concerned, he is Brighton born and bred and he will support Brighton!

47. Time added on for stoppages

On Wednesday, 3 September 1997, after another long, frustrating period of prevarication, rumour, claims and promises, Bill Archer signed the deal giving up his majority shareholding of Brighton and Hove Albion. The deal, which had been agreed in principle in April, was finally done: Archer retained a 49.5% share, Dick Knight became chairman with a matching 49.5% and Martin Perry for McAlpines held the controlling 1%. In the days before the deal was completed, Archer bizarrely stated he would invest £2m in the club. To date none of this money has been forthcoming and so the £56.25 he paid to take control is the only known money he has put into the club.

As part of the deal David Bellotti was instantly removed as chief executive. He was spotted single-handedly loading his desk into the back of his car.

Statement from the new board, 3 September 1997

All parties are pleased to announce that the shareholding restructure of the club envisaged by the FA backed mediation agreement has been finalised, all legal matters have been completed and the new board of Brighton and Hove Albion is now in place.

In compliance with the FA agreement, the employment of David Bellotti has been terminated on completion of the legal procedures and he has now left the club.

Greg Stanley has resigned as director and shareholder and all monies owed to him by the club have been repaid.

The new board comprises Knight, Archer, Pinnock and Knight consortium member Martin Perry, with former Metropolitan Police chief Sir John Smith and Richard Faulkner as non-executive directors.

The board will rapidly seek a new senior executive responsible for the day-to-day running of the club and it is intended that a supporters' representative will also be appointed.

Dick Knight added: 'Above all, we are committed to rebuilding bridges with the most important people of all – the fans – without whom none of this would have been possible.'

The night of the signing Albion drew 2-2 at 'home' in Gillingham to Peterborough United in front of a crowd of 1,215, the lowest-ever Brighton home crowd.

Ten handy hints to get rid of your club chairman

1. Identify the exact nature of the problem. Find qualified accountants and solicitors from your fans who will happily transcribe accounts and legal jargon into understandable language.
2. Unite the wide range of supporters into a broad alliance with a broad leadership. The talents of the most vociferous supporters and the usually silent seated season-ticket-holder are equally valuable.
3. Debate the developing situation openly at public meetings (as well as in smaller supporters groups in pubs and on the phone). Try and keep the inevitable rumours to a minimum and learn to spot false information.
4. Communicate your concerns clearly to the press, media, politicians and the FA. Make friends with journalists.
5. Allow imaginative ideas for protests to develop from all sections of the support. Violence against people is bad – and bad for your cause! It is a fact that 'illegal' forms of protesting often gain the most publicity, but if you are involved with illegal action, don't get caught!
6. Use every conceivable means of communication including the Internet, pen and paper, posters, petitions, leaflets, slogans, radio, TV, chanting, photographs, poetry, songs – and books!
7. Enlist the solidarity of other fans, especially fans who have had/are having problems with their chairmen or board. Phone a Seagulls fan!
8. Be prepared to make large personal sacrifices and be prepared for your relationships to suffer. (We never said it was going to be easy!)
9. Never take the word of your enemy for granted – it's not true until the document is signed.
10. Never give up. Be brave. Whatever form of action you take you may well feel stupid and intimidated; but it's better to *do* than to sit and worry. Remember the spontaneous chant from supporters of a hundred different clubs standing in Brighton's North Stand on Fans United Day: 'Football! United! Will never be defeated!'

The Albion Crisis: calendar of events
July 1995 – September 1997

1995

<u>JULY</u>

7   The *Argus* breaks the news that the ground is being sold and that 1996–97 'home' matches will be played at Fratton Park, Portsmouth. The new stadium, to be built at Waterhall north of the Brighton bypass and in an area protected from development, will be funded by the profits from a leisure development at Patcham Court Farm.

8   *Argus* reveals Brighton Council rejected the plans for Patcham Court Farm two weeks ago.

18 Greg Stanley resigns as chairman and is replaced by his business partner Bill Archer, the managing director of Focus DIY.

<u>AUGUST</u>

1   Some Supporters Club members meet David Bellotti who explains how the sale of the ground was necessary to cover debts of £4.7m.

4   *Argus* reveals the buyers of the Goldstone to be Chartwell plc and that the no-profit clause has been removed from the club's constitution.

<u>SEPTEMBER</u>

2   A local reporter is banned and a photographer escorted from the ground and some 50 fans occupy the centre circle during half-time of the home game against Notts County. Bellotti's programme notes say the Albion's debt is over £6m – more than £1m up from his meeting with fans on 1 August.

22 Stanley resigns from the board but pledges to keep his money in.

24 Away at Bournemouth, the match, live on local TV, is held up when fans invade the pitch.

29 The FA requests a dossier from the *Argus*.

<u>OCTOBER</u>

7   The board claim the removal of the no-profit clause was 'an oversight' and says it will be replaced.

20 Bellotti's programme notes state: 'The club could not be in safer hands – please trust us.'

NOVEMBER

14 Fans hold a public meeting at Southwick FC which manager Liam Brady attends in a private capacity. He tells the meeting that Bellotti had refused to pay for insurance on the youth-team minibus.

18 The Supporters Club gives Liam Brady a cheque for the minibus.

20 Brady resigns. His press statement is a thinly veiled attack on Archer, Bellotti and Stanley.

21 Jimmy Case is appointed team manager.

DECEMBER

6   Hove Council leader Ivor Caplin calls on Archer and Stanley to resign.

9   *Argus* reveals that Stanley's 'loan' of £600,000 has accumulated £381,000 of interest. Fred Oliver, the *Argus* seller inside the ground, is ejected from the stadium.

22 Bellotti unveils a £32m stadium/sports complex at Toads Hole Valley with a commercial development to fund it. Brighton Council leader Steve Bassam immediately calls it 'pie in the sky'.

30 Fans meet Bellotti for a 'clear the air' meeting.

1996

MARCH

5   League reiterate to the Albion that permission to play at Portsmouth next season will only be granted if they have planning permission in place for a new ground in the Brighton area.

12 Chartwell are granted planning permission for the Goldstone site, but not the 'all food' application which they had wanted.

14 As a result of the planning permission, Chartwell offer the Albion a lease-back deal on the Goldstone for one year for £480,000. *Argus* estimates the cost of moving to Portsmouth for a year at £1m. On TV, Bellotti says the £1m figure is a lie and rejects Chartwell's offer.

16 Before a home game, supporters distribute Hove Council-produced leaflets outlining their perspective on the financial deals available.

21 *Argus* poll shows the overwhelming majority will not go to Portsmouth.

22 *Argus* editorial demands the board should quit.

APRIL

10 With only two weeks until the last home game of the season, Bellotti announces he has offered Chartwell £200,000 to stay at the Goldstone for the next season.

11 Chartwell reveal they rejected Bellotti's offer a week previously.

16 The FA demands to know why the club has not agreed to a deal with Chartwell and why the club has repeatedly ignored requests to put the proceeds from an independent sale into an independent account.

20 After a home game against Carlisle, many fans invade the pitch and the directors box. Doors are charged in an unsuccessful attempt to find Bellotti.

22 The League now warns that the club could be expelled if it moves to Portsmouth with no plans to return. At a meeting, Greg Stanley fails to appease furious fans.

23 After defeat at Notts County, the Albion are relegated.

24 A rumoured consortium wants talks with Archer.

25 Two members of the consortium meet with Stanley.

26 Archer rejects 'half-baked' consortium.

27 York City match abandoned after fans invade the pitch and pull down the goalposts.

28 The consortium's spokesman is revealed as Liam Brady, who offers to pay the deposit on the Goldstone lease-back deal out off his own money. Archer instantly rejects interference by the consortium.

30 Chartwell's offer to lease back the Goldstone is finally signed at 11.55 a.m.

MAY

4 Bellotti ignores advice to stay away and attends the last away game of the season, at Walsall.

JULY

29 Fans meet with Archer and Bellotti. Archer agrees to step aside if the consortium, now revealed as Dick Knight and the property developers McAlpine, can agree three criteria.

AUGUST

16 The FA find the Albion administration guilty of 'failing to control a crowd' over the York City invasion: a three-point deduction is suspended for one year.

23 Archer meets Dick Knight, leader of the consortium, and demands his three criteria are met before he releases the financial accounts. When Knight meets these three criteria Archer then adds a fourth, namely that proof be provided that Knight has identified a site for a new ground to which the local councils would give approval.

SEPTEMBER

9 Archer writes to McAlpine in an attempt to divide the consortium, asking if they would be interested in a separate deal.

15 Supporters groups agree to pull out of negotiations with Archer.

22 A demonstration is held outside the Liberal Democrat conference in Brighton.

30 The FA's meeting with Archer breaks down with no positive outcome.

OCTOBER

1   In the wake of the breakdown of talks, fans, fearing violence at that evening's game against Lincoln, ask for the game to be postponed. The board ignores these fears and issues a statement saying the club will be playing at Portsmouth next year. During the game fans invade the pitch, causing ten minutes of stoppages.

5   Following the game at Wigan, a demonstration is held outside Archer's home in Mellor.

6   Fans who have stayed up in Lancashire demonstrate outside Focus DIY in Blackburn.

15 A mass walk-out of the Hereford game with 15 minutes to go is signalled by fireworks.

26 Fulham fans join Brighton fans for a march through the town before the afternoon's game.

28 Fans Forum at Hove Town Hall with Knight and McAlpine.

29 On the way to the away game at Rochdale a petition is delivered to the head office of Focus DIY.

30 Fans Forum at Eastbourne United.

NOVEMBER

4   Bellotti increases the exclusion zone around the directors box.

9   Boycott of the Mansfield game, with 400 fans breaking in towards the end of the first half. Bellotti does not return for the second half.

17 Gillingham agree ground-share for the next two seasons.

23 A new petition is organised asking the FA to charge the Albion directors with bringing the game into disrepute.

28 The FA announce they will pay for the dispute to be settled by an independent body.

30 March through London, via the FA headquarters, before the Fulham game.

DECEMBER

2   Bellotti increases the exclusion zone again: only season-ticket-holders will be admitted to the West Stand.

3   When Bellotti arrives in the directors box three minutes into the home game against Darlington, 100 fans charge from the North Stand across the pitch towards him; he leaves, never to return. After losing the game there are violent scenes around the West Stand; Jimmy Case talks to protesters.

4   Case is sacked.

7   Brighton fans protest at Stoke versus Tranmere, Leicester versus Blackburn and at Archer's house in Mellor.

9   The FA deduct two points from the Albion for the Lincoln pitch invasions: the club are now 11 points adrift at the bottom of the League.

11 Steve Gritt is appointed manager.
14 Before the home game to Hull anti-Bellotti and Gritt graffiti is daubed around the ground. Gritt receives a hostile reception. Hull fans, also suffering problems with their owners, join a whistle protest.
15 A demonstration outside Canterbury DIY is joined by fans from Watford, Wycombe, Gillingham and Dover.
18 The idea for 'Fans United' day is suggested on the Internet.
22 After the away game at Orient, a 45-minute sit-in is broken by the appearance of Gritt.
24 Paul Samrah, instrumental in exposing financial and legal irregularities, is banned from the ground.

1997

<u>JANUARY</u>
7   The first meeting with FA's mediators, CEDR, is held at Archer's offices.
13 First meeting chaired by BISA.
24 Press packs sent out announcing Fans United day.
28 Fans picket the Liberal Democrat selection meeting in Eastbourne; Bellotti is not successful.
31 Fans are invited to a CEDR meeting: Samrah's ban is lifted and Bellotti agrees to stay away from games in the interest of public order.

<u>FEBRUARY</u>
8   Fans United day.
9   'Goodbye Goldstone' debate on Meridian TV.
17 The boycott of all future games is called off indefinitely.
19 Mediation talks called off again.

<u>MARCH</u>
12 Plans are announced to contest Bellotti's county council seat. The CEDR meeting is concluded with the announcement that an agreement in principle has been reached.
14 A campaign is started for Simon Valder, charged with making threatening phonecalls to Bellotti.
15 Joint demonstration with Hull fans before away game.

<u>APRIL</u>
7   BISA meeting is attended by Knight, Perry of McAlpine and David Davies from the FA. With the final-ever game at the Goldstone only two weeks away, Davies states that unless the unsigned deal is ratified before the match the FA will take decisive action.
8   Bellotti announces plans to take the FA to court over the two-point deduction.

18 The FA meets with CEDR, Archer and the consortium to 'head bang'. The deal is still not signed.
22 A press conference announces an outline of the agreement, Archer and the new board to have 49.5 per cent each with McAlpine holding the 1 per cent casting vote.
24 Simon Valder is given an eight-month custodial sentence.
26 The last-ever Goldstone game. Knight is in the directors box. Fans take away souvenirs after the match.

MAY
1 Bellotti loses the election to the Tory candidate.
3 The last game of the season, away at Hereford.